THE QUEEN

Marguerite Jervis

THE QUEEN OF ROMANCE

Marguerite Jervis

A Biography

Liz Jones

HONNO

First published in Great Britain in 2021 by Honno Press
'Ailsa Craig', Heol y Cawl, Dinas Powys, Vale of Glamorgan,
Wales, CF64 4AH

1 2 3 4 5 6 7 8 9 10

A catalogue record for this book is available from the British Library.

Published with the financial support of the Books Council of Wales.

ISBN 978-1-912905-11-9 (paperback)
ISBN 978-1-912905-12-6 (ebook)
Cover photograph: The Gwyn Jones Papers, National Library of Wales
Cover design: Jem Butcher
Text design: Elaine Sharples
Printed in Great Britain by CPI Group (UK) Ltd, Croydon CR0 4YY

Bursaries acknowledgment

The author would like to thank Literature Wales for their Writer's Bursary,
supported by the National Lottery through the Arts Council of Wales. She would
also like to thank the Authors' Foundation for their grant assistance.

To Simon, Sian and Rachel, with love.

Contents

Contents

Prologue
A Virtuoso Storyteller

*Women's popular fiction existed in its own world far
beyond the literary canon, in the tradition of those
storytellers who want to entertain us.*
(Carmen Callil, *Subversive Sybils*) [1]

The chorus line. A dizzying whirl of blonde, bobbed, stocking-legged
dancers rush onstage. The camera pans along the faces of the men in
the front row. A toothless man leers, another mops the sweat off his
forehead, one leans forward to inspect the 'goods' onstage, while
another points his opera glass to get a close-up of the girls' legs.

This is the opening scene of Alfred Hitchcock's *The Pleasure
Garden*, his silent adaptation of the bestselling novel by Oliver
Sandys, the pen name of Marguerite Jervis. Part torrid melodrama,
part comedy romance, *The Pleasure Garden* is set in the shady
backstage world of a London chorus line. Both novel and film
centre on two young female dancers and the near-starvation wages
that push them into the beds of those 'antiques, prowlers, gilded
youths and men of the world who are out for a good time and
nothing else'.[2] Filmed in 1926 when Marguerite's career was at its
height, *The Pleasure Garden* captured the essence of her storytelling
on celluloid. Its themes of murder, voyeurism, violence against
women (all of which would become familiar Hitchcock tropes), its
seedy London variety theatre setting and its touch of Burmese
exoticism,[3] are all sprung from Marguerite's pen.

Marguerite was writing about a world she knew well. Once an
aspiring actress who couldn't find work on the 'respectable' stage,

1

she followed that well-trodden route of struggling young actresses onto the chorus line. Her experience was to spark a string of chorus girl novels: *The Honey-Pot, The Ginger Jar, Vista, The Dancer, The Pleasure Garden* and others. Beyond the cheerful boy-meets-girl plot that the genre required, they revealed the darker side of a chorus girl's life: the squalor, poverty, drug abuse and sexual exploitation. In recent years, this once-forgotten film has been reassessed and its significance as the debut of that great auteur, Alfred Hitchcock, recognised.[4] Yet at the time of its release, the film's big draw was not Hitchcock, but the novel's bestselling author. Along with its charismatic American star, Virginia Valli, the name 'Oliver Sandys' was emblazoned in eye-catching capitals on cinema billboards across Britain.

I first encountered Marguerite in 2003 during a literature festival at Aberystwyth Arts Centre. There I attended a tour and talk on local author and *enfant terrible* of Welsh literature, Caradoc Evans, led by his biographer, John Harris. Our little group climbed into a minibus that rattled us along the narrow country roads, past chequered fields to our first stop: the whitewashed stone cottage in the village of Rhydlewis where Evans was born.

On our way back we stopped at the hamlet of New Cross, some five miles south of Aberystwyth, where Harris drew our attention to a house perched high above the road, half hidden behind a tangle of hawthorn and rhododendrons. This was Brynawelon, the house where Caradoc had lived, alongside his wife and stepson, for the duration of World War Two. His wife, Marguerite Jervis, was a bestselling author, said Harris, a romance novelist, theatre proprietor and – he raised his eyebrows as he said this – *quite* a colourful character. It was the kind of *quite* that contained volumes.

We piled out of the minibus and followed Harris down the hill to Horeb Chapel. For over a hundred years, it had served the village's Welsh Methodist congregation, but recently – like many Welsh chapels – it had been converted into a private home. Harris led us through the chapel grounds (now a private garden with a right of way for walkers) and up a steep muddy bank to the old chapel graveyard. There, set in the back row of the lichen-smeared gravestones, we stopped at a squat, granite headstone bearing the inscription 'Caradoc Evans'.

We learned from Harris that Caradoc was not buried there alone; that he shared it with his wife, Marguerite Jervis, the 'colourful' bestselling author he had alluded to earlier. Yet her name was not on the gravestone and few of us had heard of her. Although Marguerite had lived in and around Aberystwyth for some twenty years, it seemed she was now little known locally. Yet this bestselling author, theatre proprietor and larger-than-life eccentric did not seem the type of woman who could easily be forgotten. Her enormous veiled hats and scarlet lipstick, voluminous layers of brightly-coloured chiffon, and her collection of Indian bangles that jangled when she walked could not have failed to have attracted attention wherever she went.

New Cross is a pretty village with majestic views of the Pumlumon mountains. But I found it hard to imagine the colourful, attention-loving butterfly that Harris had described settling for such rural seclusion. But there she lay, resting anonymously alongside a man whose grave we had travelled miles to see.

As I later discovered, her fame had extended far beyond this corner of west Wales. During the course of a career that spanned more than half a century, she had been astonishingly prolific, totalling 149 books, many of them bestsellers, with eleven adapted for the cinema.[5] She was a household name, loved and read by millions of (mostly) women readers across the English-speaking world. Her books were even translated into Portuguese for her loyal following of Brazilian readers. Yet now she was all but forgotten.

Weeks, months later, my thoughts would return to that afternoon in Horeb graveyard, as I wondered how a woman who had once been so visible could have faded into such obscurity. That gravestone, and the unmarked space where her name was meant to be, would not leave me alone. I had to find out more about this once-famous, now nameless woman.

As I began my research, one of the first lessons I learned was that it was futile to try to discover the one 'true' version of her life. Marguerite's versions of events would often pay scant regard to the boundary between fact and fiction and could be as entertaining and distorted as any fairground hall of mirrors. Her life story, as told by her, reminded me of the old Japanese puzzle box I used to play with as a child. Whenever I solved one puzzle, another, more complicated one, would always pop up. Only with Marguerite there would be no hidden drawers at the centre, to spring open and reveal her 'real' story. There would only be only more puzzles, more contradictions to solve.

Her life, I concluded, was built on a series of contradictions. One of the highest earning women in the country, she had grown rich through promoting love and romance and, ultimately, dependence on a man; having herself resolved to 'never be dependent on a man', she was later in thrall to Caradoc, despite his abusive behaviour. An inveterate self-publicist and flamboyant attention-seeker, she would shut herself up in her study for years at a time. Democratic and snobbish, fragile and tough, compassionate and ruthless, the only constant was her irrepressible ambition.

A pampered daughter of the Raj, destined solely for marriage, she turned her back on her family to pursue her dream of making a name for herself, leaving home with only the vaguest idea of what career to pursue, let alone how to survive. Incredibly she pulled it off. She tore up the rulebook for upper-middle-class girls like her – and she did it with considerable style.

Once she discovered her talent as writer, she was unstoppable. She wrote as Oliver Sandys, the masculine identity that allowed her to risk the daring and the titillating. She also wrote as Countess Hélène Barcynska, an identity that merged patrician cachet with the exotic allure her younger self had dreamed of acquiring. Writing as Sandys and Barcynska, she made not just a name for herself but two.

'Sandys' and 'Barcynska' later emerged as two different 'brands'.

The heroine of a Sandys novel would be a spirited working-class girl (usually a chorus girl) who always bounced back from whatever life threw at her. In contrast, the Barcynska heroine was an upper-middle-class girl: a ballerina or violinist, or, more commonly, one who had fallen on hard times that had driven her into – yes, that's right – the chorus line. Despite their class differences, both 'Sandys' and 'Barcynska' shared a distinctive sense of humour; their heroines were as rebellious and irrepressible as Marguerite herself, with both adored by their devoted readers.

Marguerite had not always wanted to be an author. Her earliest ambition, to be an actress, had led her to join the first cohort of the Royal Academy of Dramatic Arts. Although failing to make her mark on the theatre, she never gave up on her dream of being on the stage. She walked away from everything, at the peak of her writing career, to go to Hollywood in pursuit of an acting role. As a woman in her forties, her hopes of breaking into the youth-worshipping film industry appeared deluded at best. Yet, once again, she confounded the odds. By landing a supporting role in the silent film *Stage Struck*, she assured herself a credit in a top-drawer production starring one of the greatest stars of her era, Gloria Swanson. For this role she adopted yet another name – Marguerite Evans – the surname borrowed from her lover, future husband, and the man with whom she now rests, Caradoc Evans.

As I discovered more about her life and achievements, her talent and her sheer bloody-minded will to succeed, it felt all the more poignant to think of her lying there, namelessly laid to rest. That day in New Cross, I could not have known the years of research that would follow – years of attempting to untangle the puzzles and paradoxes that surrounded Marguerite Jervis.

My research was also leading me on a journey through the forgotten story of popular women's fiction, the silent film industry and the 'golden age' of women's film, the early Edwardian days of variety, the heyday of the repertory theatre, and the shadowy world of mediums and seances. From her Indian colonial childhood, through her early multiple careers in theatre, film and Fleet Street, to her romantic 'escape' to Aberystwyth with Caradoc, to her impoverished later years, at every turn I was stumbling upon half-hidden worlds and stories of the early twentieth century.

Over her long career she proved herself to be a one-woman dynamo who rarely stopped writing. Her occasional bouts of depression – the only thing that came between her and her work – rarely impeded her for long. Even as she grew frail and her health declined, as tastes changed and her work fell out of fashion, she never gave up.

She wrote for a multitude of reasons. After spending her savings on theatre companies, luxurious cars and clothes and a succession of kept men, she wrote because her finances demanded it. She wrote for the pleasure it gave her loyal band of readers who were growing old with her. She wrote for the thrill of receiving letters from fans, urging her to write another book as soon as she could: for the exhilaration of knowing the pleasure a new Sandys or Barcynska would give them. She wrote because writing was her life. Since the age of twenty, when her first husband Armiger Barclay had instilled her with the discipline to follow a relentless writing regime, she had forgotten how to stop and rest. As long as there were women who would read her books, Marguerite would go on writing for them.

A few weeks after that visit to her grave, I wrote an article on Marguerite for the Welsh cultural magazine *Planet*, in which I asked how someone so remarkable, who had brought pleasure to millions of readers, could be so thoroughly erased from history. But for the question to make any sense, it had to be prefaced with a brief summary of her life and achievements. It was an almost impossible task which could not begin to do her justice.

The article was published in March 2003. I had naively assumed that my involvement with Marguerite would end there; that after I had shone a light on this unjustly forgotten woman, someone else would come along and pick up the baton.

A few weeks later, a letter arrived in the post. It came from a woman in her eighties who told me how pleased she was to see Marguerite Jervis remembered. Her books had meant so much to her, she said, had cheered her up during the war and had helped her through other difficult times in her life. Later, we arranged to meet at a Welsh Writing in English conference in Gregynog, near Newtown, which we were both attending. There she told me about her large collection of Oliver Sandys and Countess Barcynska books in her house in Presteigne and invited me round to see them. She said she wanted me to have them all. Then I realised she had assumed – correctly, in hindsight – that the article was part of a larger project: that I intended to continue my research on Marguerite.

As I was moving house and in no position to take up her offer, I urged her to donate the books to the National Library of Wales.[6] But before she did, I said I would love to accept her invitation to browse through her collection. Sadly, she passed away soon afterwards and the visit never took place. Yet to hear first-hand from one of her readers of the delight that Marguerite's books had given her filled me with a renewed conviction that she deserved to be remembered. One day, I told myself, someone would put that right and make her work and life more widely known. It was not until 2014, when I learnt that Honno was publishing an occasional series of biographies of unjustly forgotten women, that I began to think of Marguerite as a suitable subject for a biography. I was also beginning to realise that if I didn't write it then maybe no one would.

My research for the *Planet* article had previously led me to the sizeable collection of Marguerite's works, along with an archive of her correspondence and press cuttings, at the National Library of Wales. Although, it has to be said, it is unlikely that any of it would have survived if it had not been for her notorious and (in Wales, at least) well-remembered husband.[7] (This realisation is, I suspect, common among biographers of women married to well-known men.)

I began reading her works in the wood-lined hush of the National Library's North Reading Room. There I discovered that her publishing career had begun sooner than imagined: that five years before World War One the young Marguerite was already turning out risqué stories for dubious magazines. I discovered too that she continued to write into the 1960s: that her last novel – the hospital romance she completed on her deathbed in Shrewsbury Hospital – was published posthumously in 1964 as *Madame Adastra*.[8]

I also discovered that at the height of her career during the 1920s, her Sandys and Barcynska books were together averaging sales of more than 200,000 copies a title. When her publishers wanted her to complete at least one Sandys and one Barcynska a year, Marguerite obliged by becoming a one-woman production line, churning out the works of not one, but two prolific authors. Inevitably, such an arduous regime affected the quality of her work. Yet what was surprising was not that some of her work was uneven, but that despite working under such intolerable pressures, so much of it was so vibrant and engaging. Her publishers pushed her (and other women authors like her) to the limit. They viewed romance fiction as a frivolous product, of little value beyond the sales figures of her latest title, with little thought given to her need for rest and recuperation.

Her books were as loved by her readers as they were despised by anyone with intellectual pretensions. As literature they were considered fair game for detractors, even those who had not actually read them – especially those who had not read them. While some critics were more polite, there was no one who championed books like hers or recognised their cultural significance in the way that, say, George Orwell did with boys' comics.[9] Romance novels were read and adored by millions of women, yet were never considered to be of any lasting value. They were ephemeral: sweet islands of leisure and luxury, heady escapes from housework or shop work. To the maids, the shop assistants, the office and factory girls who read them, a romance novel meant a few hours of indulgent pleasure. They were consumed like boxes of chocolates, or, indeed, trips to the cinema. Romance was a genre that attracted a mix of gender- and class-based snobbery like no other. Even its readers had internalised the message that the books they loved were trash and the pleasure they derived from them was marred by feelings of guilt or even shame. And yet they continued reading.

Although romance was central to the story, books like Marguerite's also appealed because they offered the fantasy of female agency. In her stories the heroine might earn her own living, work on her own terms, as a dancer, or an actress, or musician, or simply spend each day charging up and down the North Circular in a sports car. She also had the freedom to pick and choose her future husband – a duke or a lord, perhaps, or simply the boy next door – so long as they were in love and her journey to marriage had been thrilling and glamorous, with her hands firmly on the steering wheel the whole time.

Marguerite was a virtuoso storyteller. She had to be. Holding the attention of her frequently tired, overworked readers, keeping them turning page after page until the end, demanded all the talents of a Scheherazade: talents that Marguerite possessed in abundance. As Caradoc once said of her, she could 'write like the Angels sing – without effort'.[10]

Marguerite had come of age reading sensation novels like *Lady Audley's Secret* by Mary Elizabeth Braddon. Scottish author Mrs Oliphant's heady mix of the domestic, the historical and supernatural also made its mark on her eclectic subject matter. Like Marguerite, Mrs Oliphant wrote unceasingly to support herself and her family – a habit that later prompted Virginia Woolf to bemoan the fact that she had sold 'her very admirable brain' and 'enslaved her intellectual liberty' to earn her living and educate her children.[11] Although Marguerite never mentions her by name, the eccentric Marie Corelli, a major influence on generations of romance authors that followed, would have certainly left an impression. Corelli, a bestselling romance author and inveterate performer, was adored by fans but reviled by critics as 'the favourite of the common multitude'.[12] From her, Marguerite would have imbibed an important lesson: that a carefully-constructed glamorous image would get a woman writer noticed.

But glamour alone was not nearly enough. Marguerite had to

work phenomenally hard to keep her readers coming back, producing story after story that would charm and delight, surprise and titillate. Nor did she shy away from the controversial: prostitution, illegitimacy, adultery, miscegenation and, most of all, the indignities endured (from a loveless marriage to a loveless kept-woman 'arrangement') by women with no economic independence were among the many 'social' themes in her work. The term 'romance novel' was itself a cosy euphemism for stories that dealt frankly with all of those themes. No wonder Marguerite claimed she wrote the kind of books that women would hide under the cushion.[13]

Despite her phenomenal success as an author of a maligned genre, she could not expect any recognition beyond the money she earned and the pleasure it gave her readers. Had she written for audiences other than working-class women, would she have been overlooked in her time, or so quickly forgotten after her death? This book is an attempt to make visible a woman who has all but disappeared. It is an attempt to shed light on an author who deserves not just to be remembered but celebrated.

Chapter 1
From Raipur to Reigate

Since as a small five-year old child sent home to England
... I had been lost ... feeling that I belonged nowhere.
(Oliver Sandys, *Full and Frank: The Private Life*
of a Woman Novelist)[1]

Tilbury Port, Essex, 1892

Two months had passed since she had boarded the steamer at
Mumbai. Yet its warm evening air, its street vendors' cries, its heady
scent of garlic and ginger would never leave her. Now, as she stepped
off the gangplank onto the foggy quayside, she carried her memories
of India with her. This was five-year-old Marguerite's entrance to
England: the country she had been told to think of as 'home' but a
place she barely knew.

Marguerite Florence Laura Jervis (known to her family by her pet
name Daisy and to her *ayah* back in India as 'Daisy Baba') was born
on 7 October 1886 in Henzada, Lower Burma (now Myanmar).
Then under British rule, it was deemed a region of India. Like all
colonials, her family would have thought of Britain – or England, as
they usually called it – as solid, unchangeable. But in reality the home
country was changing rapidly. The year before Marguerite's arrival,
St Hilda's College in Oxford had become the fourth women's college
in the country to open its doors. In the same year, Wales' first
university in Aberystwyth (the town where Marguerite was later to
live), with its declared intention to educate the sons (and daughters,
too) of coal miners, was incorporated by Royal Charter. With the

11

aim of improving literacy for the masses, the Elementary Education (School Attendance) Act had raised the school-leaving age in England and Wales to eleven. The year 1893 also marked the launch of the Independent Labour Party, chaired by Keir Hardie: a few months later, after troops fired on striking miners near Wakefield, killing two, the ranks of the party swelled. In the world of literature, Arthur Conan Doyle shocked his readers when, in a dramatic scene at the Reichenbach Falls, he sensationally 'killed off' Sherlock Holmes along with his serialised adventures in *The Strand Magazine*.

Back in colonial India, life carried on as usual: its British officials abiding by their own, increasingly anachronistic, version of British life. Following Britain's recent acquisition of Uganda, Marguerite's family and others who served the British Empire would have felt secure in its invincibility and certain that England, whenever they chose to return, would welcome and honour them accordingly.

There are no pictures of Marguerite as a child. In her memoir, *Full and Frank*, she describes herself as 'a tiny, dark-haired girl, young-looking for her age'.[2] Like the sickly, neglected Mary Lennox in Frances Hodgson Burnett's *The Secret Garden*, Marguerite's diminutive appearance was the likely result of fevers she had suffered in India. Also like Mary, she had arrived in England without her parents. The role of carer had fallen on her mother's older sister, Charlotte Chapman, Marguerite's Aunt Tots, who accompanied her on the passage.

A photograph of Tots from around this time reveals a pale, still young, woman with tightly curled hair and the beginnings of a premature stoop. The passage from India would have served as her initiation into the role of maiden aunt. Approaching her thirties and still unmarried, Charlotte had been charged by her sister and brother-in-law with the task of accompanying her niece to England. As a spinster (or 'surplus woman', as some would have unkindly called her), she had little choice but to attach herself to her married sister and strive to earn her keep by making herself useful.

From Tilbury, Marguerite and Tots caught the train to London's Charing Cross Station. In her memoir, Marguerite recalls a waiting room with a fire burning in the grate – the first time she had seen such a thing. She was so intrigued, that before anyone could stop her, she had put her hand in the flames to see what would happen. This, and the terrible pain that followed, would be her earliest memory of England.[3]

During those early years, she found little in England to comfort her. A flower uprooted from a sunny garden, she could not see how 'cold, grey England' could ever become her 'home'.[4]

Tots put her niece's unhappiness down to her missing her parents. In her attempts to console her, she would tell Marguerite that her Mama and Papa would be joining them soon, once they had 'tied up affairs'. Marguerite did not understand what these 'affairs' were or why they needed to be tied up. Perhaps they were dangerous, like the snakes that would invade their garden, or even the cobra she had once discovered coiled under her pillow in the nursery. Or were they mischievous, like the monkey who would swing on the branches of the tree by her verandah, or the Indian green parrot that would sing and chat outside her window and bathe in her foot pool when the servants' backs were turned? Or perhaps they were fierce, like the tigers that prowled outside the compound; only safe when shot, their heads securely mounted on the wall.

Unsurprisingly, Marguerite, who had spent little time in her parents' company, hardly missed them at all. It was Mootima, her *ayah*,[5] for whom she pined. She had been a constant presence in her life, accompanying her daily from first thing in the morning, when she would dress Daisy Baba, to the end of the day when she would lull her off to sleep with a story or lullaby in Hindi (a language that Marguerite was to later forget). If Mootima was her mother, then Yaseem and Suliman, who played games with her every day on the verandah, taking turns to fan her to sleep, were her brothers, and Francis, the Goanese butler who would smuggle bowls of half-melted ice cream to her from her parents' dinner parties, her favourite uncle.[6] Her servants were her world: her family, friends and playmates. But to Tots and others of her class, servants – Indian servants especially – were useful, but otherwise invisible.

With Mootima, Yaseem, Suliman and Francis as her willing, adoring satellites, Marguerite had been the star of her own orbit. It was all she had ever known and losing them was a shock from which she would never completely recover. Their absence left a void which neither Tots, nor anyone else, could fill. With her Indian servants, the infant Marguerite was the princess of her nursery; while in the company of her parents, she felt shy and insignificant. As was the custom of the English upper middle classes, she would only see them during their daily visit to the nursery at teatime, when Mootima would have to coax her into a starched dress, persuade her to sit upright at the table, and on no account scratch her prickly-heat rash. Her father, Colonel Henry Pruce Jervis, a surgeon in the Indian Army, demanded nothing less than impeccable behaviour from his daughter. For Marguerite, his visits felt like some cruel parlour game in which she had to second-guess the behaviour that was mysteriously expected of her. The punishment for getting it wrong – which she did often – was a severe scolding; or worse, the force of his hand.

Henry Pruce Jervis and Florence Mary Dorinda Chapman were married two days before Christmas in 1884, at St Thomas' Cathedral, Mumbai.[7] Florence was eighteen and Henry twenty-nine. The time and place would suggests it was a small and hurried affair, perhaps carried out soon after Florence's arrival in India, or possibly out of fear that any delay might prompt her to change her mind and board the next steamer back home, as sometimes happened. The cathedral was well known for its weddings of British colonial couples. Set inside the fortified walls of the British settlement, protected by the lookout post above the towering church gate, it felt solid and secure. To a young bride newly arrived from Britain, it gave the misleading impression that India was immutably secure under British rule – a little England beyond England. It was an illusion that was maintained by the most brutal means. Just beyond the church gate entrance, on the square the British called Bombay Esplanade, the dozen cannons defending the British settlement were also sometimes used for the execution of Indian insurgents. In a practice known as 'blowing from guns', the condemned would be strapped to the end of the barrel and the cannon fired directly through their body.[8]

There is no record of how Henry and Florence met, although it is likely that theirs was a perfunctory courtship. It is possible the couple had not met before Florence's arrival in Mumbai and had become engaged based on an exchange of letters and photographs. Maybe Florence sailed out with the 'fishing fleet', the unflattering name associated with those young unmarried women who travelled to India in search of a husband. It is more likely, however, that she was introduced to Henry in Britain, where he may have gone in search of a bride to take back to India, as was the custom among colonial men with established careers. As a surgeon of the 7th Bombay Infantry, having already risen to the rank of colonel, Henry would have made a distinctly eligible match – a fact that would not have been lost on the young bride's family. It was also well known that as an officer in the Indian Army he was likely to continue his rapid progress through the ranks. India was considered a land of opportunity, where a young man (and his bride) could rise up the social scale in a way that would have been impossible at home. Nor would Florence have been the first young woman to have fallen for the glamour of an officer and been swept away by the romance of an adventure in the Indian Raj, her head crammed with tales of giant rubies and tea in a maharaja's palace.[9]

Whatever her motives, they would have been considered of secondary importance to her family's desire to see their daughter safely married off to a man of means and status. Up until then, her life would have been sheltered and cosseted. Beyond learning to read, write and carry out basic calculations, her rudimentary education might have also taken in a little French, embroidery and just enough piano for her to entertain guests when required. Sheltered from the facts of life, she would have gone to her marriage bed knowing little about sex, pregnancy or childbirth.

Henry was among the tens of thousands of British men who, during colonial rule, had gone to India for a position in either the civil service, the police or, as he did, to take up a commission in the army. He went there during the height of the Raj, more than twenty years after the British had established their direct rule, in search of a higher rank and a lifestyle superior to anything he could have expected in Britain. Yet as those who went to India soon discovered, opportunity often came at a heavy price.

There is only one remaining photograph of Henry: a standard-issue regimental portrait, taken around the time of his marriage. He is wearing the full dress uniform of the Indian Army: the high collar and heavy woollen fabric, so ill-suited to the tropical climate it could almost have been carefully selected to make him look and feel as hot and irritable as possible. Having sat perfectly still for the photographer for fifteen minutes in the Burmese heat, time enough for the chemicals to etch his image onto the glass plate, it is no wonder that he looks ill-tempered. His thick, dark hair and smooth skin suggest a youngish man. His pince-nez glasses, straight-winged English moustache and formidable frown combine to create an impression of a perfect *pukka sahib*: the role demanded of an officer in the Indian Army. In India, even the humblest *chota sahib*[10] arrived straight off the boat would be expected to take on the responsibilities of someone ten years his senior back home. As George Orwell observed, the British officer in Burma 'wears a mask, and his face grows to fit it'.[11] Colonel Jervis' mask looks so firmly in place that it is difficult to imagine it slipping, even when off duty or at home with his family and his emotional, headstrong daughter with her febrile imagination. It is also easy to imagine him before his marriage, in sordid bachelor lodgings so common in imperial India as to have been a cliché, finding his comforts in gin and the clubhouse; to picture him taking part in those sports – tiger shoots, playing tennis, cricket or polo, or in the forest pig-sticking or jackal-shooting – so adored by the English in India. Like many officers, he might have followed the custom of the 'polls' and taken a local 'wife', with an understanding that, in lieu of a marriage certificate, the young 'bride' could expect a house for her family and, if children resulted, that the man would provide for them.[12] Perhaps, along with the majority of his colleagues, he had frequented the brothels in Bombay's red-light district, notorious among British soldiers, not least for the cases of syphilis that were associated with it.[13]

After the wedding, Henry and Florence would have travelled four thousand miles – almost certainly by rail – across India and into Burma.[14] A year later, a twenty-three-year-old Rudyard Kipling was to describe a similar journey in a series of letters to the *Pioneer* newspaper in India. In rapturous, lyrical prose he enthuses about this 'pleasant damp country where rice grew of itself and fish came up to be caught' and where 'two-thirds of your girls were grinning, good-humoured little maidens and the remainder positively pretty', concluding that any visitor would find Burma 'quite unlike any land you know about'.[15] It would certainly have been unlike any land that Florence would have known about. Nothing in her cloistered life could have prepared her for the beauty, or the dangers, of Burma.

Henry had been posted to the region during the tense run-up to the Third Anglo-Burmese War, which eventually flared up in November 1885 and was quickly suppressed by the British, who also seized on it as an opportunity to annex Upper Burma and overthrow Theebaw (Thibaw), the last king of Ava. Yet this did not mark the end of the Burmese armed resistance, which continued long after the war had ended, so lending weight to Marguerite's claim that she had been born 'under fire'.[16]

For the final stage of their journey, the couple would have taken the paddle steamer from Mandalay. Then, as safety demanded, they would have joined the British flotilla down the Irrawaddy River, sailing past a haze of rice fields, gleaming pagodas and majestic timber-carrying elephants onto the plains of the Irrawaddy Delta and to their marital home in Henzada.

During those early months, Florence would have encountered first-hand the well-known hazards of Burmese life: the blistering heat, the relentless humidity and the interminable buzz of mosquitoes and the ever-present threat of fatal diseases. She would have learnt to be vigilant against snakes, poisonous spiders, the occasional tiger, or, most terrifying of all, a rampaging elephant. More frightening still was the threat of attacks by local insurgent forces.

A threat of a more insidious kind was boredom. While Henry attended to his duties by day and his club by night, his young bride was expected to stay at home and preside over the retinue of servants on whom she now depended – a chasm of language, culture and snobbery dividing them. Even in her relatively modest bungalow, she would have had at her disposal a bearer, a *khitmagar* (butler), a *khansamah* (cook), a *messalgie* (pantry boy), a *bheestie* (water carrier), a sweeper, a gardener, a *chowkidar* (nightwatchman), and a number of *chokras* (boys). The birth of her first child would herald the arrival of an *ayah* and a host of nursery servants.[17] With staff on hand to carry out every conceivable task, there was little opportunity to distract herself with meaningful work. Other than arranging dinner parties for visiting officers and officials, there was little to do but supervise her servants and wait for sundown (or any earlier time deemed appropriate), when she could indulge in a *chota peg* or two of whisky or gin. Aged nineteen, this was her initiation into the role of *memsahib*.

While Marguerite wrote about her father at length, she had little to say about her mother. When she does mention her, the flesh-and-blood woman all but disappears in her misty-eyed accounts. In Marguerite's memoirs, Florence is largely absent. When she does appear, it is as a shadowy, elusive presence: a 'scent of lilies of the valley' or a pair of 'blue forget-me-not eyes'. She was a 'darling', concludes Marguerite, for whom 'the tending of children was just not her metier'.

That Marguerite, a writer who is normally so adept at describing characters, paints only the sketchiest of portraits of her mother, is revealing. Even by the standards of Florence's class and times, where the children of the upper middle classes were routinely raised by *ayahs* or nannies, she was an absentee mother. This Marguerite puts down to 'the strain of having a baby almost every year in that dreadful climate', which had made her 'very delicate'.[18]

But does this fully explain why Florence was so emotionally distant from her daughter? And in what way, exactly, was she so 'delicate'? As is often the case with Marguerite, she reveals more of her life in her fiction than she does in her memoirs. Pauline, the heroine of the part-comedy, part-psychological drama *We Women!*[19] – published around the height of Marguerite's career in 1923 – is a successful violinist who suffers from blackouts just before she is about to go onstage. When the attacks grow more frequent, she fears she has inherited them from her mother, who was committed to an asylum when Pauline was an infant and too young to remember. Eventually, she becomes convinced that she has inherited her mother's insanity. She also reflects that she has seen her mother so rarely that she cannot remember her face. This loss finds expression in recurring dreams in which she finds herself reunited with her mother. Increasingly, her waking self is overwhelmed by 'one long yearning for a mother's love':

> [T]he love that only a mother can give. As a child she often wept for the goodnight kiss that other children received, as a girl she had hungered for the maternal companionship she saw everywhere around her – envied it.[20]

Parallels between author and fictional heroine are not difficult to find; like Pauline, Marguerite battled with a lifelong depression which at times would lay her low and unable to function. Although she had been brave in revealing her periods of 'nervous exhaustion' (a term that would have been instantly recognised as code for a nervous breakdown), to expose also her mother's 'fragile' nature as mental illness may have been a revelation too far.

The shock of India after Florence's sheltered middle-class upbringing, combined with her marriage at eighteen to a cold and distant older man, would have been enough to crush the spirit of any sensitive young woman. Later, she endured the ordeal of losing a succession of children in infancy – four in total. It would have been surprising, after her experiences, if her mental health had *not* been affected.

All the privileges enjoyed by the British in India were not enough to shield their children from the threat of fatal illness. Whether it was cholera, typhoid or smallpox, parents of the Raj lived in the shadow of those 'dreadful scourges' that could snatch their children away from them overnight. The death of a child was a tragedy that left few families untouched.

Marguerite was one of the lucky ones: lucky to have been born at the start of the 'cold' season, arriving just after the monsoon and the fevers that came with it: luckier still to have been born stronger than her elder sister (and the family's first-born) who had died eighteen months previously at nine days old.

Marguerite's father was away in Raipur, the capital of Chhattisgarh, when she was born. As a soldier of the Raj, he was inured to being shunted from posting to posting, often with only a week's notice. Florence decided to remain in Henzada and have her second baby there. For the heavily pregnant Florence to remain behind, rather than join her husband on the gruelling two-thousand-mile journey by river and overland, would have been a sensible decision.

Tots, who had joined her in India, was also on hand to help. Although only in her mid-twenties, she would already have been consigned to the unenviable role of family spinster, to be pitied at best and, at worst, treated with contempt. It was rarely acknowledged that women like Tots were essential to the running of many middle-class families. Whatever sadness she may have felt about her new role, to judge by Marguerite's account she performed it with grace and dignity, as well as love. In the years that followed,

Tots became the linchpin of her family, the glue that held together the brittle, unhappy bonds between Florence, Henry, Marguerite and the surviving children that followed. To Marguerite, she was 'mother to us all, my own mother being such a girl'.[21]

Tots would also have been on hand to help and soothe during the family tragedies that followed. Three years after Marguerite was born, Florence gave birth to twins – a boy and girl – who both caught a fever and died in infancy. Just over a year later, Marguerite's sister Kathleen was born. She fell dangerously ill and died when only a few days old. Marguerite recalls in her memoirs how her parents had called for the padre to christen her: 'I couldn't understand why she should need a name if she was going to die, nor could I understand what death was.' When her mother explained that without a Christian name her sister could not be buried in a Christian cemetery and would not be able to go to heaven, it added confusion to her grief. 'It took me years to sort this out,' she said, 'and it made me think of God as someone not quite fair.'[22] Then, on learning that the 'small white box' that she saw the servants carrying had her sister inside it, she grew hysterical. 'Kathleen inside! Shut up and how could she breathe? I screamed and shrieked and kicked.'

In place of kindness, her father scolded her and pronounced her the 'child of the devil'. It was a name he was to call her many times over the course of her childhood, until she began to half believe it.[23]

Later, Marguerite added a codicil to her nightly prayers: 'Please God, don't let my mother have any more children.' Her prayers were not answered: a baby brother, Charles Arthur Bree Jervis, was born in 1892, less than a year after Kathleen's death. He was soon followed by another brother, Edmund Alfred Bree Jervis, who arrived the following year. Both survived.[24]

Then Marguerite caught a fever: a bad dose of malaria which made her delirious. It was then, she writes, that she first heard the 'Whispering Voice' that was 'quite real' and 'went on throughout the night and day'. It was this voice, she claimed, that dictated all her stories to her, to which she attributes her gift for storytelling.[25]

Like many lonely children, she had also found an imaginary friend – a girl who would appear in the mirror and hold long conversations with her. Marguerite called her 'Maggy Oliver', a name that later found an echo in the 'Oliver' of her most-used pen name, Oliver Sandys. Maggy also popped up as the heroine of her first bestseller, *The Honey-Pot*.[26]

She later claimed that 'Maggy' was named after her fictional heroine: the clever, wilful Maggie Tulliver in George Eliot's *Mill on the Floss*. It is easy to see how Marguerite would have identified with bright and wayward Maggie Tulliver. Both Marguerite and Maggie's parents feared the effects their daughter's intelligence and love of books might have on future marriage prospects. Yet as the lengthy, sophisticated *Mill on the Floss* would have proved too much of a challenge for even a precocious six-year-old reader like Marguerite, the Maggie Tulliver connection was probably made in retrospect.

Later, recovering from her illness, Marguerite left Raipur to recuperate. Along with her mother, brothers and a collection of servants, she joined the annual exodus of British women and children from Raipur to the nearby hill station of Panchgani in the Sahyādri mountains, reaching her destination by means of a 'three-day mule ascent, up the winding mountainside, changing mules at every stop'.[27] The uncomfortable journey proved worth it. With its 'beautifully cold and perfumed air', the 'wild roses in the hedges', and its abundance of strawberries, Panchgani was idyllic. For its British visitors, the gentle breezes and mild climate invoked bittersweet yearnings for English summers. In more practical terms, it served as a refuge from the heat and humidity of the monsoon and all the unwelcome diseases that accompanied it.

In her later years, these mountains remained imprinted on Marguerite's memory. When comparing her home in rural west Wales – with its sweeping view of the Pumlumon mountains – to 'the India of my childhood',[28] she would not have had in mind the bustling India of Raipur, or the rice paddies of the surrounding plains, but the green, majestic Sahyādri mountains.

When the season was over, Marguerite left the resort and returned with her family to the plains of Raipur, only to be struck low with malaria again. She claims it had prompted her parents to decide she had 'outstayed the health span for a child in India' and make plans to send her back to Britain as soon as she was strong enough.[29] There would have been nothing unique about this: most families of the Raj sent their children 'home' between the ages of five and seven. As the physician, Sir Joseph Fayrer, who had spent his career in the Bengal Medical Service, noted:

> It has long been known to the English in India that children may be kept in that country up to five, six or seven years of age without any deterioration ... but after that age, unless a few hot seasons spent in the hills should enable parents to keep their children in India until a somewhat later age, to do so is always a doubtful proceeding.[30]

Yet the patterns of infant mortality (and the four infant deaths in Marguerite's family alone) would contradict Fayrer's advice. A child's fifth birthday was a cause for celebration: a marker that, having outlived their infancy, they were far more likely to survive. So why would this highly-regarded physician recommend that British parents remove their children from India when they would have already outlived their most dangerous years?

This apparent paradox would have been readily decoded by Fayrer's contemporaries, as would his warning that children who remained in India beyond their fifth birthday might deteriorate 'physically and morally'. British parents in India did not send their children home so much on health grounds as they did out of fear they might pick up local customs or, worse still, 'go native' and adopt a local 'chee-chee' accent. To avoid this fate, parents sent children as young as five to live in England with relatives, or in a boarding school of often dubious quality, or to one of the commercially-run foster homes for children whose parents were posted overseas. Such were the values of the Raj.

Marguerite waved goodbye to her ayah, not knowing she would never see her again. In England, where she 'fretted and cried' all she had to remember her 'pretty Mootima' by was her parting gift of a pair of brightly painted glass bangles she had pulled off her wrist to give to her charge before she left. These treasures were too chee-chee to be worn in public and had to be hidden away. Only at night-time, under the cover of blankets, could she slide them on her wrist, shake her arm and listen to the brittle jangle that reminded her of Mootima.

For the adult Marguerite, the textures, smells and colours of those early years in India found expression in her love of flamboyant clothes and bold, clashing colours and, of course, the colourful Indian bangles that adorned her arms. She transformed her many homes – from manor house to red-bricked terrace – into shrines to her Indian childhood, with bright orange walls, statues of Buddha, bunches of marram grass and the heady scent of incense. Yet she never returned to the subcontinent, not even as a visitor. Her declared love of India never showed signs of being anything more than a taste in clothes, jewellery and decor. Nor is there any evidence in her writing of her interest in India beyond its mountains and the shaded verandah of her nursery, those jasmine-scented evenings and her mythologised, eternally adoring *ayah*.

Marguerite and Tots sailed to England by 'P. & O. in a great big liner'. The Peninsular & Oriental Steam Navigation Company carried almost everyone – soldiers, civil servants, shopkeepers, maharajas and missionaries – to and from India. Now that its liners travelled via the Suez Canal it had shortened the journey by more than a month, while the perilous waters of the Cape of Good Hope were avoided. Yet the dangers that accompanied any long sea crossing had not gone away. Only earlier that year, the disappearance of the White Star steamship *Naronic* en route from Liverpool to New York had been a salutary reminder of the perils of sea travel.

As members of an officer's family, Marguerite and Tots travelled first class, in one of the larger cabins on the cooler, shaded side of the ship. Yet even their first-class tickets could not protect them from the daytime heat and the hot humid nights which accompanied them, when everyone was forced to sleep on deck to keep cool.[31]

In the evenings, there was plenty of on-board entertainment – Egyptian magicians, snake charmers, Indian dancers, musicians – to help distract from the heat, or endless rounds of bridge or poker, or cricket, or sack races, while a few would be swept up in a shipboard romance.

While the children on board would entertain themselves by playing hide-and-seek or blind man's bluff or British Bulldog on deck, Marguerite would watch from a cautious distance. She was used to playing with adult servants, and her peers and their loud, boisterous games intimidated her.

Pampered yet homesick, spoiled but lonely, Marguerite must have made a difficult charge for the inexperienced Tots. Nightly she would cry for her *ayah*, only to be comforted by her aunt with a shy pat on the hand or an uncertain 'cheer up'. Reserved and undemonstrative, Tots was as different to Mootima as it was possible to be. Despite this Tots persisted. When Marguerite flew into yet another rage, her aunt would come and sit beside her, waiting for it to pass.

In England, their first stop was Bayswater, west London. With its grand houses and elegant white terraces, it had once been fashionable. But as the rows of peeling stucco now signified, the area had declined into a state of dreariness. Tots had taken a couple of rooms in one of the area's many lodging houses. It was the type of accommodation that catered for what Marguerite described as 'the not-quite-so-well-off middle classes',[30] most of them single women. The area was frequented by the kind of women that Saki (Hector Hugh Munro) observed in his Bayswater short story 'Cross Currents' – ones who busied themselves 'making laundry lists, attending bargain sales, and, in ... more adventurous moments, trying new ways of cooking whiting'.[32]

Had Tots been expecting something grander? In London, the fortunes of an area could change so rapidly that families in India would have little hope of keeping up. In Bayswater, she learned not to expect anything like the luxury she had enjoyed in India. Although it was only temporary, lasting no more than a couple of months, the lodgings hinted at more reduced circumstances to follow. Marguerite thought the boarding house 'hideous', 'full of stairs and dark, and I hated it'. While she may have sounded petulant, they were also childish expressions of a deeper distress. Later, recalling that period as an adult, she was, she said, a 'petrified child' wandering alone through a 'cold fog'.[33]

A few months later, Marguerite moved with Tots to one of London's more salubrious fringes: a place where they could live more cheaply, and so in grander fashion, than in central London. In the still-rural town of Bushey Heath, they secured what was to be the first in a series of rented homes. A succession of what Marguerite (perhaps generously) refers to as 'big commodious houses' soon followed – first in Southampton and later Reigate in Surrey – as they followed the relatively comfortable, yet itinerant trail of so many ex-colonials. They also had to adjust to having few servants with their retinue of dozens in India now reduced to an all-purpose housemaid, a 'good, plain' cook, and a versatile man who could serve as gardener, handyman and, eventually, chauffeur.[34]

Like the fictional Mary Lennox, Marguerite expected the same attentiveness from her new servants as she had received from those in India. With her surrogate family gone, it was hardly surprising that she directed love and attention towards their equivalents in England. When they rejected her, scolded her for being 'spoiled', it only added to her anger and confusion.

It was two years before Marguerite's parents joined her and Tots in England. Always distant figures, now, after their separation, she had all but forgotten them. Nor did their arrival do anything to improve her loneliness. Her mother was as remote as ever. Now with more time on his hands, her disciplinarian father imposed the strictest of regimes. Rather than viewing Marguerite's imaginary friend as a child's creative response to loneliness, he thought it an aberration. Concluding that his daughter had 'too much imagination', he decided on boarding school as its 'cure'.

Henry enrolled his daughter as a boarder at Miss Cowper's School for Girls in Herne Hill. Aged eight, and the youngest boarder by far, Marguerite recalls a 'great big house' with lawns and tennis courts and a cohort of some ninety girls. She was one of only sixteen boarders –and the youngest by six years.

Whatever Tots' or Florence's feelings on sending Marguerite away at such a young age, their views would have held little sway. No longer an officer in the Indian Army, or resident in a country where his race alone ensured a superior status, his home became his last bastion of authority. His life of luxury in India now over, ahead lay years of struggling to maintain the appearance of an upper-middle-class lifestyle on his modest military pension. Nor was the Britain he had returned to the country he had left, but a new, more upwardly-mobile place, where merchants and shopkeepers could leapfrog over ex-colonials like Henry. He had become a fossil, a 'Colonel Blimp', a figure of youthful ridicule. Yet among his family he could still command – and demand – respect.

Although her school days had not got off to a promising start, Marguerite recalls them with fondness. She also recalls her headmistress, Miss Cowper, if not with warmth exactly, then with respect and admiration. A strict disciplinarian she may have been, but she was also 'so absolutely just'. Under Miss Cowper's watchful eye, and away from her father's iron rule, Marguerite began to flourish and to 'work very hard'. She notes with obvious pride how, despite her poor grammar, she was soon coming top in examinations and that her essay 'The Tiger', which reimagines a tiger in the zoo as roaming free in its natural habitat of the Indian forest, was awarded a prize. Although the essay has not survived, it chimes with

Marguerite's lifelong love of animals and her passion for animal welfare. (In Wales, for instance, her insistence that dogs should be left free to roam drove a neighbouring farmer to almost shoot her beloved fox terrier Jock.)

Miss Cowper's also instilled in her a love of the stage. It was there she made her acting debut with a recitation of 'The Requital', with a recitation of 'The Requital', a popular, sentimental monologue by the Victorian poet and philanthropist Ann Proctor. 'Somehow,' she writes, 'a local reporter was present' to review it in the press. Even at eleven, it seems, she had a natural flare for making the press 'somehow' appear. Throughout her career, this extraordinary, unselfconscious instinct for self-promotion was to serve her well.[35]

Although Marguerite was getting into her stride at Miss Cowper's, she still missed Tots and would count the days to her next Sunday visit, when they would have tea in town together. It was during one of these visits that Tots sat her down and told her that her parents were to return to India for a year. Worse, Tots was to go with them. First Mootima, now Tots. Marguerite remembers a barrel organ playing in the street as she absorbed the news; how it made her feel as if it were 'grinding out my heart'. The year would pass quickly, her aunt tried to reassure her. There was little else she could say.

Marguerite's later claim that she spent the following summer with some 'very rich relatives' in the fashionable Welsh resort of Tenby suggests an attempt to paper over the truth. It was more likely that she simply stayed put at Miss Cowper's. Stories like hers were not unusual; Marguerite had joined those 'orphans of the Raj' who were deposited in boarding schools or foster homes, many of them inadequate, negligent or downright abusive. She was lucky, at least, to have been placed at Miss Cowper's, with its more enlightened approach to girls' education. Keen to nurture her girls' talents, Miss Cowper encouraged Marguerite to gain qualifications and eventually, perhaps, even go to university. Although smaller and, presumably, cheaper than the new progressive schools for girls, Miss Cowper's was modelled on the groundbreaking Cheltenham Ladies'

College. The school's aspirations for its pupils were in line with its grander counterparts, and the girls were encouraged to sit examinations that until recently had been the preserve of boys.[36]

This modernisation of girls' education had its opponents, many of them claiming that sitting examinations might cause a girl to overstrain herself or even damage her health. Perhaps the biggest obstacle to girls' educational advancement was complacency from many of the girls themselves. When a girl had been brought up to see getting engaged as soon as possible as her primary ambition, to persuade her to take examinations and qualifications seriously was often an uphill struggle. Although she later became a pioneering feminist, Vera Brittain recalls in her memoirs how her progressive headmistress struggled to convince not only her mother, but the young Brittain herself, that university was worth the effort.[37]

When Henry returned from India to find that Miss Cowper's had turned his daughter into a studious, 'bookish' child, far from being pleased, her academic progress troubled him. Convinced that few men would marry an 'over-educated' woman, intelligence was a quality he did not approve of in his daughter. Fearing that Marguerite was in danger of 'wasting' those fleeting marriageable years between the ages of sixteen and twenty on education, he decided to act. Even though she was still only twelve, Henry was keen to remove any thoughts of exams and university from his daughter's head. There was only one certain way of doing this – to remove her from Miss Cowper's immediately.

There was also another motive behind Henry's actions, one which his bright daughter had surmised. His limited resources were already committed to her brothers' school fees. To also have a daughter with academic aspirations was the last thing his finances needed.

While her brothers were sent to prep schools and primed for public school, their sister was to be, as Marguerite bitterly remarked, 'finished off more cheaply' at a boarding school a few miles from their current home in Radlett, spotted by Henry in the local paper:

Two Educated Gentlewomen (daughters of Army officer) will receive into their large private house a strictly limited number of girls, ages 10-16, whose parents are abroad and who require healthy home conditions combined with social advantages. Foreign languages, music and dancing. Social references given and required.[38]

The classified columns of the press – especially those papers that catered for an overseas readership – were filled with advertisements like this: from the boarding school in Devizes in Wiltshire, for 'Girls whose Parents have to live Abroad', which listed 'Bracing air, Garden, &c.' as its main attractions,[39] to St Kilda's Home School for Girls in Bath, which offered board and lodgings for 'limited numbers of the Daughters of Gentlewomen to educate with their own'.[40] Few of them listed among their attractions any examinations or academic qualifications.

Often unregistered and run by unqualified staff, some were not so far removed from the nightmarish boarding schools that had gripped the mid-Victorian imagination. As their readers would have known, the gothic horrors of Dotheboys Hall in *Nicholas Nickleby* and Lowood's regime of terror in *Jane Eyre* were barely fictionalised accounts of real-life atrocities.[41]

Although it was fifty years later, Marguerite's account of her time at the school of the 'Educated Gentlewomen' would not have seemed out of place on the pages of Dickens or Brontë. The contrast between her new school (which Marguerite does not name, presumably for reasons of libel) and Miss Cowper's could not have been more marked. She had just stepped out of a new, more enlightened age, and into all that was worst about Victorian education: a nightmare of a place where pupils existed on a semi-starvation diet of bread and 'something that was perhaps dripping or lard' – a diet that kept pupils 'subdued into a state more abject than timidity'.

Iris James, a contemporary of Marguerite's who had also been sent 'home' from India as a child, testifies to a strikingly similar experience when she was left at a vicarage at Potten End, run as a home for children of the Raj. Just like Marguerite, James' overriding memory was one of permanently feeling half-starved. For James, it was a torture that she endured for two years, until her mother came to visit and, finding her in an emaciated state, removed her immediately.[42] Marguerite's new school quickly turned her into 'a wreck of a child', with conditions so unbearable that at one point she even considered suicide, although fortunately she couldn't 'summon up the courage to sever an artery with a pair of blunt scissors'.

Marguerite's nightmare school narrative reaches its climax when, in desperation, she crept out of bed one night and climbed out of the first-floor window. Despite falling and spraining her ankle, she claims to have endured a five-mile walk through a blizzard until she reached the family home. 'Though it was painful,' she offers, 'I would have gone on my way even if it was on my hands and knees.'[43]

Given the documentary evidence of that period, the school's brutal regime is all too believable. Yet with no other evidence to hand, it is impossible to unravel the fact from the fiction behind her gung-ho escape, which reads a little too like a girls' adventure story to be entirely credible. As likely as it is that she embellished the story, or even that it was fictional from start to finish, the unquenchable spirit of the little girl prepared to walk five miles through a blizzard is characteristically Marguerite's.

She writes that, on her return, her father had not been 'so angry after all' at her escape.[44] Finding his daughter in an emaciated state would have, after all, been enough to soften the heart of even this strictest of fathers. It might even have made Henry feel guilty. Perhaps he was also secretly pleased at his daughter's homecoming. Newly retired from the Indian Army, yet still only forty-seven, his daughter's return gave him a new role as her self-appointed tutor. And so Marguerite's haphazard education continued at home. Aged fourteen and starved of educational rigour at the gentlewomen's house, she struggled to adapt to her father's methods of teaching

Latin and arithmetic by rote. 'He was impatient and no wonder,' she writes, 'for howsoever hard I tried I could not master compound fractions or get my declensions right.'

It was then that Marguerite saw another, surprising, side to her father's personality. Having 'abandoned all hope' of teaching his daughter maths or Latin, he turned instead to the more esoteric subjects of palmistry and graphology. Such interests were common among his generation. Rosa Baughan's ever-popular book, *Character Indicated by Handwriting*,[45] for example, could be found on the shelves of thousands of middle-class homes. While Baughan's book sensationally analysed the signatures of luminaries from William Shakespeare to Marie Antoinette, the London-based 'celebrity palmist' Cheiro (the professional name of Irishman William John Warner) was renowned as palm reader to a dazzling list of living celebrities, including Oscar Wilde, Thomas Edison, the former prime minister William Gladstone and even the Prince of Wales.[46]

Her otherwise rational father's expertise in such esoteric arts did not strike his daughter as strange or surprising. Nor did she see any contradiction in a retired officer of the Raj, with an unquestioning belief in British superiority, now revealing himself as a devotee of palmistry, a craft rooted in Hindi culture and one that Cheiro himself had learnt from a Brahmin guru. The teenage Marguerite was too captivated by the heady promise of mystery and allure to concern herself with such contradictions. Her father's lessons were to ignite her lifelong fascination with the occult. In turn, this developed into her idiosyncratic blend of spiritualism and Celtic mysticism which became a recurring theme in her later works. This new, peculiar, brand of education also marked a turning point in her relationship with her father. With this fascination in common, the remote, sometimes frightening patriarch of her childhood now appeared not so stern after all. As his rigid mask slipped, Marguerite began to see the human face beneath it.

Yet she had no illusions. Henry's objective to get her married off as soon as possible held firm; his belated interest in her education was also a way of keeping her amused until she had secured a suitable match. He and Florence were already making enquiries to that end among their circle of family and friends.

Horrified at the prospect of getting married and doing 'nothing at all except have babies', Marguerite resolved she would do anything to escape that fate. Yet she had no illusions. Escaping that 'backwater oblivion where one spent the rest of one's life as "some man's Mrs Someone"' would not be easy. She must plan it carefully.[47]

Her midnight dash from boarding school was nothing compared to the elaborate getaway she was now plotting. This time her escape, she had decided, would be to the stage and a career in acting. She had loved performing at Miss Cowper's, had thrilled at having an audience, and had adored holding the attention of an entire room. What could be better than repeating that moment over and again by performing for a living? Surely it would feel almost as warm and joyous as those times back in India, where her doting servants would stop their chores to watch and applaud her antics. Acting, she hoped, would give her all the love and attention she craved.

Marguerite was not the first middle-class girl to have dreamed of escaping her stultifying home for the glamour and freedom of the stage. For most it remained a dream. For Marguerite, it was a serious and urgent plan. The stage would be her route to success and, more importantly, to independence. She knew that persuading her father, who viewed the theatre as a young woman's surest path to damnation, would not be easy. Yet she *would* persuade him – she *must* persuade him. The dispiriting prospect of a 'bed and board marriage', the tiger trap that she knew was being set for her, made failure unthinkable.[48]

Chapter 2
From 'Cage' to Chorus Line

One hears a lot about the chorus-girl being on the make-haste and living you-know-how. One doesn't hear how she's driven to it, like cattle into a dirty pen.
(Countess Hélène Barcynska, *The Honey-Pot*)[1]

The boarding house could not have been more convenient. Set in one of Bloomsbury's Georgian tree-lined streets, it was only a five-minute walk from the newly established Academy of Dramatic Arts, where the nineteen-year-old Marguerite was about to enrol.[2] The landlady, a pleasant middle-aged woman, led Marguerite and her aunt upstairs to a small attic bedroom. With a pretty rose-patterned eiderdown and a charming view of the back gardens, Marguerite thought it quite delightful. Now all that was left for her to do was to wait for Tots to approve it and then leave her alone to thrill at her new-found freedom. This was the culmination of years of dreaming, weeping, plotting, wheedling and cajoling: years when she felt 'as wild for freedom as any wild bird in a cage': the result of the promise she had made to herself that she would never marry or live the confined life that came with it.

The year was 1905 and Marguerite was just emerging from her chrysalis. With the Victorian taboo against middle-class women travelling alone having recently melted away, it was now acceptable even for 'respectable' women to travel, unescorted, by bus or train, while the most daring of them rode around on the new, affordable passport to freedom: the bicycle. In recent years it had even become possible, in theory at least, for a woman to earn her own living. Seeing how the weather was changing, Marguerite wanted her place in the sunshine. To achieve it she had determined to gain her father's permission to pursue her dream of a stage career. Yet it seemed impossible that Henry – the strict, Victorian-minded father – would ever agree to his daughter embarking on a career which he saw as only a step or two away from prostitution. As the clock ticked and the prospect of the marriage her parents had planned for her grew ever closer, Marguerite treated this as the fight of her life – which, in a way, it was.

Marguerite had already broken the news to her father that she had no intention of marrying. If she wasn't going to marry, he told her, she would train as a hospital nurse. Nursing – in the world view of the retired army surgeon – was the only noble occupation for an unmarried woman. But there was only one kind of theatre for Marguerite and it was not a surgical one.

Not daring to confess her acting ambitions to her father, she confided in her mother instead. Florence's response was not encouraging; she said that Henry would rather see his daughter dead in a coffin than acting on the stage. Daisy going to London alone? Was she mad? Did she want to end up a 'white slave'?[3] But nothing – not even the perceived risk of enforced prostitution – could steer her away from her fixed ambition.

Marguerite knew if she was to overcome her father's resistance, she had to be audacious. She also decided that she needed a professional mentor: a woman who had carved out an illustrious career for herself on the stage. Undeterred by fame or celebrity, she wrote to the leading grande dame of the theatre, Ellen Terry, seeking advice on how to achieve her ambition to become an actress. In her sixties and the proprietor of London's Imperial Theatre, Terry was that rare thing: a woman who had succeeded not only as an actor, but also the proprietor of her own theatre.[4]

Terry replied. Although it was not the answer that Marguerite had been hoping for, but a stark warning that she should not pursue a career on the stage unless she was prepared to trudge 'pilgrim-like', for many years, 'over stony ground'. It was the same dose of harsh medicine that Terry had administered to decades of aspiring actors, most of them female. Marguerite did not swallow it. Instead, she chose to dwell on the glamorous letterhead on Terry's letter, with its fashionable Chelsea address embossed in gold, as if it were a talisman of her future success. Perhaps to sweeten the pill, Terry's letter ended with a vague invitation to 'come and see me in London'; Marguerite interpreted her words as a firm appointment that might lead directly to an acting engagement. There was just one problem: how could she go to London without her father's permission?

She was to find the answer in his copy of *The Daily Telegraph* – in an article about the launch of the new Academy of Dramatic Art, founded by the renowned actor-manager Herbert Beerbohm Tree. 'If Paris can boast of her conservatoire, London, at length, is able to point to her Academy of Dramatic Arts,' it began, before listing the theatre aristocracy – J.M. Barrie, W.S. Gilbert, Irene Vanbrugh, H.B. Irving and others – who had attended the glittering opening ceremony at His Majesty's Theatre in London's Haymarket. The acclaimed playwright and director Arthur Pinero, who could not be there, sent a telegram: 'Pray count me an enthusiastic supporter of your school,' he wrote, adding, 'I beg you to call upon me for any practical help you may think me capable of rendering.' Pinero was to number among the theatre celebrities who served the Academy as visiting lecturers. Terry herself sent a telegram, which was read aloud on the evening: 'Our art like any other cannot be practised without training,' she wrote. 'I hope that your training ground will produce many fine personalities, fine imaginations and fine industry.'[5] Marguerite determined to become one of their future 'fine personalities'.

While persuading her father was never going to be easy, at least the Academy had the benefit of being a respectable route to the stage. It should, given its illustrious supporters, be a place where middle-class parents might send their star-struck daughters without undue fear of molestation. Later she was to find another argument to back her cause: Beerbohm Tree's daughter, Viola, was to study at the Academy. Surely, Marguerite reasoned, no father would send his daughter to a place where she would be seduced, let alone kidnapped or sold? But she knew that persuading Henry would be no easy task. There was also another obstacle to her ambition – the Academy's 'very thorough stage grounding' did not come cheap and Henry's army pension did not stretch as far as he might have hoped.

Then along came an unlikely saviour in the flamboyant form of the tea and grocery magnate Sir Thomas Lipton, at fifty-seven all of seven years older than her father. Marguerite had met him, she tells us, via a friend in Southampton 'who had a racing yacht'. The cage of her home, as she carefully explains, 'was a cage against which another cage was set so that I could flit from one cage to another' – perhaps hinting at a social life somewhat livelier than the impression she had given.

Apart from her own unreliable account, there are no other records of her association with Lipton. Yet his reputation as an inveterate socialite who surrounded himself with young people adds credence to her story. Lipton was also known for being generous to the point of extravagance. His astonishingly large donation of £25,000 to the Princess of Wales' Diamond Jubilee Fund in 1897 to provide a Jubilee dinner for the poor made him a well-known figure in the newspaper society columns.

Was Lipton the model for the expansive generosity that caused Marguerite much hardship in later life? It would not have been the only characteristic the two had in common. Both were mavericks who lived and breathed contradictions: Marguerite a fervent patriot and equally fervent pacifist, and Lipton, an Ulster Protestant tturned Irish nationalist, who had made friends with everyone from royalty to revolutionaries.[6] Both were dazzling weavers of stories and irrepressible self-publicists with a cavalier approach to the truth. Both had a gift for inventing, and reinventing, their personas.

Marguerite, adept at slipping in and out of different identities, was to become in turn actress, author, theatre producer and spiritualist mystic; Lipton 'quite literally invented himself' by adopting a persona that was 'nothing like the real person'.[7] No wonder they were so drawn to each other.

Although Lipton was also known as a womaniser, Marguerite insisted there was no more to their relationship than friendship. 'I suppose my appearance interested him,' she teased. 'I was a spectacular-looking girl and I dressed in a style that caused my father to rave – in anger. Enormous hats, highest heels, vivid colours, feather boas, silk petticoats (the kind that rustled). I was very slim and graceful.' While 'Sir Thomas did have an eye for a pretty girl', Marguerite insists that 'he was no ogre or baby-devourer', just a man who 'liked the society of young and gay people' and 'enjoyed most the society of chorus girls and stable boys'.[8]

Lipton had indeed entertained the bright young things of his day, boasting Princess Patricia of Connaught, King Alfonso of Spain and Kennedy Jones 'the newspaper man' among his regular guests. Yet despite her teasing hints to the contrary, Marguerite's assertion that 'he never made any silly overtures' may well have been true. Lipton's carefully cultivated reputation as a playboy provided a convenient smokescreen for his sexuality. Around the time he met Marguerite his thirty-year relationship with one of his former shop assistants, William Love, was coming to an end. Rumours of Lipton's numerous other affairs with young men – including an orphan he met when on a cruise around Crete – were rife among those who knew him well.[9] However, it was a closely guarded secret that few beyond his inner circle were aware of, least of all Marguerite's mother, who wholeheartedly approved of her daughter's new friendship.

When Lipton's open-topped sports car (an Itala, as the car-loving Marguerite, who later indulged herself with a succession of expensive sports cars, was keen to point out) turned up at Marguerite's house with instructions for the chauffeur to take her for dinner with its owner at the South Western Hotel, her mother was delighted. Nor did she appear concerned that her seventeen-year-old daughter was being pursued by a man approaching his sixties with a reputation as a playboy. Lipton was a millionaire, and a titled millionaire at that: enough, it seemed, to blind her to everything but her daughter's golden ticket into high society – and a glittering world of yachts and villas.

When Lipton later accepted their invitation to tea, it caused great excitement in the Jervis household, particularly as he had also requested an audience with Henry. To Florence and Henry, this could only mean one thing: a request for their daughter's hand in marriage.

Picture it. A tall, greying, but (as her mother would no doubt have insisted) still handsome millionaire: top hat on head, silver cane in hand, sipping tea from one of the family's best bone china cups, sitting on the best (although somewhat faded) chair, surrounded by the newly polished teak and rosewood. Lipton was indeed planning to seek her father's permission, but not in the way her mother was so eagerly anticipating.

Henry's audience with Lipton did not go well. While he felt an innate 'contempt for shop people howsoever rich they might be', he was also more than willing for Lipton to marry his daughter. But Lipton had come with a different proposal: an offer of paying Marguerite's fees so she could attend the Academy of Dramatic Arts.

A tight-lipped Henry 'thanked him very much and declined'. Instead of this wealthy bachelor wanting to marry his daughter, he had come to set her on the most undesirable of paths. And what of Sir Thomas's relationship with his Daisy? If he did not intend to marry her, what was she to him that he was offering to keep her in this way? And how dare this upstart, this jumped-up shopkeeper, assume that he, Henry, who had served the Queen in the Indian colony, was unable to support his own daughter in her chosen occupation. This attitude would have come as no surprise to Lipton, whose humble background and vast wealth sometimes attracted a toxic mix of envy and snobbery. As a tradesman, he had never been fully accepted by his wealthy peers. Although one of the leading yachtsmen of his time, his local yacht club had recently refused his application for membership on the grounds that they did not accept tradesmen.

Henry had returned from India to find a very different Britain from the one he had left, with social mobility the order of the day. Now, in front of his own fireplace, in his small, overstuffed parlour, this jumped-up shop clerk was a striking signifier of his family's – and his class's – fall in fortunes.

When Henry was serving in India, Lipton had gone there to buy and sell tea – the commodity on which he was to build his fortune. Eventually purchasing 5,000 acres of plantations in Ceylon, he grew his business to become one of the largest tea, coffee and provision dealers in the world. This, and the chain of grocery stores that he had also established, combined to make him one of the richest men in Britain.

Back in India, Lipton would have been called a 'box-wallah' – a tradesman, and so at the bottom of the white social hierarchy; someone Henry might have to tolerate in his club, but would never invite home. Now he was Henry's social superior. Worse still, Lipton had humiliated him by implying that he could not afford to support his daughter. How dare he wave his money around like some overexcited shopwalker at a Whitsun fair! If his daughter wished to take the road to perdition, well, that was her affair, but he would not allow that man to treat him as if he were another of his charitable causes.

It is likely that this was exactly the response that Sir Thomas – who had not grown wealthy without a good helping of shrewdness – had anticipated. It was also likely that Lipton's visit was a ruse to help his amusing, wayward, star-struck young friend get her own way. If this was the plan, it had worked like a dream. Marguerite's father relented, giving his permission for her to sit the Academy entrance examination and agreeing to pay for the course if she passed. While Marguerite compared her father's sudden change of heart to 'some sort of miracle', it was likely to have been prompted by nothing more miraculous than a simple attack of wounded pride.

Bloomsbury, London, September 1909

Tots' departure was accompanied by a series of predictable warnings: Marguerite was never to flirt and was not to trust any man, 'however nice he may seem'. As Marguerite nodded, she would have struggled to hide her mounting excitement. London! At last! The city where she would 'Make a Name' (always with capitals): where a determined, ambitious and beautiful enough young woman could succeed. From now on, she would no longer be plain old Marguerite Jervis and she would certainly not be Daisy. She had already selected her stage name: Olive Bree. It was short, modern and would sit well in large letters at the top of a theatre billboard. 'Olive' was a nod to Olive Schreiner, the archetypal New Woman who, in her novel *The Story of An African Farm*, had railed against the limited life-choices that women were given. Author, anti-war campaigner and role model for any self-respecting rebellious young woman, Schreiner was revered by Marguerite.[10]

After Tots had left, a tapping at the door jolted Marguerite from her reverie. It was her new landlady, freshly made up, with a cup of tea in hand, come to see how she was settling in. 'If there's anything you want, my dear – anything at all – just ask. Think of me as another aunt.' Just broken from her family's clutches, Marguerite had no interest in finding another aunt. It had been a long, exciting day and who knew what might happen in the morning. But for now, all she wanted was to go to sleep.

She sat up with a jolt. In the darkness she could make out a figure, crouching over her bed. It was a man: an old, grey-bearded man and he stank of whisky. It must be a nightmare. She knew it wasn't.

'Get out!' she cried.

He agreed he should go, but not before he had told her exactly what kind of 'boarding house' she was staying in. After he left, he insisted, she must lock the door, then she must leave first thing in the morning. His voice was severe, reproachful, as if the incident were somehow her fault.

41

Marguerite decided she would not tell Tots, at least not for a while. She didn't have the heart to tell her that 'she had so carefully selected a brothel'.[11] This type of scenario, where an innocent girl accidentally stumbles into prostitution, would later become a common motif in Marguerite's early writing, most strikingly in *The Pleasure Garden*, *The Honey-Pot*, *Vista the Dancer* and her other 'showgirl' novels. Given that her parents had been eager to pair her with the much older Lipton, in exchange for a comfortable, although loveless, bed-and-board marriage, this preoccupation with prostitution is not so surprising. To Marguerite, the prospect of a woman selling her body outside of marriage, instead of within it, was not such a huge conceptual leap.

Marguerite joined the Academy of Dramatic Arts in 1907. She was among the first cohort of sixty students (forty-eight women and twelve men). From its inception, she had eagerly followed its progress in the press, yet had not stopped to consider how demanding the training would be. Its celebrity founder, Beerbohm Tree, insisted on nothing less than complete dedication from his students and would daily put them through an intensive drilling in elocution, recitation, movement and mime. Marguerite, stunned by this strict regime, decided she would skip a couple of classes. But Beerbohm Tree would not tolerate absenteeism. Summoning Marguerite to his room, he warned her that if she missed any more classes she would have to leave. It worked. The prospect of being sent back home jolted her into taking her lessons more seriously. Yet her star was never fully to shine. Despite her doubtful claim that, during their first-year production of Pinero's *The Second Mrs Tanqueray*, she was cast in the lead role of Paula Tanqueray, there is nothing to suggest that she had demonstrated any exceptional talent for acting.

Fortunately, she was imbibing other skills – skills she was not yet aware of. Beerbohm Tree's eclectic repertoire was instilling in her a feeling for plot and character, an understanding of the importance of mixing humour with pathos. In Du Maurier's *Trilby*, she discovered the bohemian world of Paris and a heroine who was happy to be a 'bachelor woman'; in Ibsen's *An Enemy of the People* she met a hero who dared to expose hypocrisy and follow his own moral code. But it was *The Second Mrs Tanqueray* that resonated most strongly. This highly charged drama about the upper-class Tanqueray's marriage to the much younger, sexually experienced, working-class Paula (a name that Marguerite was to later adopt for a number of her heroines) puts social class and sexual hypocrisy (the double standards for men and women in particular) at centre stage. This 'woman with a past' theme, beloved of Victorian theatre and literature, was to find its way into Marguerite's fiction – only with a twist – beginning with her first Oliver Sandys novel, *The Woman in the Firelight*,[12] where in place of the required tragic ending (as retribution for her past indiscretions), Marguerite decides to give her heroine another chance of happiness. Through Ibsen, Pinero and other playwrights, she learned that morals change according to the times and that the job of an artist is to challenge current morality, especially as it applies to women. Taking these values from the bohemian world of the theatre, she eventually imported them into the far more conventional genre of romantic fiction, where traditionally a heroine was either innocent or, if she had a past, would ultimately pay for it with her life.

In her final year, Marguerite performed at His Majesty's Theatre, where she was cast as a slave girl in Herbert Beerbohm Tree's *Nero*. This was a professional production in which Beerbohm revived the title role for which he was famous, but he also produced it for the benefit of his students, for most of whom it was their first taste of being on the professional stage. Marguerite was required to perform a 'wriggle-stomach' sort of a dance, her costume 'a gold brassiere and a flowing transparent skirt'. (Fortunately for her, her easily outraged father did not attend, claiming that he lived too far away.)

At the end of her second and final year, she landed another minor role in *The Merry Wives of Windsor*. This time she found herself performing alongside her heroine, Ellen Terry, who only two years previously had replied to Marguerite's fan mail, warning her of the pitfalls of a career onstage. Now suffering from the early stages of dementia (a disease which was to haunt her later years), Terry's memory was beginning to fade. Marguerite recalls how she would pin her lines on the back of scenery and props then, forgetting where she had hidden them, would dash around backstage searching for them. Despite this, writes Marguerite, 'she was always at her entrance in the nick of time' and no one in the audience would have guessed the difficulty she was labouring under.

As the Academy course drew to a close, some students had already found paid engagements and were taking their first steps into successful careers. Marguerite's fellow student, Muriel Alexander, was to return to South Africa, where she forged a career as an actress, producer and founder of the Johannesburg Repertory Players. Another alumna, Dorothy Holmes, found leading roles in the burgeoning silent film industry: a career that also survived the arrival of the new 'talkies'.

Marguerite was not so fortunate. With no work lined up, she faced the prospect of having to go back to her parents' house with nothing to show for her training but 'one medal, a few prizes and no job'. It was hardly the shining route to success that she had been dreaming of. True to form, she had a contingency plan: she had been saving up her father's weekly allowance in order to support herself, at least for a few months, until she landed a theatrical engagement.

Marguerite had also used some of her father's money to pay to put on a solo performance at Steinway Hall in London's Marylebone. To promote it she had deployed sandwich men to tramp up and down the West End streets, with her stage name of Olive Bree emblazoned on billboards. Marguerite concludes, cheerfully but briefly, that the venture was a success, with the concert enjoying a full house and good press.

Other findings suggest that the reality was not quite as Marguerite recalled it. While the concert was indeed in Steinway

Hall, it was in one of the tiny concert rooms – one among a warren of rooms available for hire. She also fails to mention the less than effusive *Daily Telegraph* review. The 'reciter, Miss Olive Bree', performed to an 'audience of moderate numbers' a repertoire ranging from Shakespeare to a piece by the poet Adelaide Procter.[13] While praising the young performer for her 'taste and commendable restraint', along with her audience that 'extended no lack of encouragement', it concludes that the event was 'scarcely marked by any distinguishable qualities'.[14]

Although she did not admit it, at least not directly, it seems that Marguerite fell victim to confidence tricksters. Naïve and ambitious to the point of delusion, she would have made easy prey for criminals. One of the stories in her crime caper, *Chicane*[15] – a picaresque romp involving the adventures of a duo of female confidence tricksters – hints at her first-hand experience, with one of the ruses employed by the confidence artists (the morphine-addicted Lady Weybridge and her young female accomplice) bearing a striking resemblance to Marguerite's Steinway Hall episode. Posing as theatrical agents in search of fresh talent, they place a notice in the press, inviting hopefuls to book an audition. The fraudsters then flatter their victim, assuring them their talent is so exceptional they will arrange a solo concert for them at a prestigious location. The concert will, of course, involve an upfront fee, but this, the victim is assured, will be an 'investment', as a flurry of producers' offers will be sure to follow. The scam is described in such intimate detail, right down to the Steinway Hall venue, that it is not a huge leap to imagine that those details were gleaned from Marguerite's own hard experience.

It was a cruel trick: one that would have been enough to crush the hopes of all but the most determined. But Marguerite was not to be defeated. The dispiriting prospect of returning home as a failed actress only sharpened her determination. Daily she would catch the omnibus to Garrick Street near Covent Garden to haunt Blackmore's Theatrical Agency in search of an elusive appointment, inuring herself to Charles Blackmore's daily refrain of 'No dear, I've got nothing for you today' and becoming adept at sidestepping the secretary in order to see him in person. She had acquired that essential attribute of the theatrical profession: an exceptionally thick layer of skin.

During one of her daily visits to the agency, Marguerite struck up a conversation with the beautiful teenage girl sitting next to her, who told her she had found work as a film actress. Marguerite was intrigued. Film was barely in its infancy and she had never considered it as a means of earning a living. Then the secretary called the girl to her appointment: 'Miss Gladys Cooper, Mr Blackmore will see you now.' Soon afterwards, the girl in the agency would move to Hollywood, where she rose to become one of the biggest stars of the silent screen. Cooper was one of the few agency hopefuls who did not need to listen to the polite brush-off that Marguerite would get every day. It was difficult enough for male actors to find work, Blackmore would tell her, but when women outnumbered them by around nine to one, with far more roles for men available, her chances were slim. Blackmore may have been too polite to add that for female performers of no exceptional talent, like Marguerite, the chances were virtually nil. Instead, he suggested she try her luck on the chorus line. With its troupe of beautiful young women singing and dancing their way through a series of set routines, the chorus line had sprung up with the new musical comedies of the Edwardian era. It proved a popular formula – one that has endured to this day.

Marguerite would have met chorus girls at the agency; heard them laugh at the diaphanous 'bathing suits' they had to wear, designed to reveal as much flesh as was legally permissible; heard them describe how they would run through their exhausting, gyrating, high-kicking routine night after night. She would have also heard talk of near-starvation wages and of those unsavoury 'stage door Johnnies' who would skulk in wait for them after the show.

She knew that the chorus line would be a major climbdown from her serious theatrical ambitions. The public's love for the 'glitter, glare and gaiety' of variety theatre meant far more openings for performers, especially for pretty young women like Marguerite, than could ever be found in 'serious' theatre. In the Academy, however, chorus girls were pitied at best and despised at worst, with one of its founders, the leading playwright Arthur Pinero, even branding them 'a menace to society'.

Even in the more reputable variety theatres, a chorus girl's life was one of relentless hard labour and hand-to-mouth struggle. Despite her meagre pay, she had to maintain a wardrobe, and support herself during her inevitable bouts of 'resting' between engagements. For many, their day-to-day struggle was such that finding a 'sugar daddy' from among those 'stage door Johnnies' was not just viewed as part of the job, it was encouraged and enabled by the theatre proprietors, who, like De Freyne in *The Honey-Pot*, procured girls for his 'wealthy stage door dilettanti' in return for:

> admittance to elevated circles; a select club, a shooting party, a cruise on a big yacht. Sometimes it was an invitation by a young and indiscreet member of the peerage to his country house and a photograph in the illustrated papers to proclaim it ... But what gave him most satisfaction was to be able to put an important City man under an obligation. It often resulted in special information concerning stocks and shares that brought him large profits. He would sacrifice any girl's reputation for a one-fourth per cent turn of the market, and frequently did so.[16]

As any new recruit quickly found out, the chorus line made for a precarious, demeaning and short-lived existence, its members 'trained by methods similar to those used in schooling performing animals'.[17] An industry that fed on youth and beauty, it rapidly devoured its steady supply of eager, fresh-faced girls.

Marguerite could not have failed to have heard tales, reported in salacious detail in the Sunday papers, of the latest body found in a South Kensington or Somers Town boarding house – another chorus girl who had committed suicide or taken an accidental overdose of morphine or cocaine. She had heard all the warnings, was prepared for all the dangers that lay ahead. She would have chosen it a hundred times over returning home to her parents. For her, anything was better than that stifling, oppressive house with her nervous mother and volatile father. After tasting freedom, the thought of sipping tea in her father's front parlour, making polite conversation with a potential suitor of her parents' choosing, was too awful to contemplate. It would also have put her out of call for the stage and ended her theatrical ambitions.

Although Marguerite never admitted to having worked as a chorus girl, her detailed descriptions in novel after novel of such work suggest strongly that she is drawing on first-hand experience. This interpretation is strengthened by the fact that Marguerite was the kind of writer who preferred to draw from life rather than research. As the critic Clement Shorter noted in his review of her Oliver Sandys novel *Garment of Gold*, 'Miss Sandys evidently knows a great deal about the theatre outside of the range of the successful actor and actress, and can describe its lesser stars exceedingly well.'[18]

She could dance too and had boasted of her 'wiggle stomach' dance in Beerbohm Tree's *Nero*. A job in the chorus line in the musical comedies of the Gaiety Theatre on the Strand or the Empire on Leicester Square, or, if she was not so lucky, one of the lesser-known theatres, would at least have allowed her to hold onto her hard-won independence.

Such experiences would later have proved invaluable to Marguerite when writing her chorus-line novels – a collection of gritty tales, told from the point of view of the high-kicking, scantily-dressed girls in the footlights. Written for titillation, the stories amount to something more. They tell of chorus girls who suffer, and sometimes overcome, the daily indignities and humiliations that come with the job. They throw the spotlight on the dark corners of show business – beyond the prurient headlines in the Sunday papers – few of her readers would have been aware of.

While newspapers and popular fiction peddled myths of stage girls marrying lords, as almost everyone knew it rarely happened in reality. Far more commonly, the girl would have a relationship with a wealthy (sometimes titled) 'patron', but only as long as it took for him to tire of her and exchange her for a younger model. Instead of stepping up to play lady of the manor, she would be handed a notice to quit her Piccadilly apartment. Marguerite's fiction merged both narratives. Her 1916 novel *The Honey-Pot* (Barcynska) is described by its publishers as 'a stage novel that deals with the tinsel, its temptations and its strivings and', as the cover copy delicately puts it, 'with an ebullient girl who loves a man of the world too generously'. While it duly delivered the fairy-tale marriage-to-a-lord ending that the publishers required, with a heroine who has an illegitimate baby by the 'wrong man' yet still goes on to marry a lord (who is not the father), it also slyly subverted popular fiction's moral code. Marguerite's version of romance merged lurid accounts of the seedier realities of a chorus girl's life with the happy, romantic ending the genre demanded. She also slyly imported the New Woman, complete with her demands for independence and sexual freedom, into romance fiction. Snatching her from the works of H.G. Wells, Olive Schreiner, George Bernard Shaw and others, Marguerite gave her a happier, more conventional ending (with a Mr. Right, of course) than that of her literary counterpart.

The revelations in her later showgirl novel *The Pleasure Garden* (published under the name of Oliver Sandys) are even more sordid. Written in 1923, just as Marguerite's writing career was beginning to fly, the novel was later directed by Alfred Hitchcock as his debut feature film. Yet even the arch-voyeur Hitchcock shied away from the novel's motifs of prostitution, cocaine- and morphine-addiction, and suicide. He also sidestepped its overt portrayal of those theatre proprietors who saw taking their pick of girls to sleep with (and sacking anyone who refused them) as just another perk of the job –

a perk which, as the #MeToo movement has so starkly revealed, has continued unabated.

Marguerite knew all too well that the life of a chorus girl lasted only as long as it took for a new, rosy-cheeked girl, fresh in from the provinces, to replace her. From the start, she would have been plotting her most likely route out. She was to find it just one mile away from London's theatres, among the burgeoning newspaper and magazine presses of Fleet Street.

Chapter 3
A New Woman on Fleet Street

*I would borrow [my mother's] silk petticoats from
the wardrobe without telling her [and] help myself
to her scent, her veils, her gloves, and go off all
decked up to vamp the editors.*
(Oliver Sandys, *Unbroken Thread*)[1]

'Journalism is not a game and in journalism there are no excuses.'
This cautionary piece of advice was given in Arnold Bennett's 1898
handbook *Journalism for Women*. He was writing for a small but
rapidly-growing, cohort of women journalists, as well as the women
who now aspired to journalism as a career. As the editor of *Woman*
magazine, Bennett was all too aware that the industry needed a
ready supply of women journalists. His own less than convincing
attempts at producing articles on fashion, cookery and other
'women's issues' had taught him that writing for a female audience
was not as easy as it appeared. In any case, his women readers wanted
authentic female voices and preferred advice that came from other
women – ones they might even come to regard as friends. The
problem, as Bennett saw it, was that few women writers were equal
to the task. Even fewer, he claimed, took their profession seriously.
He added that it was not a matter of biological destiny, but a
problem created by an educational system that left women ill-
equipped in spelling, grammar, punctuation and attention to detail
and, worse still, endowed them with a tendency towards 'shrillness,
a certain quality of multiloquence'. While his tone was patronising,
his intentions were perhaps more laudable, claiming that he wished

to provoke women journalists into taking their profession more seriously.[2]

As Bennett knew all too well, women's magazines, and that new phenomenon of women's pages in newspapers, were on the ascendancy. For women writers who understood this market and how to meet its demands, the door was open like never before. By 1897, the *Newspaper Press Directory* listed at least one female writer on the staff of every London paper, but the majority of women journalists were freelancers.[3] As a discreet means of earning money at home, the prospect of finding work in freelance journalism was appealing. This emerging new breed of women freelancers also owed a debt of gratitude to their groundbreaking Fleet Street predecessors of the previous century: women like Isabella Beeton (better known as Mrs Beeton, for her book of household management), who in 1861 had dreamed up the first ever glossy magazine, *The Queen*, and Mary Billington, a staff writer on *The Daily Graphic*, who in 1890 rose to become the paper's India correspondent, later moving to a column of her own in *The Daily Telegraph*, which she used as a platform from which to conduct a tireless campaign for women's suffrage. In the hard-drinking, masculine world of Fleet Street, these pioneers laid a solid path for the women that followed.[4]

By 1904, two years before Marguerite's first feature appeared, *The Englishwoman's Review* printed a letter from a man who had 'just returned to Britain after thirty years abroad' and was struck by the number of women working in Fleet Street, where today 'women reporters are almost as numerous as men'.[5] The letter was hyperbolic: women on Fleet Street were still far outnumbered by men, although, in recent years, their ranks had certainly swollen. The women who filled column inches with features, essays, opinion pieces and short stories were no longer viewed as curiosities but had become part of the fabric of Fleet Street.[6] Along with teaching, nursing, clerical work or stenography (typing), women, in theory at least, were also free to enter the field of journalism. Most of the new female arrivals worked freelance, finding themselves at the sharp end of the industry. Paid as they were by the article, it made for a precarious and unpredictable living. Yet for women like Marguerite, whose work was in demand and whose temperament suited the erratic lifestyle and tight deadlines demanded of them, journalism offered the thrilling prospect of freedom and financial independence.

Marguerite began writing for women's magazines when they were just coming of age. Modern, chatty, breathless, sometimes titillating, they were always irresistible. Titles like *Health and Home*, *Lady's Pictorial*, *Ladies' Review*, *Forget-Me-Not* (edited by another woman pioneer, Winifred 'Biddy' Johnson, later to become Marguerite's friend and her editor on *Woman's Weekly*) and *Woman's World* (edited by Oscar Wilde from 1888 to 1890), as well as Bennett's *Woman*, covered between them almost every conceivable topic that could be of interest to their readers. Articles on celebrity and fashion, crafts and homemaking, sex and love, women's suffrage, education and employment, plus plenty of fiction, all vied for the attention of the liberated New Woman. A recurring figure in novels and plays over the last decade of the previous century, the term 'New Woman' was applied to any (usually young) woman who did not want to be defined solely as a wife and mother: who sought a career and financial independence, as well as legal and sexual equality. In women's magazines, she was ubiquitous and hungry for advice on how she might take her rightful place in the fast-moving world around her. As Marguerite was soon to discover, publishers were eager for new eye-catching articles, short stories and serials that would appeal to her. When Marguerite began writing for Fleet Street, the New Woman was being hotly discussed and debated. In 1909, H.G. Wells's latest novel *Ann Veronica* railed against the middle-class woman's 'functionless existence varied by calls, tennis, selected novels, walks, and dusting her father's house'.[7] Although by then the theme was no longer original, the fact that Wells's heroine was able to live happily with her lover, despite not being able to get a divorce from her husband, reflected a significant shift in attitude, as more liberal attitudes towards marriage, divorce and extra-marital relationships were absorbed into the mainstream.

Even so, few middle-class women would have been keen to follow in the footsteps of Ann Veronica, who, when her husband died suddenly, was disinherited and (together with her daughter) left to face a future of hardship and exclusion from society. While for many young women, living outside of wedlock held a fleeting romantic appeal, in reality few would risk the social stigma it carried. Most women also rejected the prospect of living without a man. While the New Woman may have been a figure of seemingly endless fascination, few women were prepared to turn their backs on marriage and children and the financial support that came with becoming a wife. The prospect of a woman having to support herself in a career for which she was likely to have been ill-prepared was daunting. While the appetite for tales of those New Women who had 'got away' was voracious, most had no intention of following them. There were also those determinedly conservative women who agreed with anti-feminist campaigners like Frederic Harrison, who, in his misleadingly titled 'Emancipation of Women', rehearses the old chestnut of a woman being best employed 'as mother, as wife, as sister, as daughter, as friend, as nurse, as servant, as counsellor, as purifier, as example, in a word – as woman'.[8]

For Marguerite, the New Woman was more than just an interesting concept, but a model she knew she had to follow. Her combination of ambition and desperation to escape made her a rare pioneer. Venturing out – first as an actress and then as a writer – she was among that tiny minority of women who dared to live independently.

Although a decade had passed since Bennett's polemic, Marguerite would have almost certainly read it: his excoriating advice had become a touchstone for any woman who held journalistic ambitions as she now did. If she had read it carefully, she would also have noted Bennett's observation that there was a 'busy market for short melodramatic stories – stories for which "action" and a certain ingenuity of plot are the only essentials'.

She had gained enough experience of stage life to have learned – as her novels later made clear – that it could offer her nothing but the most precarious of livings. Her limited acting ability, as she was shrewd enough to realise, made her prospects worse still. She found that writing, unlike acting, came to her quite naturally. With her career in the theatre ending almost before it had begun, she saw writing as a field that could at least offer her a second chance of earning her own living. Like Alexandra, the chorus girl in *The Honey-Pot*, she knew that after leaving the stage her career options were limited:

> She could not do office work: she knew nothing of shorthand or typewriting. She might apply for the post of children's governess or companion, but would she be acceptable for either? There would be questions as to her previous experience. All she would be able to cite would be [her] stage work in the chorus, hardly the right qualification for a guardian of youth or companionship to a lady![9]

Yet freelance journalism was no easy option – especially for a woman. It is no accident that in the literature of the era, the female journalist is invariably portrayed as a down-at-heel, somewhat desperate, figure. In Stephen McKenna's *Sonia* they are portrayed as a breed of 'faded women, no longer young, with shabby boots and carefully mended gloves' who haunt editors' offices;[10] while those 'third-rate lionesses' in 'tumbled gowns' who haunt London's 'dubious journalistic gatherings', in Dolf Wyllarde's *The Pathway of the Pioneer*, are a little more louche, the portrait is hardly any more flattering.[11]

Yet for Marguerite, it was a career that came with distinct advantages: not least that it could give her more flexibility and autonomy than any other 'female career', allowing her to set her own schedule. It also gave her the freedom to visit theatrical agencies in the afternoon, where, like an addict, she would go daily to chase – just one more time – that dream of a stage career.

Women's magazines were not the only growth area on Fleet Street: during those boom years of publishing, new newspapers and periodicals – aimed at everyone from grocers to vicars to podiatrists – were springing up like mushrooms. With their bold, eye-catching headlines, they covered fresh new topics like crime, sports, gossip, human interest and celebrity. 'Spurred on by the rush of new technology in the late nineteenth-century' – the electric telegraph, the telephone, the typewriter and the high-speed rotary press, which made newspapers cheaper than ever to produce – an all-out circulation war was raging. Among its victors were *The Pall Mall Gazette*, with its sensationalist campaigns on child prostitution and other previously unheard-of scandals,[12] and *The Star*, which carried breathtakingly lurid reports of the 'Jack the Ripper' murders. Alfred Harmsworth (later to become the newspaper baron Lord Northcliffe) gave his readers a more comforting mix of readability and jingoism in the *Daily Mail*, while his other paper, the *Daily Mirror*, caused a sensation of a different kind as the first to employ the new halftone block technology to print photographs on its front page.

Yet Marguerite's debut in print was not in any of these new titles, but in a letter to her father's favourite paper, the thirty-year-old *Daily Telegraph*: 'I am only a girl of eighteen, but I have read the correspondence in your paper with the greatest interest', she wrote. The letter was her contribution to the paper's long-running debate about organised religion, which had dominated its letters page for months. It also revealed a deeper, more philosophical side to the future author of books that she would cheerfully dismiss as 'light and frothy':

When old enough I read all the scientific journals I could get hold of, and very gradually a light began to dawn, and I saw how foolish had been my attitude of atheism, and, latterly, agnosticism. By degrees I worked out a belief of my own, which could fit in with the Bible and science, and since then I have been happy.[13]

This preoccupation with spiritual matters, and her accompanying unease over organised religion, were never to leave her. As young as eighteen, she was already showing signs of her idiosyncratic mix of spiritualism and mystical paganism. The letter also foreshadowed her later belief in a world where the living communed with the dead, where fairies lived in bluebell-dotted hedgerows and 'wise men' – the possessors of stones holding magical powers to heal the sick and distressed – could be found on Welsh mountainsides.

Three years later, she had another letter published in *The Daily Telegraph*. This time, the subject was of a more worldly nature, complaining of the difficulties she had experienced in finding work after graduating from the Academy of Dramatic Arts. Her former principal at the Academy, Herbert Beerbohm Tree, responded with some pointed advice; instead of a career in acting, she might instead earn her living as a writer. Marguerite chose not to see it as a comment on her ability as an actress, but rather as praise for her talent as a writer. With this as her cue, she wrote her first article, 'A Day at the Academy of Dramatic Arts', then proceeded to tout it around Fleet Street.

Treating it as she would an audition, she took great care in selecting her outfit: 'a white muslin frock' or a 'blue sash and a hat adorned with blue ribbon',[14] in order to best 'vamp' an editor. As her brief experience as a chorus girl had taught her, 'vamping' was an important part of the game; attracting the eye of the agent, shrugging off rejection and tactfully deflecting unwanted advances were all in a day's work. The hard knocks she had received in the theatre had inoculated her against any fear of rejection. Besides, in comparison to the predators that prowled the variety theatres, magazine editors seemed a tame bunch. So began her daily walks from her lodgings in Bloomsbury to Fleet Street, where she would tramp up and down that long, dark road, up and down endless stone steps to the top floor editors' offices. Soon she had memorised every editor's name, had learnt their movements during the day, and knew she had to catch them before lunchtime, when they disappeared into Bower's Wine Bar or Ye Olde Cheshire Cheese.

'How it happened I don't know, for usually there are forms to be filled in before one sails into editorial presences, but this was my lucky day.'[15] It was indeed. She had marched into the office of Hamilton Edwards, the editor in chief of the Amalgamated Press. She proceeded to read her article aloud as if she were at an audition.

Her unconventional approach paid off. After she had finished her reading, Hamilton, a 'broad squat man with a brown moustache and the worst squint I have ever seen', said he could use it. The article was subsequently published in a new magazine, *Answers: The Popular Journal for Home and Train*. As the title suggested, the journal was aimed at the growing market of London commuters. On reading her article, 'Miss Answers Spends a Day at the Academy of Dramatic Arts',[16] Edwards paid her three guineas (£3.15) – one guinea for the delivered article, plus two in advance for two more. Such a large payment, with two commissions thrown in, made Marguerite feel 'slightly intoxicated'.[17] It would have taken her more than a month of high-kicking on the chorus line to earn the same amount.

As with all the magazine's pieces, her 'Miss Answers' features were unattributed. Her contributions also included 'Answers by a Pretty City Miss', detailing a romance between a waitress in a tea shop and one of her customers. 'Confessions of a Lady Swindler',[18] claiming to be 'published exactly … as it came in', was later in her career recycled as 'The Adventures of a Lady Companion', which appeared in *Sievier's Monthly*, under Marguerite's old stage name of Olive Bree.[19]

These were soon followed by the publication of her first two short stories: the first a sentimental love story and the other 'a grim tale about Russia and a knout and a woman disguised as a man'. Both were accepted by *Smart Novels*, a penny magazine produced by Shurey's Publications, earning her fees of five guineas (£5.25) and thirty shillings (£1.50).

Those early cheques meant more to her than a much-needed cash injection. They were proof that she could earn a living on her own terms. Had Marguerite read Adeline Sergeant's 1902 novel *The Work of Oliver Byrd*? Whether she had or not, the parallels between her and the novel's heroine, Eleanor Denbigh, are unmistakeable. The fictional Denbigh's first cheque (thirty shillings for an article in the *Phonograph* magazine) marks a turning point in her life, as she realises that she is capable of earning her own living and so escaping the 'good offer of marriage' that her mother had been pressurising her to accept.[20]

Galvanised by a similar prospect of independence, Marguerite determined to adopt a professional approach to her work. Like Bennett, she was acutely aware of the shortcomings of a 'young lady's education' and resentful that her own education was one where good grooming and housekeeping were considered more important than perfect grammar. Resolving not to let her idiosyncratic grammar and punctuation get in the way of a promising writing career, she became a quick and eager learner, ready to drink up every drop of editorial medicine she was given. Isabel Thorne of Shurey's (one of Marguerite's few women mentors) helped to iron out her punctuation and also instructed the talented, yet naïve, young writer – whose early work was submitted as one unbroken lump of text – on the necessity of paragraphs. Marguerite credits Clement Shorter, the founder and editor of the popular *Sphere* magazine, for giving her 'no end of sound advice about writing', along with 'the handsome Mr. Huskisson' [*sic*] (Peter Edward 'Teddy' Huskinson) of the *Tatler*. Ralph Blumenfeld, the American-born editor of the *Daily Express*, whom Marguerite describes as 'the most courteous and charming of beings', rewrote one of her early efforts to coach her on the paper's house style.[21] They were not helping her out of altruism but nurturing a promising young woman writer at a time when women writers were in short supply and high demand.

Marguerite did not disappoint: ideas and stories came tumbling out of her. It was as if they had been locked away and were now finally set free. The only problem was getting them all down quickly enough, catching the words that galloped from her imagination before they slipped away.

In her memoirs, Marguerite recalls the 'Whispering Voice' that first came to her in India during a childhood bout of malaria.[22] She also remembers how at school, despite her lack of paragraphs, she had been head and shoulders above the others at essay writing and still had the clutch of medals to remind her of it. She still loved the stage, but it had not loved her back. She no longer had any illusions that it might provide her with a livelihood. Now she had found another path to independence: her longed-for escape from a future of 'doing nothing at all except have babies like my mother'.[23]

Like Magda Burke, the heroine of *The Pathway of the Pioneer*, Marguerite adored her walks down Fleet Street; loved wondering what commissions would come her way that day; found it thrilling to belong to 'that great living force ... the electric sense of being behind the scenes in the world's drama, of knowing how the machinery works'.[24] She made it her job to get to know Fleet Street intimately, becoming familiar with every building, paper and magazine, every editor, assistant editor, subeditor and secretary. In turn they got to know her. Although not her dream of 'Making a Name' on the stage, she was making a name of a different kind.

At lunchtime, after the male editors adjourned to the pub and the tiny clutch of women editors to the coffee shop, Marguerite would head off to Charing Cross Road. There – still tugging at the rags of a stage career – she would do the rounds of theatrical agents. At night, instead of sleeping she would work on tomorrow morning's copy. The money would tumble in, then tumble out again just as quickly. Cheque in hand, she would take the bus from Charing Cross to Regent Street, where she would browse through the satins and silks at Liberty's. Perhaps not wanting to join the ranks of those struggling women journalists in their 'tumbled gowns', she would carefully select outfits with which to vamp an editor. But it was the writing that was best of all: it seemed to emerge from some infinite source, as if the Whispering Voice had returned and was now dictating endless stories to her. Soon, her ability to invent stories through the night began to feel as natural to her as breathing.

Then she held her breath. Arriving home one evening she felt exhausted and, instead of heading to her writing desk as usual, fell straight into bed. The next day, feeling 'shivery and peculiar', she could not get up. It was all terrifyingly familiar; malaria, her old childhood enemy, had returned to strike her down. Aunt Tots was sent over to nurse her niece back to health. She also carried instructions from Marguerite's father to take her home as soon as she was well enough to travel. Henry, putting his daughter's illness down to 'late nights and dissipation', was at least correct about the late nights.

Marguerite's family had moved again – this time to Reigate in Surrey. She told herself that at least it was within commuting distance of London. As soon as she was feeling stronger, she would purchase a season ticket and travel into Fleet Street four days a week. Soon she returned to her old routine: vamping and charming, with a brown envelope under her arm containing her latest supply of glittering copy. Only this time it felt different. As midday approached, the sinking feeling would return. Her frantic morning behind her, it was time to walk to London Bridge and board the train home. In a compartment that smelt of leather, paint and sweat, she would gaze out of the window as it rattled south past the Southwark slums, through green fields and church-spired villages and the newly-built semis and terraces that were springing up along the line. At the end of it was the house she shared with her parents and Tots, where her victories of the day were of no significance.

She remembered how, bursting with pride, she had presented her first article in print to her father and how he had responded with 'Trash! Trash!'[25] When she tried to write late at night, he complained that she was using too much electricity. When she continued, he switched it off at the mains. Her output diminished, her trips to London fell to three times a week, then twice, then once.

She had stepped out of the Edwardian parlour and into a new world where she could earn money of her own and was free to meet men as she pleased, without an introduction. Now she was being pushed back into her old cage. If her fledgling career was not to shrivel and die, she had to escape and be free to resume her old pace. She also needed to keep in touch with her editors. But her father's attitude had hardened. He had already given her more than enough leeway, he told her, had been a fool to let her pursue an acting career. And now she was writing trash! But this time it would be different. If she left again, he would wipe his hands of her. She would no longer be his daughter. It was a step that Marguerite did not feel brave enough to take.

Her marriage prospects took centre stage in the Jervis household. She had had her fling on the stage and was now twenty-three. Marguerite claimed her parents found what they saw as a 'good match' for her: 'Reggie', the eldest son of some distant relations. Both sets of parents had always said they would marry their children to each other. He was apparently 'very rich', on an income of £10,000 a year, and also 'fairly young'. The trousseau had been purchased, she tells us, and a 'superb ring' had appeared on her finger. She also claims the engagement was announced in the society pages of the solidly conservative *Morning Post*. Yet with no record of this, it is unclear if the engagement – or indeed Reggie – existed at all.

More likely, he was a composite of the type of man her parents would have considered a perfect match for her. A Reggie would have hated art and would have found Marguerite's twin loves of literature and the theatre insufferable. Instead, he would have lived for hunting and hunting only, while Marguerite viewed 'chasing a frightened hare across country' as the height of barbarity. Worst of all, she dreaded that a Reggie would have echoed her parents in refusing to take her career seriously, would see her 'writing mania' as just another of her 'mad girl crazes'. This 'mania' would soon pass, her family would tell her, as soon as she was married and a mother. It was the very last thing she wanted to hear.

Marguerite's *Peggy Day-by-Day*, a romantic comedy serialised by Amalgamated Press and later published as a novel, drew on her experiences – either real or imagined – with Reggie. The series is written from the point of view of a somewhat dim suitor who is continually baffled by his loved one's resistance to matrimony and her 'mad notions about independence and [...] earning money'. Why, he wonders, when he is 'decently well-off' and 'ready to lay all my worldly possessions at her feet', is she 'always harping on about a career for herself'? [26]

Each episode finds Peggy (a diminutively disguised Marguerite), still searching for her right vocation. The stories also have a more serious subtext: as the clock is ticking, this ill-prepared young woman, educated only just enough to make a good middle-class wife, is desperately seeking a way to earn a living that would allow her to live independently. In her increasingly frantic efforts to avoid matrimony, she tries her hand at everything from modelling hair oil to playing the piano (badly) as a silent film accompanist, with each attempt ending in comic disaster.

The series concludes with Peggy finally 'surrendering' to her beau. *Peggy Day-by-Day* marks a fresh, comic response to the New Woman, although ultimately, it comes with a conservative message: the headstrong heroine, incapable of taking care of herself and earning her own living, needs a husband to provide for her. And so the New Woman is placed safely back in the domestic sphere as order is restored.

It is ironic that a successful, well-paid woman writer like Marguerite created a heroine who was far too 'giddy' to become independent. In Marguerite's defence, as a commercial writer, and a writer of popular romance at that, she would have had to follow the Amalgamated Press's editorial guidelines or not get published at all. The newspapers and periodicals she wrote for were, after all, highly conservative. Like many comedies, *Peggy Day-by-Day* addresses a contemporary anxiety, only for it to be mocked and so rendered less threatening. Marguerite, who was in no position to afford the luxury of principles, would have had to either reinforce her newspaper clients' world view or, like Peggy herself, give up and give in to marriage. With far more determination than her fictional

Peggy, Marguerite had no intention of giving in so easily. Unlike Peggy, she had found her true vocation. The threat of a future with a Reggie, or whatever match her parents were about to choose for her, filled her with horror.

Escape came in the unlikely form of a man more than twice her age and for whom she felt little affection, let alone love. Bernard Armiger Barclay was a journalist best known for his series of satirical articles in the *Daily Mail*. He had also recently published his first book, *The Kingmakers*, a historical novel set in the nineteenth century about a cabal of financiers who, for personal gain, attempt to place a king on the throne of the fictional Balkan country of Sergia.

Marguerite (who loathed sport of any kind) claimed to have met him at Reigate Tennis Club through an introduction by a mutual friend. It was more likely, though, that they had met in Fleet Street, perhaps in one of the pubs where contacts were made, information shared, and stories pitched and commissioned. They were places few women would enter – at least if they valued their reputation. But an ambitious young Marguerite would likely have put the advancement of her career before her reputation. Compared with the prospect of career and independence, her reputation was a commodity that held little value for her, beyond securing a marriage she was desperate to avoid.

She said she found Armiger 'interesting' for his 'personality, suavity and distinction'. He would regale her with stories of his adventures: his claims of having escaped from prison in Russia or, when in New Zealand, of Maori villagers making him their chief. As a one-time theatrical producer who now wrote a theatre column for *The Fortnightly Review*, he also appealed to Marguerite's abiding love of the stage.

Most importantly, Armiger took a keen interest in her work. He would read her writing carefully, telling her that her stories were good, very good, that she should write a full-length novel. He initiated her into mysteries of the *conte* and *feuilleton* and the difference between serial and third serial use of a story. This arcane knowledge of literature and the publishing business was more delightful to the ambitious young author than any lover whispering sweet nothings in her ear. He told her (truthfully) how lucky she was to get her work read, let alone published, considering it was not typewritten but had all been submitted in longhand. When it came to the business side of writing, he declared her completely naïve, assuring her that he would take her in hand and guide her towards a successful career. This appeal to her ambition was enough to make her overlook his greying beard, hooded eyes and bald head, although she could not entirely forget that she did not find this older man attractive, 'not in any way at all'.[27]

Then she received a letter from Armiger, assuring her that he had her best interests at heart and would help her succeed as a writer. He was not a rich man, he said, but he could make her comfortable in a country cottage where she could write to her heart's content. Lacking any declarations of affection, let alone love, she took it for a business proposition. She had to read it many times over before she realised that this 'curious document' was a proposal of marriage or, rather, a proposal that they live together. Marguerite's account of their meeting does not mention that Armiger was already married.

Nothing could have prepared Marguerite for the force of her parents' disapproval, who viewed her living with a married man as nothing short of scandalous. Their daughter was sacrificing not only her own reputation, but her family's good name along with it. And all of it for what? For a man of no rank or standing and who was almost as old as her father? Armiger was also Jewish. With all the prejudices of their time and class, this made them doubly distressed.

Henry's response was to promptly declare his daughter 'dead to him forever' and to cut off all contact. He also terminated the monthly allowance that had smoothed out her rocky path when living in London. Although secretly keeping in touch with a dismayed Aunt Tots, and, through Tots, with her even more disappointed mother, Marguerite had, as far as Henry was concerned, made her pact with the devil and must now be cast out.

Chapter 4
Tabasco Tales

We get used to everything in this world,
especially when the result's pleasant.
(Oliver Sandys, *Chicane*)[1]

Armiger Barclay, born Bernard Armiger Barczinsky in Sunderland in 1858, was the son of Jewish Polish immigrants and proprietors of a small private school, Eliza Crawcour and Samuel Barczinsky. When he met Marguerite in 1907, he had recently become estranged from his wife, Caroline Elizabeth Wright, the painter and suffragette known as Ethel Wright, whose portrait of Christabel Pankhurst still hangs in the National Portrait Gallery.

Armiger and Marguerite set up home together in Yew Tree Cottage, a rural retreat in the then remote hamlet of Bierton, near Aylesbury in Buckinghamshire, on which Armiger had taken out a short-term lease. Surrounded by lush meadows, beehives and a white-blossomed orchard, it made a romantic setting for their distinctly unromantic relationship. However much Marguerite tried to console herself with the cottage's pastoral charms, they were overshadowed by her lonely, loveless relationship with this peculiar older man. From the start, she claims, they slept in separate rooms.

On their first evening together, Armiger raised his glass for a toast: 'To our long life together and our success and plenty of it.' This at least was something she could concur with. Later, as life with Armiger grew increasingly difficult, she would tell herself it was just a business arrangement: one that allowed her to pursue her writing career. Her desire to 'Make a Name' was such that she was prepared to tolerate this strange collaboration, if that was what was needed for her to achieve it. Besides, wasn't the idea of the 'bed and board marriage', that she so despised, nothing more than a business arrangement of a different kind? At least this one allowed her to follow a career.

From day one, Armiger wasted no time in coaching Marguerite in his strict writing regime. They would keep daily office hours, begin work early in the morning, break for a light lunch followed by a walk at 2 p.m. Then, at 2.45, they would return to their respective desks to write until teatime. He also instructed Marguerite to write a chapter a day during the week, then 'rest' over the weekend by tackling a short story. Above all, his protégée must write every day, regardless of how she felt. She must, on no account, wait until the mood took her. At first, Marguerite did not take to these methods. While her previous habit of writing through the night had made her ill, it had, in its own rickety, erratic way, proved productive.

Under Armiger's control, Marguerite was forbidden from taking a break during the working hours he had set for her. Even when the sun shone and the garden beckoned, Armiger insisted she stay at her desk. The rebel who had fought and broken free from her father's iron rule was now held captive by a man who controlled her every waking hour.

She tolerated it because she wanted to study the craft of writing, which Armiger had promised to teach her. Under Armiger's instruction she learnt that a novel is very different from a short story: that a short story is compressed, the writer must decide what to leave out, while with the novel the writer must find enough to put in. Armiger also drilled his new protégée on the importance of planning her work in advance and not leaving anything to chance.

While Marguerite found Armiger's lessons useful, she was beginning to discover that when it came to the *practice* of writing, her pedagogue was less assured. Armiger struggled with writing fiction, while Marguerite took to it almost effortlessly. Bubbling over with ideas for novels and short stories, she was discovering she had a talent that her self-styled tutor lacked. While initially in awe of Armiger's status as a published author, on actually reading his work she found she detested it. She thought it too long, overly descriptive and, worst of all, lacking any kind of story. Unlike Armiger, she loathed 'tedious' purple passages, preferring her stories to rattle along without pausing for breath. With a likeable, worldly-wise and, of course, beautiful heroine at the wheel, her stories twisted and turned at breathtaking speed. When it came to narrative technique, she concluded, Armiger had little to offer her. Disregarding his instructions, she preferred to write intuitively, almost spiritually, listening to her other mentor: the Whispering Voice that had been with her since childhood. Despite this, Armiger's severe regime of undeviating adherence to set work hours imbued her with a discipline and focus that was to serve her well throughout her prolific career. This combination of disciplined routine and intuitive writing was one she was to draw on, copiously and productively, for the next fifty years.

Writing became her only escape from Armiger's jurisdiction: a respite of productive, pleasant labour. When she walked into her study and closed the door behind her, she was also closing the door, for a few hours at least, on Armiger. Evenings were more difficult, especially when Armiger decided to read aloud from his work. When Marguerite tried to escape to the spare room to play on an old out-of-tune piano, he took it upon himself to join her, beating out the time as he instructed her to play Chopin *mazurkas* the Polish way. As early as she decently could, she would excuse herself and retreat to her room for the night, her sleep disturbed by remorseful thoughts. Why had she run away with him? What had she been thinking of ?[2]

A few months into this 'arrangement', Armiger asked her how much money she had in her account. It was only ten shillings. Well, in that case, came the thunderbolt, they were only a few cheques away from starvation.

Sailing close to the wind financially was a way of life for Armiger. A one-time gunmaker, theatre producer and cook to a prospecting party in New Zealand, he was inured to living from cheque to cheque. There was also the possibility he was lying: that his savings were not so depleted and that it was a ploy to pressurise his surly young partner into writing and selling her stories. As much as she resented Armiger, his misleading her in this way was a possibility she never suspected – not even in retrospect. Perhaps it would have been a betrayal too far, even for Armiger.

Marguerite had been brought up to assume that, as if by magic, all men had some private means at their disposal. She had never imagined being with a man who apparently had no fixed income, and next to nothing in the bank. Even when working as a showgirl in London, with spells of living off tinned sardines, her father's monthly allowance had shielded her from any serious financial hardship. Now, with even that gone, she had no idea how she would cope. To face it with a man she did not like, let alone love, made it doubly intolerable.

Once she recovered from the shock, the necessity of earning a living spurred her on. She set to work on the first of what she (and Armiger, no doubt) hoped would become a series of short stories for the popular family magazine *The Word*. Completing her first in a day, she gave it to Armiger to check, as he had instructed. He read it and approved then 'got out a bottle of red ink, crossed out a few commas, added some, changed a few to semicolons, deleted a few quotations and broke up a few paragraphs', then typed it up (as Marguerite could not type) and handed it back to Marguerite to read. Apart from these few minor amendments, only one detail had changed – Marguerite's name had been removed from the title page and in its place was 'Armiger Barclay'. He was only 'lending' her his name to help her, he told her. He was well known, he said, established. He could command higher fees. Armiger became a Willy to Marguerite's Colette: an older man who forced his talented wife to write. Just as Willy would lock Colette in her room until she had completed her daily quota of *Claudine à l'école*, so Armiger would force his young partner to produce her daily quota. Like Willy, Armiger insisted that her work was published under his name, although his contribution was little more than pencilling a few corrections in the margin.[3] Marguerite obeyed and continued for years to write under the name of her 'otherwise non-collaborating taskmaster'.[4] As unpleasant as it was, the experience taught her how to live and work under the threat of insecurity: to hone her commercial instincts and to keep a few steps ahead of the market.

Despite the impression he had given when he first met Marguerite, Armiger had not enjoyed any notable success as a writer. While his satirical right-wing column in the *Daily Mail* had met with some success, he had recently been sacked for revealing the real name of one of his subjects, so exposing the paper to libel charges. He also found writing in English – his second or even third language (he had spent much of his childhood in France) – something of a struggle. *The Kingmakers*, written before he met Marguerite, was to be the only novel he ever produced.[5] Greeted as it was with a trickle of lukewarm reviews, it gave him little encouragement to write another. 'The story is told with vigour, and makes interesting reading,' said one, 'but the writer has something yet to learn in the handling of English.'[6] With Marguerite now the sole author of 'his' stories, Armiger's only recent contribution to the household income was an appearance in a newspaper advertisement for Sanatogen tonic wine, in which 'the distinguished author' Armiger Barclay commended this 'valuable preparation' for its 'remarkable recuperative powers'.[7]

Now 'his' writing had suddenly become more vivid – and far more prolific – editors were taking an interest again. As his bank balance (which was solely in his name) grew accordingly, he ignored Marguerite's pleas to allow her to use her own name, even jointly with his. In the end, this growing demand for what she knew was really her work gave Marguerite the confidence to issue Armiger with an ultimatum: if he wouldn't give her a credit, she would stop writing for him. As the goose who had been uncomplainingly laying his golden eggs threatened to go on strike, Armiger found himself outmanoeuvred.

Marguerite's next series was the romance-cum-crime caper *The Activities of Lavie Jutt*, which featured the various 'activities' of the (anti-)heroine Lavie (Lavinia), a headstrong American heiress living in London. When Lavie (like Marguerite) finds herself suddenly faced with the shocking prospect of having to earn a living, she runs into the decidedly shady Lady Loamington, who entices her into carrying out a variety of dubious undertakings or activities. These turn out to involve assisting with a rigged gambling den, pistol-toting, manipulating the press to save a teetering theatre production, and saving the ailing hat-making business run by Eveleigh (Lady Loamington's son and heir). Later she rescues the feckless young man from the clutches of an actress who is pursuing him for breach of promise before helping him get elected as a Tory Member of Parliament by kidnapping a carload of Liberals. In the final (least convincing) episode, Lavie foils a gang of murderous criminals who attempt to steal a priceless pink diamond. Its picaresque style and cynical, worldly tone mark a shift from the lighter, more 'innocent' comedy romances of the time. The series was published in 1910 by *The Word* magazine, then in book form by publishers Stanley Paul, who placed it within its new six-shilling series of popular sensationalist books with eye-catching titles like *The Woman-Hunter* and *Maids in Many Moods*. While Lavie Jutt's political theme and right-wing leanings may have been influenced by Armiger's satirical columns in the *Daily Mail*, the rattling plot and the wit and audacity of its young heroine were distinctively Marguerite's. Both versions were credited to 'Armiger and Marguerite Barclay' and, although Marguerite was its sole author, gaining any credit, even if only a half one, at least marked some kind of victory on her part. 'A perfect literary collaboration,' declared Armiger. To Marguerite it still felt less like a collaboration and more like theft.

71

Marguerite's next series was centred on the adventures of Babe, 'a very beautiful woman who has led a bad life'. Although she may have behaved badly in the past, 'that didn't make her a bad woman'. And thus we encounter what is to become a familiar and recurring theme of Marguerite's writing – the woman with a past. 'There is a young man who admires her very much and whom she loves,' the introduction continues, 'and she will tell him all the high-light episodes of her life – twelve of them.' Scheherazade-like, the storyteller device framed a series of short stories – beginning with the adventures of Babe's sixteen-year-old self, arriving in London following the death of her father – each one engineered to teasingly postpone the possible seduction of a young man by an older woman:

The Boy glanced up at her. She had chosen her frock well. It was a kind of flame-coloured filminess. Her eyes shone. Her whole body, though tensely still, seemed vibrant with magnetism.

The next moment she had her arms wound round him... Dazed he could not push her from him. Her lips, red and tremulous were close to his. The manhood in him stirred, suddenly awoke and clamoured.[8]

Marguerite would have been all too aware of the growing popularity of the 'sex novel' and the growing demand for 'sex excitement' among women readers. Novels such as *The Visits of Elizabeth* (1900) and *Three Weeks* (1907) by the flamboyant, scandalous and hugely successful Elinor Glyn, fuelled the craze for romances involving risqué content, luxurious settings and improbable plots.[9]

Borrowing the 'older woman' theme of Elinor Glyn's *Three Weeks*, Marguerite even went as far as adopting Glyn's trademark leopard-skin rug motif. Yet she went further than Glyn in pushing the boundaries of acceptability by adding the younger man's willingness to abandon his young fiancée for the older woman who so obsessed him. Although Marguerite would insist that her stories were 'highly moral' and not at all daring, even during this early stage of her career she was too shrewd an author not to know exactly what she was doing. The promise of something in the style of Elinor Glyn, only a touch more daring again, was to prove a successful formula.

She had also unwittingly stumbled on a solution to her authorship problem. 'It wouldn't have a family reading market,' Armiger critiqued, somewhat unnecessarily. 'I don't think I can lend you my name for this.' Considering her stories too risqué for his name to be attached to them, Armiger told her to submit them under her own name. Perhaps following Armiger's wish to completely dissociate himself from the series, Marguerite adopted a new pseudonym for the purpose: Oliver Sandys. The 'Olive' – an echo of her stage name, Olive Bree – came with the added benefit of a being a man's name – chosen in the belief that risqué content would be considered more acceptable, and even taken more seriously, if penned by a man. The stories were published in *The Winning Post* in 1909 – a magazine notorious for its salacious content. In 1911 they were combined and published by Long as the novel, *The Woman in the Firelight*.

Although Marguerite was now asserting herself as a writer on her own terms, she remained under Armiger's control. When payment from editors grew sluggish, as it often did, he would instruct Marguerite to 'run up to London' to collect payment and chase up commissions and stories that were awaiting publication. For work written in Armiger's name, she was to introduce herself as his secretary and not reveal her true identity. In her autobiography, Marguerite recalls how Armiger told her to wear her best dress 'and the Tuscan straw hat with the purple feather [and] your prettiest shoes, the ones with the silver buckles'. Pronouncing her 'delightful', he would tell her there was no need to hurry back if she was 'seeing people and getting on with them'. She would leave, she says, with a heavy heart.[10]

After a jolting ninety minutes' ride, she would step off the omnibus at Charing Cross, then walk up the Strand toward Fleet Street. She was returning to Fleet Street, *her* Fleet Street, but no longer as her own woman. What was she, then? Armiger's 'secretary'? His pupil? Or, as his words had implied, was she to be his whore? Before meeting Armiger most of her Fleet Street visits had been spent running up and down narrow stairs, in and out of swing doors, knocking on the doors of editors' eyries, always with a brown envelope under her arm containing her latest story. Now she was here at Armiger's bidding. Her old luck, she writes, had deserted her and she found it difficult to win commissions – although truthfully, she had not been trying. When selling her own work she had become adept at tricking, charming or wheedling her way past any gatekeeper. From the spotty boy behind the counter to the groomed secretary at the reception desk, she'd been able to persuade them to open the door to the inner sanctum of the commissioning editor's office. Face to face with the editor, she had known how to play the game, flirting just enough to get what she wanted. And if her flirting gave rise to certain expectations, she would resolve the situation satisfactorily, depending on how high the stakes were. The power ratio was unbalanced, of course – but at least she was playing for herself. Now it was solely for Armiger.

On one visit, she decided to make a call on her own account, to chase up a cheque from *The Winning Post* for her latest risqué Oliver Sandys story, and, for the first time, met its editor. With 'his silk hat tilted to one side, a pink carnation in his buttonhole, a big cigar between his teeth', he made a startling impression on her. Looking around forty-two or forty-three, he was, she writes, 'a real man'. This 'real man' was Robert Standish Sievier, the one-time bookmaker, racehorse owner, professional gambler and serial bankrupt, whose latest venture was in magazine publishing. He was also a notorious womaniser: a doe-eyed charmer and just the sort of man who could sweep Marguerite off her silver-buckled feet.

The Winning Post made a perfect home for those 'Oliver Sandys' stories that Armiger found too shocking to be associated with. Its claim to publish 'literature suitable for all tastes' belied the blue jokes and double entendres of such regular features as its Paris column titled 'Our French Letter'. Its mix of racing news and tips, celebrity gossip, and, of course, risqué stories, plus its affordable one-penny cover price, combined to make it an instant success. Sievier – who at first wrote the copy almost entirely single-handedly – named his cheeky stories 'tabasco tales', so called because the spicier they got, the more their popularity grew.[11] The eventual ban of the paper on grounds of public decency by W.H. Smith & Son only increased its popularity further as, in fewer than three years, it had achieved an impressive circulation of over 50,000.[12] Most popular of all was Sievier's 'Celebrities in Glass Houses' column. Its scurrilous attacks on the characters and sexual fidelity of the rich and famous were adored by the public and, of course, loathed by high society, many of whom feared they would be his next victim. The column turned Sievier into a pariah of high society and a hero to his public. Unlike his victims, Sievier made no attempt to hide his liaisons with women. Even when standing for Parliament in Shoreditch as a Unionist candidate, he boasted that, with seventeen illegitimate sons having served during the Great War, no one could accuse him of not doing his bit for his country.

Marguerite thrilled at Sievier's scandalous reputation and delighted in his nickname, Robert le Diable. Whatever his faults, he was no hypocrite. Unlike the prissy Armiger, who would not have racy stories published under his name yet pressurised her to sleep with editors in order to secure commissions, Sievier did not lay claim to any moral high ground. Marguerite claims that Armiger, far from being concerned that his young partner was seeing a notorious philanderer, gave her his blessing, telling her, 'You ought to know your way about.'[13]

Despite Sievier's reputation, Marguerite (herself not averse to a bit of selective hypocrisy) insisted he had not made any advances beyond 'seducing' her into authorship. It was Sievier, she claims, who encouraged her to write for a predominantly male readership those stories that men would hide 'hastily beneath cushions when female members of their family were about'. Later, as she switched to writing for a mainly female readership, she boasted that she wrote the kind of books 'that girls read in their bedrooms and married women stuff behind their sofa cushions'. It was a formula that was to serve her well for decades to come.[14]

Whatever the nature of the relationship between Marguerite and Sievier, he recognised her potential as a journalist, offering her the job of subeditor on a new journal, *Sievier's Monthly*, with a generous salary of £500 per annum – a sum which would secure a comfortable middle-class lifestyle. The first issue was launched in January 1909, with Marguerite's job to select between eight and ten stories (including Sievier's own serialised contribution) for each number.

As she soon discovered, her role involved a great deal more than subediting. When she couldn't find contributors, or when a contributor didn't deliver on time, she would end up filling the gaps by writing articles and short stories herself. For these she adopted a variety of pseudonyms: Olive Bree (which she had previously used as her stage name), Oliver Sandys, Claudia Rayne (sometimes spelt Raine), and possibly Constance Romanné-James. This suited her perfectly; it was a chance to try on and take off different personas as easily as new clothes. [15] So began her lifelong habit of using multiple names. This was good business – different names could be used for different genres. It was also fuelled by her desire to try out different identities and personas, apparently in response to a need to fictionalise her own life as well as those of her heroines. 'My light and frothy stories happened to suit the magazine very well,' she says. Yet they were far more than simply 'light and frothy'. Full of powerful men and cunning women, sinister murders and political satire, they were worldlier than Marguerite cared to admit. [16]

Marguerite's spell at *Sievier's Monthly* coincided with the height of the suffragette campaign. Tired of being ignored, the Women's Social and Political Union began their campaign of civil disobedience with their rush on Parliament in October 1908. Under the leadership of mother and daughter Emmeline and Christabel Pankhurst, they undertook a series of headline-grabbing protests such as smashing shop windows, burning letterboxes and vandalising paintings in art galleries. It was a battle which Marguerite generally did her best to keep out of – except for a couple of fleeting references. An exception to this was the Oliver Sandys satirical series 'Letters from Space', which featured a series of fictional letters from the deceased Lady Tubmouth. In one episode, she expresses her fear of being reincarnated as a suffragette, which she sees as worse even than coming back with a squint or as a member of the working class.[17] But Lady Tubmouth – an outrageous caricature of an ancient high Tory – was clearly intended as parody.

In another issue of *Sievier's Monthly*, a story credited to a Constance Romanné Jones (although given its distinctive fast-paced wit and comic pay-off, it is more likely to have been written by Marguerite) also makes light of the suffragette cause. It features the reactionary Lord Charles and his surprising recent conversion women's suffrage, although this was later revealed to have been solely motivated by his designs on a beautiful suffragette. 'I will study the suffragette question,' he leers. 'If you will undertake my education I can promise a very willing pupil.'[18]

It was common for the press to make light of the women's suffrage movement in this way. The popular magazine *Modern Society and Answers*, for instance, coined the then-popular saying 'meek as a Suffragette's husband'.[19] Trying to turn suffragettes into figures of fun offered reassurance to readers, male and female, who may have felt threatened by their demands.

Marguerite's passionate belief in a woman's right to independence and a satisfying career did not translate into support for the women's suffrage movement. Even if she had sympathised with their cause, while working for Sievier she may have thought it expedient to keep it to herself. Unlikely to have been a supporter of women's suffrage, Sievier also preferred to avoid the topic, at least in print. Once, when standing for Parliament,[20] a heckler challenged him to give his views on votes for women. 'I would never refuse anything to a lady,' he quipped.[21]

Marguerite insisted that her relationship with Sievier was purely platonic and her generous salary was motivated solely by friendship and the quality of her writing. 'If I were his lady love it would be understandable,' she writes, 'but I wasn't.'[22] Yet while her memoirs can be highly unreliable, her fiction often appears closer to the truth. In the early Oliver Sandys novel *Chicane*, we find Lady Weybridge (a female Sievier figure) sharing her philosophy with her new companion in crime. 'Surely what I offer you is better than selling yourself or starving in the streets? There's not much else left for a pretty girl who's penniless.' Asserting that women no longer need to marry in order to survive, Lady Weybridge tells her young accomplice to put on her sexiest fishnet stockings in order to trap her latest (male) victim. 'You've got to weave a web to catch a fly.'[23] Was this also the means by which Marguerite contrived to win her place in a man's world?

In her *Sievier's Monthly* serial 'Closed Chapters' (which she penned under her onetime stage name of Olive Bree), the heroine decides to be a romance writer, but is distressed to find that without any experience of romance she has little to draw from. She resolves to correct this by living 'a year of amorous experiences', regardless of the consequences. 'Should notoriety ... come to me,' she says:

> I can hide behind my pen name and laugh up my sleeve at the crude emotions my novels awaken in their thousand readers ... I shall have given the public what it wants, and paid for my mess of potage with – myself.

To try to untangle Marguerite's life from her fiction would be futile. Over the course of her long career, her 'light and frothy' romances had darker edges in which prostitution, kept women, the showgirl's 'casting couch', depression, fraud, as well as morphine- and cocaine-addiction (*Chicane*'s Lady Weybridge is 'as needle-pricked as the business end of a seamstress's index-finger'), are all on display. This seedier side is also described in such vivid detail that it would be difficult to believe it sprang from her imagination alone. In particular, *Chicane*'s fictional *Whispers* magazine, that 'exposed scandals, hypocrisies, and drew aside the veil from much that had hitherto been left in obscurity by a libel-haunted Press', reads almost like a piece of investigative journalism revealing the murky dealings that lay behind Sievier's façade as a publisher.[24] From the femme fatale of *The Woman in the Firelight* to the honeytrap fraudsters of *Chicane*, Marguerite's early fictional heroines were at odds with her later self-styled image as the innocent, somewhat naïve, purveyor of romance. They were more likely to have been a reflection of her own experiences, especially her youthful struggles to succeed as an actress and, later, as she struggled to gain a foothold in Fleet Street. When she felt her very life depended on her success, men like Sievier and Armiger held the key to her future.

The fantasy that many of her stories embodied held a potent appeal for her female readers: that of a woman using her sexuality not just to 'win over' a man, but (as with Lady Weybridge and her accomplice) to defraud and humiliate him. Or, as in *The Woman in the Firelight*, where an older woman is imbued with the power to tempt a young man away from his betrothed, that of a woman even capable of disrupting the institution of marriage. This was escapism of a new and daring kind – a kind that the other 'sex novels', with their alpha males and helpless heroines, did not provide. However carefully she dressed up her early heroines in chiffon and lace, all of them – in varying ways – use their sexuality as power: a means of making their way in a man's world. This combination of sex and power, under the guise of 'frothy romances', played a big part in her enduring success and her acquisition of a loyal female readership.

While Marguerite wrote her scandalous stories, Sievier was on a hunt for real-life scandals. Becoming an unlikely habitué of the British Library, he would scour back copies of *The Police Gazette* in search of transgressive celebrities to blackmail. To his victims he would offer a choice – pay him a large sum of money or see their past indiscretions advertised on *The Wining Post*'s notorious

'Celebrities in Glass Houses' page. The ploy proved lucrative, until one of his victims, the racehorse owner and diamond merchant Jack Joel, called the police and had Sievier arrested for blackmail. Charged with demanding £5,000 in exchange for not publishing a defamatory article on Joel, the trial promised to be a humiliating defeat for Sievier. While the press predicted his downfall, Sievier used his ill-gotten gains to acquire the best legal defence that money could buy. He found it in Rufus Isaacs KC, the son of a Jewish importer of fruit for east London's Spitalfields Market, and a star of the legal world. His recent prosecution of the fraudulent company promoter Whitaker Wright – who, after his conviction, committed suicide by swallowing cyanide in a court anteroom – had secured Isaacs' reputation as one of the most brilliant barristers of his generation. For Sievier it was an opportunity to perform. His display of outrageous disregard for his accuser and the authority of the court delighted his public. His biographer John Welcome writes:

> On the day the trial opened all the approaches to the court were crammed with a crowd struggling to get in. Sievier, turned out immaculately as usual ... in top-hat and morning coat, drove his carriage to the Old Bailey.[25]

Isaacs made the case that Sievier had been entrapped by the Metropolitan Police, whose officers had hidden behind a curtain during his visit to Joel's house (a situation that sparked a great deal of lampooning in the press). This unexpected defence confounded what had promised to be an open-and-shut case, resulting in a verdict of 'not guilty'.

His fame and popularity now sealed by the trial, both *The Winning Post* and *Sievier's Monthly* went from strength to strength. Yet the court case had taken its toll. Beneath his persona of playboy and raconteur, Marguerite thought him 'full of anxieties and sorrow and worry' and noted that, during the trial, he had grown 'intensely irritable' and took to 'storming violently at anyone who came into his line of fire', as Marguerite often did.

What Marguerite does not mention is that Sievier, no longer able to use *The Winning Post* for lucrative blackmailing purposes, was rapidly losing interest in publishing. During his frequent trips to Monte Carlo, Pau, Baden-Baden, Biarritz or Deauville, he would leave his new magazine in the hands of the inexperienced Marguerite. Inevitably, she made mistakes. One day, returning from one of his trips, Sievier exploded into an uncontrollable rage, with Marguerite taking the brunt of his furious words. Yet she placed the blame on her own shoulders. 'I got more stupid and stupid,' she writes, 'and he grew more and more impatient, and with just cause.'[26]

Although Marguerite left her role as subeditor after only a few months – she was not suited to the precise nature of subediting, she writes – it was not the end of her relationship with Sievier or his journals. She continued to contribute to *Sievier's Monthly* for a few more months until he abruptly closed it down at the end of 1909, after only twelve issues. Given Sievier's erratic reputation, the closure would not have come as a great surprise – least of all on Fleet Street, where the deaths (and births) of publications were routine events. It was a death for which Marguerite appeared to have been prepared. Freed from the responsibilities of editing, she had been building up regular commissions with a number of magazines, including Sievier's original journal, *The Winning Post*, which she continued to contribute to until 1913.[27]

In 1910, when Armiger's divorce came through, he and Marguerite agreed to make their marriage of convenience legally binding. They married the following year, at Aylesbury Register Office on the 17 July 1911, after having lived together for almost two years. Marguerite was twenty-four and Armiger, claiming to be fifty, was fifty-three. Their marriage certificate lists Armiger's occupation as 'journalist', while Marguerite was, in the custom of the times, listed only as a 'spinster'.[28] The delay following Armiger's divorce would suggest there was some contention over the issue.

Perhaps he had only agreed to marriage following pressure from Marguerite – more for her legal and financial protection than for reasons of propriety. Maybe Marguerite, now earning her own income as Oliver Sandys, had relented to pressure from Armiger, who viewed their marriage as a means of securing his tenuous claim over Marguerite's work.

With only two witnesses present (the legal minimum), the wedding was a perfunctory affair. It was during this joyless ceremony that Marguerite discovered not only Armiger's real age (at fifty-three, he was only two years younger than her father) but also his real name of Barczinsky. Barclay – the name she had known him by – had been unofficially adopted by him as an anglicised version of his Polish name. She had now to adjust to being Marguerite Barczinsky, or its feminine form of Barczinska, not Marguerite Barclay as anticipated. Was it when she was making her desultory vows, or when Armiger was placing the doubtlessly cheap ring on her finger, that she decided to use Barcynska (as she had mistakenly taken its spelling to be) as another pen name? She needed a Christian name to go with it: something exotic, not overly Polish – French perhaps, like Hélène. But Hélène Barcynska was not quite enough. It needed something else – a title, perhaps. And so a new alter ego for Oliver Sandys (author of popular, racy romances for shop girls, showgirls and maids) was born: Countess Hélène Barcynska, a feminised, ennobled version of her new married name. And what would this grandly-titled author write? Something more sophisticated, perhaps, than the oeuvre of Oliver Sandys: something more literary, for an audience that would be further up the social scale, yet who might still relish a racy tale or two.

She had hated writing as 'Armiger Barclay', or even sharing authorship with him. Now 'Oliver Sandys' was not big enough to contain her literary ambitions. She was already writing more than could be published or, more importantly, more than could be stocked by commercial lending libraries, especially Boots or W.H. Smith, who would refuse anything over their two titles a year from a single author.[29]

How to overcome this problem had been occupying her thoughts for some time, but there was a simple solution: she would create a second pseudonym for herself. She would be Oliver Sandys and the Countess Hélène Barcynska, the stagehand and the aristocrat. Between them, they had seen all sides of life; together they could tell a myriad tales.

Chapter 5
Making a Name, or Two

The elusive Jervis always seems to be hiding behind a
pseudonym ... playing the leading role in her own story.
(Elaine Jackson, 'Sievier's Monthly',
Book Trade Connections)[1]

He is in his fifties, wears a neat, grey beard, and is sporting a tweed three-piece suit with matching cap. On his feet are a pair of what look like spats: shoes that a gentleman of leisure might wear when in town, visiting his club or attending a formal dance, not with country tweeds. His legs are crossed and his eyes look outwards, as if fixing on an object in the middle distance. To his left sits a young woman, her face partially covered by the floppy brim of an oversized hat, arranged at just the correct angle to the side of her head to create a stylish effect. The hat's playful voguishness is belied by its wearer's demure Edwardian skirt and white frilled blouse, as it is by the pensive expression on the wearer's face. Her head is half turned towards the older man to her right, as if seeking his affection, or at least an acknowledgement, but is resigned to receiving neither.

The photograph was taken in June 1914, in the garden of Old Roses, the large Jacobean house in Bushey Heath into which Marguerite and Armiger had recently moved. The photographer was their new neighbour Malcolm Dunbar. He and his wife Nell had befriended Marguerite. Just two months later, Britain would declare war on the German Empire. Dunbar's daughter Monica, just ten years old when the photograph was taken, recalled how the threat of war had put Marguerite in a state of near permanent anxiety. Armiger, on the other hand, was unmoved by the events in Europe, secure in his belief that everything would blow over in six weeks or so.[2]

It was not just the threat of war that made Marguerite anxious. Trapped in a loveless marriage, with only her black spaniel (ironically named Cupid) to console her, she was, in Monica's words, 'a young girl with an old man she didn't love and a spaniel she did love'.[3] Later, when Cupid began shedding his hairs on his beloved rose-pink Persian carpet, Armiger insisted she get rid of him. Malcolm and Nell came to the rescue, offering Cupid a home and allowing Marguerite to visit him regularly. For Marguerite, it was the beginning of a 'friendship of a lifetime', particularly between her and Monica.[4] In later years the two were to maintain a long correspondence, only ending with Marguerite's death in 1964.

Despite her claim of having 'relations galore all mixed up in this', Marguerite was relatively unaffected by the war.[5] Armiger, now approaching his sixties, was too old to fight, while her brothers Charles and Edmund (aged twenty-two and twenty-three respectively) also avoided active service. Both teachers, they were among those 'certain classes' exempted from military service.[6] Despite the war, Marguerite's professional life continued to flourish, with journals and books being published as usual. She was also developing a new strand to her repertoire, one which was quieter and more reflective than her earlier work, with an emphasis on the domestic.

This new tone can be seen as early as 1914 in *The Little Mother Who Sits at Home*, a series of fictionalised letters said to have been 'edited' by Countess Barcynska and serialised in the popular family magazine *Nash's*.[7] The series is framed as a collection of unsent letters from a mother to her only son, revealing her hopes and fears for his future. As it progresses, the sacrifices the mother makes for the sake of her son – her struggle to put him through public school and college, the penny-pinching and, at times, near starvation – are revealed. In an echo of Marguerite's own 'unsuitable' match with

Armiger and the family rift it sparked, the mother chides her son for his choice of fiancée and begs him not to marry her. This marks a major departure from her previous mix of the risqué and the satirical. With a moralistic melodrama, she was once more adapting her style for a new readership. No longer was she writing for Sievier's racy journals, but for a more respectable, middle-class readership. Yet, lacking the sauciness and wit of her earlier work, these stories feel strangely flat. Later, in 1915, the series was published in book form by T.C. and E.C. Jack, to a mixed reception, praised both for its 'interesting and sympathetic' account, while censured for an 'emotionalism [that] jars a little at times'.[8] Yet, as an early attempt at developing Barcynska as a mature and serious voice distinct from that of Sandys, it marked a significant departure in style. T.C. and E.C. Jack must have been satisfied with its sales, as they also published the book in the United States, under their New York imprint of Dutton. It was to be the first of many American publications for Marguerite.

By September 1914, Marguerite and Armiger were on the move again: their next stop the small market town of Sudbury in Suffolk, some seventy miles away from Bushey Heath. This was Armiger's idea. Perpetually restless, he would lurch between large, salubrious houses and then – unable to keep up the rent – more modest accommodation. A lover of luxury, he tended to live above his means. He also relished haggling over rent and then getting into disputes with landlords when, at the slightest pretext, he would withhold payment.

Their new home, which Marguerite dismisses as a 'semi-detached monstrosity',[9] was a far cry from the Jacobean splendour of Old Roses. The 'dreadful little villa'[10] made her miserable, she complained. Yet her unhappiness had other causes, not least her dreadful marriage to a man who acted more like her agent (and an exploitative one at that) than her husband. The move had also taken her away from her new friends, the Dunbars, and her beloved Cupid who now lived with them.

Then she made a new friend: Captain Walter Preston Lovell, a 'handsome, reserved' army officer and a bachelor of forty. Too old for active service, he had been posted to a desk job in Sudbury.[11] Monica Dunbar, who met him when visiting Marguerite, thought him a 'very delightful man, rather in the style of David Niven'. Marguerite appeared less smitten. Instead, she liked him for his 'kind and gentle character' and relaxed manner. He was as different from the controlling Armiger as any man could be. She and Walter also had a lot in common. Walter had served in India like her father and, as Marguerite soon discovered, knew many of the same people. Their common country of birth helped forge a special bond between them.

Marguerite claimed Armiger did not object to her seeing Walter. 'We three became very friendly,' she says. 'Perhaps I should say he and I became very friendly as Armiger was working on a detective novel which he was hoping to get published and left us alone a great deal together.' The detective novel was never published, but the scene was set: a lonely woman and a handsome, single man who 'looked in most evenings after dinner', ostensibly to teach her card games.

On 13 January 1916, Marguerite gave birth to a son: Nicholas Barczinsky. Armiger – perhaps at this stage hoping to avoid paternal responsibilities – claimed that the baby did not look the least bit like him. While she stops short of admitting that Nicholas was not Armiger's child, She also made it clear that her marriage to Armiger was sexless, as well as loveless.[12] If Marguerite's claims were true, their relationship had also been an exploitative one, with Armiger pressuring her into giving sexual favours to other men in return for commissions. If so, the father could have been one of any number of men.

Nicholas would later claim that his biological father was a 'military man named Parry' who was 'possibly Irish', whom he 'liked' and would visit from time to time.[13] It is also possible that Nicholas's father was Marguerite's one-time editor – and, most likely, lover – Bob Sievier, although she was no longer working for him at that time. However, the most likely candidate for paternity was her current lover, Walter Lovell. Here, once again, Marguerite's fiction might reveal more of the truth than anything in her purportedly factual accounts. In the Barcynska novel *Tesha, A Plaything of Destiny*, the heroine is trapped in an unhappy marriage with an emotionally withdrawn, shell-shocked man. Falling in love with his friend, she eventually has his child and decides to leave her husband to go and live with the baby's father.[14]

Following the birth of her son, Marguerite writes that her 'old loneliness' returned, and she grew 'very frightened'. In an account that is infused with hints of depression and agoraphobia, she writes that she 'loathed' going out in the daytime and 'hardly ever did'. Apart from the blessing of Aunt Tots, who came to help after Nicholas's birth and stayed for four weeks, she was cut off from everyone, including the rest of her family, and felt imprisoned in what she could only see as 'a depressing little house in the middle of town'.

As the breadwinner of the house, Marguerite had to keep on working. There was no time for her to recover from the birth or to get to know her new son. When Nicholas was only three days old, she was already busy correcting proofs. 'I resented this,' she said. 'I was well enough, but I wanted to be left in peace with my baby.' Try as she might, she found that being a mother was sapping her energy and she was unable to sustain the long hours she had worked previously, finding that 'baby had used up all my creative power'.[15]

It was not only the baby that was sapping her energy. Before she met Armiger, when she was writing for herself, it had felt almost effortless. Now, writing for him, it had become an unspeakable chore. The more pressure Armiger applied on her, the more she struggled to comply; it was an unconscious rebellion, but an effective one. When she failed to produce the output that Armiger required, she claimed he ordered her to pay a visit to Lipton or Sievier to try and 'obtain' money off them. Marguerite refused. Eventually Armiger decided there was nothing else for it but to rake though their possessions for valuables to hock.

The young Marguerite with her beloved cocker spaniel Cupid. Later, Armiger forbade her to keep him.

Chorus girls, 1913.

Filming of *Tesha* (Dir. Greenwood & Saville, 1918).

Marguerite and Armiger Barclay (Barczinsky) in 1914.

Marguerite, Walter Lovell and Nicholas with Cupid.

Sir Thomas Lipton.

Robert Standish Sievier.

Charlotte Chapman,
Marguerite's Aunt Tots.

The only known photograph of Marguerite's father,
Colonel Henry Pruce Jervis.

Poster for the Quarry Theatre,
Aberystwyth, 1936.

Pleasure Garden film poster.

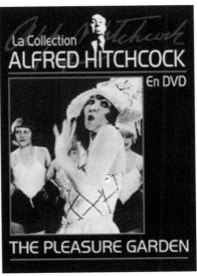

Pleasure Garden (Hitchcock: 1926),
cover of Spanish DVD.

Marguerite and Caradoc in Maidenhead, a few months after their wedding in June 1933. © Topfoto

News of the war on the Western Front was also adding to Marguerite's distress. At first, news of its progress and its great battles came to her censored, leavened by a generous helping of jingoism, via *The Daily Telegraph* or the *Daily Mail*. As an upper-middle-class product of the British Empire, she had little cause to disbelieve their reports; however, she did not swallow them whole.

Then reports of the horrors of the 1915 Battle of Neuve Chappelle, where over nine thousand men died, many of them found hanging on the barbed wire 'like washing',[16] belatedly reached the public. Marguerite must have wondered whether, if the war continued, this might be the fate of her own baby son. Her anxiety found voice in her serial *From Dug-Out and Billet: An Officer's Letters to his Mother*. Initially published in weekly instalments over 1916 in *Nash's Magazine* (alongside contributors such as the young Enid Blyton and one of Marguerite's literary heroes, Rudyard Kipling), it also came out in book form later that year. The 'letters', said to have been written by an unknown infantry officer calling himself only 'Chota' – Hindi for 'small or young' or, more pertinently, 'of lower rank or importance' – reveal the conflicting emotions of a soldier grappling with doing the 'right thing' by king and country as he also ponders the ethics of war. He writes of his homesickness and his confusion over why he is fighting at all: 'You'll make sacrifices, you'll smile, but when you put the sword in your hand you drive another into your own heart as well.'[17]

Intended as a companion piece for *The Little Mother Who Sits at Home* (also 'edited' by Countess Barcynska), *Dug-Out and Billet* is more emotionally complex than its predecessor. Although undoubtedly sentimental, it also conveys a picture of war that is quieter and more ambivalent than any other popular literature of the time.

Fellow romance writer Berta Ruck produced propaganda thinly disguised as wartime love stories, but Marguerite had no appetite for such flag-waving. While Ruck's *Khaki and Kisses* (1915) castigated those 'degenerates' who refused to fight and valorised those 'brave men' whose sweethearts waved them off to the front,[18] Marguerite would have nothing to do with enticing young men to go to battle. In general, she avoided the topic altogether, with *Dug-Out and Billet* her only work that dealt directly with the Great War. She preferred instead to stick to light-hearted mixes of fast-paced comedy and sizzling romance, escapist entertainment for the mothers, wives and sweethearts left behind.

Most successful of these was *The Honey-Pot*. Published in 1916 as one of Hurst and Blackett's new 'six shilling novels', it was to be her breakthrough Barcynska novel. Although one of the smaller publishing houses, Hurst and Blackett had successfully tapped into a lucrative niche market with their new, low priced 'yellowback' editions – the soft cover novel and forerunner of the paperback.

The novel's plot of a chorus girl who has an illegitimate child by another man, yet *still* marries the handsome Lord Chalfont, caused a minor sensation. Marguerite had taken the 'good girl ruined by a bad man' theme, so beloved of Victorian melodrama, and had revived it with a blast of twentieth-century oxygen. Before the year was out, *The Honey-Pot* had already gone into its third edition, totalling sales of over 100,000 for that year alone. It also marked the beginning of her four-decades-long partnership with Hurst and Blackett.[19]

Its success had also taught her that when writing as a 'countess' she was given more licence to break the rules. (Apparently conventional morality did not apply to the aristocracy.) 'Countess Barcynska' was a name that also commanded a certain amount of prestige to win over those critics who might otherwise have ignored it, among them *The Daily Telegraph* reviewer who lauded it as 'a story that never flags, a story which reveals an intimate knowledge of stageland [where] every character ... rings true'.[20]

Its spirited heroine, Maggy, became so popular with readers that Hurst and Blackett commissioned Marguerite to write a sequel, *Love Maggy*. Published in 1918, *Love Maggy* picks up where *The Honey-Pot* leaves off, describing the adventures, misunderstandings and faux pas of its much-loved cockney heroine, now elevated through marriage to the role of Lady Chalfont.

In the rapidly changing world of publishing, women's popular fiction was a lucrative, fast-expanding genre. As literacy continued to grow in the wake of the educational reforms of the late nineteenth century, popular markets rushed to keep up with their growing readerships, not least the burgeoning working-class female readership. At a time when sales of over 100,000 copies of a book conferred the status of bestseller on an author (unlike today's bestsellers which can total several million),[21] Marguerite was propelled from her just-scraping-by existence to being one of the highest-earning authors of her day.

Yet, for Marguerite, having to use the Barcynska pseudonym, which legally still belonged to her husband, took the shine off her achievement. Armiger had also used his status as the legal author to sell any claim to future royalties on *The Honey-Pot* in exchange for a higher flat fee. He had also agreed it without consulting Marguerite. Given its growing sales figures, it was an ill-judged decision.

A few months later, Armiger's fortunes appeared to have changed. He had 'somehow' raised the money (probably borrowed on future sales of 'his' Barcynska books) to take out a lease on the red-bricked eighteenth-century Manor House in Royston, Hertfordshire. It was an imposing house that marked a rise up the social scale, although not quite as grand as Marguerite's description. Set in the middle of a busy thoroughfare, not in its own substantial grounds, as Marguerite liked to imply,[22] today it is a Grade II listed building and a Wetherspoon's public house.

Perhaps the move was a sign of remorse on Armiger's part, an attempt to win back his wife, or, as Marguerite would have seen it, an attempt to hold on to the goose that laid his golden eggs. Perhaps he thought that if Marguerite, who had so loathed their house in Sudbury, was transplanted to more salubrious surroundings, she would be happier and so more productive. If he had also wanted to move his wife away from Walter, the man most likely to have been her baby's father, it was to have the opposite effect.

Missing Walter's company and sinking into depression, Marguerite had an attack of writer's block. With Marguerite unable to write, and an annual rental of £40 to pay, Manor House quickly proved too expensive. Almost as soon as they had moved in, Marguerite moved out to live with Walter, taking Nicholas with her. In Marguerite's version of events Armiger, unable to support his family, suggested she should move in instead with the more solvent Walter. 'I have often thought what was in Armiger's mind at this time,' she wrote, before reaching the 'uncomfortable conclusion' that, now viewing his young wife as a liability, he wanted to pass her on. Yet it is difficult to piece together exactly how events unfolded, especially as there is little to go on except an account in which Marguerite, probably to defend her reputation, presents herself as an innocent victim – although it is perhaps more plausible that Marguerite, unable to tolerate Armiger any longer, left him for Walter. Or maybe she and Walter had found their separation so unbearable that it galvanised them to live together and sacrifice respectability for happiness.

Once removed from Armiger's sphere, Marguerite's writing flourished again. Her magic touch restored, she was soon producing more of 'the selling stuff' – and selling it as Oliver Sandys, the pen name that was entirely hers. 'I wrote an Oliver Sandys short story,' she writes, 'and sold it for twelve pounds and kept it. I bought baby some lovely woollies and silk socks and a folding pram.'

When Armiger got wind of his estranged wife's revived career, he wrote to her, urging her to 'get on with the next Barcynska'. It was to be the first in a series of 'elegantly typed' and coolly manipulative letters: blaming Marguerite for deserting him while at the same time leaving the door open for her return. She was young, he would tell her, and had been through a great deal of worry. He was willing to forgive her on the condition she returned to him and did not see or communicate with Walter again. He would find a furnished cottage for the two of them. But it was too late. Although not exactly in love with Walter, Marguerite had found in him an agreeable companion. Importantly, he allowed her the freedom to write at her own pace. With him she could be her own woman again. Now she had tasted a kinder, gentler form of partnership, the prospect of living again under Armiger's iron rule was unthinkable. Knowing that Armiger would never grant her a divorce, she resolved to leave him without one.

More letters from Armiger followed; their tone growing more insistent. In no circumstances, he warned, was Marguerite to use the name Barcynska for private or literary purposes, and all rights to her entire literary output belonged to him. However, if she was reasonable, and agreed to this, then he would allow her half of all the income that accrued. Marguerite knew how tenacious he could be. She knew he enjoyed nothing better than a good legal battle, that he had no fear of acrimony. She had witnessed his battles with landlords, seen how he had browbeaten others into submission. She felt she had little choice but to agree that he should receive half the income on all her Barcynska novels.

'One day the sirens sounded,' writes Marguerite, 'and people ran in the streets and some were laughing and some were crying. It was the end of the Great War.' Walter was demobilised and, like many former soldiers of the time, especially the older ones, he struggled to find work. For a while, the couple got by on a combination of his savings and Marguerite's earnings. Then Walter's savings began to run low. Writing as Countess Barcynska, Marguerite became a regular contributor to a number of magazines, including a new up-and-coming title aimed at the modern woman: *Woman's Weekly*. But with yet another man to support, she bitterly resented having to pass on half her income to Armiger. Writing as Oliver Sandys – a name that belonged to her and her alone – Armiger had no legal claim over her work. When Marguerite submitted her latest commissioned serial to Winifred 'Biddy' Johnson, the 'editress' of

Woman's Weekly who had already published a number of Barcynska stories, she asked if it could be published under the name of Oliver Sandys. Johnson – well aware of Armiger's belligerent reputation on Fleet Street and most likely guessing the reason for Marguerite's request – readily agreed.

There was not much on Fleet Street that went unnoticed by Johnson. One of the most successful women editors of her generation, she was also one of the shrewdest editors on Fleet Street.[23] Taking over the reins of *Woman's Weekly* in 1915, the formidable Johnson set about moulding it to her vision. Out went the old dusty 'R&R' (religion and royalty) and in came fiction, human interest and practical articles such as recipes and sewing patterns – so setting a format for the magazine (and others that followed) that has changed little to this day.

Johnson's career began in 1891 as editor of *Forget-Me-Not* magazine, the fourth title of Alfred Harmsworth's[24] Amalgamated Press. There she quickly made a name for herself by identifying the rapidly growing market of shop girls and domestic servants and giving them the fiction and beauty and human interest articles they wanted to read. Johnson was so respected that, like Marguerite, she was among a small band of women who could break the rules and get away with it. Married to a stockbroker and a mother of two, she continued to work at a time when most women were forced to give up their jobs following marriage. She was also known for helping other women journalists. Like Arnold Bennett before her, she argued that it was a positive benefit to have women writers who had first-hand experience of marriage and motherhood. Over her long career, she stuck firmly to Amalgamated Press, where she became one of the first women to join the directorate in 1945.

Yet Johnson's style of running a magazine was not to everyone's taste. As one contributor put it, she was known for being 'a trifle dictatorial'.[25] Under Johnson's rule, love stories had to be moral and serious in tone, with strictly no humour allowed (a rule that Marguerite, a naturally humorous writer, found particularly difficult). While the hero and heroine would meet frequently over the course of a romance serial, she strictly forbid any embrace between them until the final episode. Her other rules were more stylistic than moral: the reader must never learn what is going on in the hero's head and all stories should be written entirely from the woman's point of view.[26]

Despite Marguerite's reservations about her choices as an editor, Johnson was to become Marguerite's ally and mentor. One of those early lessons was keeping her eye fixed firmly on the reader. 'If I dressed one of my heroines too expensively,' writes Marguerite, 'Miss Johnson would tactfully suggest that I didn't, as it might convey an air of superiority.' Marguerite also credits Johnson with advising her on how to negotiate a more favourable deal with Hurst and Blackett – one where she could retain the rights on her work while also receiving an advance for royalties on sales. Unlike the deals that Armiger had negotiated, keeping the rights meant that Marguerite owned her own work and could potentially receive an income indefinitely.

In 1921, Marguerite published *Garment of Gold*, her first Oliver Sandys novel since leaving Armiger.[27] At last, she had a book that was entirely her own, one on which Armiger had no claim. Reviving the formula of *The Honey-Pot*, it again features an eternally cheerful, yet naïve, chorus girl heroine who falls into the clutches of Parfitt, an unscrupulous stage manager. One reviewer, dismissing it as 'an unpretentious piece of pretty sentimentality [which] will probably appeal to the class of readers for whom it has been written', was perhaps revealing more of his own snobbery than he was of the novel.[28] A more generous review appeared in the popular illustrated weekly newspaper *The Sphere*, where the influential critic and author Clement Shorter praised it for its 'very effective defence of the life which is led by hundreds of girls associated with the theatre'.[29]

Following this success, Johnson commissioned her to write another Oliver Sandys serial for *Woman's Weekly*. The story, a melodrama about a jealous woman who spreads malicious rumours about a lord's gypsy wife before finally confessing after the gypsy cures her baby of diphtheria, marked yet another change in style for Marguerite. In 1922, it was snapped up by Hurst and Blackett, who published it as *The Green Caravan*. The film version, produced by the UK company Master Films, was rushed through during the same year.[30] Oliver Sandys was flourishing.

This success attracted the attention of Armiger, who resumed his letter-writing campaign. Every other day Marguerite would receive a neatly-written envelope containing a demand that in future she publish no more work as Oliver Sandys, but solely as Countess Barcynska. Marguerite consulted Winifred Johnson, who insisted that Armiger hadn't a leg to stand on. Spurred on by this advice, Marguerite decided to fight back. If she didn't, she knew she would never be free of him. Replying to Armiger, she told him that she could not agree to his demands, nor did he have any right to make them.

Then another letter arrived. This time, it wasn't from Armiger, but from her Aunt Tots. Her father, whom she had not seen since she left home, had suffered a cerebral haemorrhage. 'It seemed strange to me that I should mind so much,' she writes, 'considering that he had never been an affectionate father to me or I a dutiful daughter to him.' Despite her habit of subterfuge when writing about her life, in moments such as these, she could be insightful and disarmingly frank. Tots wrote again. Her father had improved a little and was asking for 'Daisy'. Could she possibly come and pay a visit?

She arrived to find her father weak and debilitated. She also found the family finances were 'in a complete muddle'. Her father had never discussed money with her mother, keeping her as an 'eternal girl'. As Florence did not have the first idea of how to manage a household budget, the role of family banker now fell on Marguerite. Soon all Henry's petty deceits and cover-ups, his decades of wishful thinking and denial, came out. Marguerite had to break the news to her mother that Henry had spent all their savings in order to maintain the illusion of status.

Even with her father unwell, she decided they had no option but to leave their grand house on Bournemouth's Fisherman's Walk. She found them a new, more modest home in the form of a bungalow in New Milton and dismissed their staff of eight servants, replacing them with a single maid-of-all-work.

Marguerite and Walter moved to nearby Southbourne to be near them. This time her parents were not scandalised that their daughter was living with a man out of wedlock. After all, it was the 1920s and times had changed. 'They all knew about Walter and how I left Armiger,' she claimed, 'and no one blamed me.' Perhaps she was reflecting her own feelings when she added that her parents were relieved she was now with a man who was 'one of their kind'. It's also likely her parents were grateful for their daughter's help, which, given her writing schedule, was more likely to have been financial than practical.

'Are you aware you have not done a stroke of Countess work for six months while all the time in my consideration for you, I have been waiting to give you an opportunity to continue as before, but you have been deceiving me by writing as Oliver Sandys.' Another letter from Armiger. As Oliver Sandys, she was now earning £200 for first serial rights, plus a £200 advance on each book, and had no intention of sharing a penny of it with Armiger. The thought that 'every penny went into my own bank account and not through Armiger Barclay' delighted her.

She was also revelling in the material trappings of her success, describing in loving detail her new 'architect-designed house', the Lych Gate. A light and airy house in the Arts and Crafts style, Marguerite enthused about its 'central heating ... charming garden, copper and pewter chimney pieces with iridescent tiles, a square hall and a staircase that was something more than ascent'.[31]

Her pleasure was marred by Armiger, who was still bombarding her with menacing letters. Only now their tone appeared more conciliatory, saying he wanted to meet her so they could reach an agreement. Marguerite knew him well enough to realise that an 'agreement' could only mean her giving in to all his demands. She also knew just how much he relished a battle.

Finally, she agreed to meet him at her home. Marguerite describes, with obvious satisfaction, how her new home with its *famille rose* and *famille verte* plates, its Sheraton and Chippendale chairs and Queen Anne bureau, impressed him. Although it may not have been the wisest negotiating stance, she appeared to enjoy provoking his envy.

Although she claimed their relationship had been little more than a business arrangement, she was a young woman when she met him and he was her first love. Even now, she was keen to win his approval. She wrote of love and romance while receiving little, if any, from her husband. His lack of interest in anything except her earnings potential would have been enough to hurt anyone, let alone a young inexperienced woman. She had been rejected by her father and cast out from her family to follow Armiger into the unknown. Instead of nurturing her talent, as he had promised, he had tried to steal it from her. He even coerced her into prostitution. Despite everything, she wanted to see him, was eager to impress him. If she could not win his love, then at least she could win his admiration. For all his unpleasantness, Armiger had left his stamp on her. He had shaped her taste in clothes and her love of antiques, and, above all, had shaped her career as an author.

She offered to let him maintain his rights to all the Countess Barcynska books, on the condition she could continue to write as Oliver Sandys. It was a more than generous offer. Yet Armiger would not hear of it and no agreement came out of their meeting.[32]

He found another card to play. The agents Curtis Brown had sold the film rights to *The Honey-Pot* along with the sequel, *Love Maggy*, for a total of £1,600 – a life-changing amount. As owner of the Countess Barcynska name, Armiger signed the contract and promptly wrote to Marguerite informing her that he would give her half. As Marguerite had anticipated, there was a catch: she would receive her share of the fee only if she agreed to write solely in the name of Barcynska. With £800 of film royalties dangled in front of her, Marguerite was left with little choice but to agree to his demands.

Yet no amount of coercion by Armiger could make Marguerite write if she did not feel motivated. As her Barcynska labour slowed down, then almost came to a halt, Armiger resorted to writing a Barcynska himself and submitting it to *Woman's Weekly*. It was so markedly different from (and inferior to) Marguerite's work, that Johnson spotted it immediately and alerted Marguerite, telling her to seek help from the Society of Authors. Its secretary, G. Herbert Thring, told her that Armiger had no claim on her work. He said he could not help her directly as Armiger was also a member, but recommended a solicitor who could help.

It was Armiger's turn to be on the receiving end of a threatening letter. It was sent by Marguerite's solicitor, advising him that his client wanted to sever all connection with her estranged husband. He was silenced at last.

A few months later he left the country and decamped to Menton on the Côte d'Azur. He did not go there for the sunshine: Menton was a well-known tax haven. As Marguerite soon discovered, Armiger had fled there to avoid paying tax on the film royalties, leaving her with a parting gift of a demand for unpaid tax from HM Customs and Excise. Although he had already deducted her share of tax from her payment, he left Marguerite shouldering the tax bill for both of them.

Already supporting two households – her father's as well as her own – it came as a hard blow. Worse still was the feeling that Armiger would never stop tormenting her. He was living in a different country, but still threatened to ruin her. How many more bills for his unpaid tax demands would she be liable for? Resolving to break his hold over her work, she appointed solicitors to threaten him with the full weight of the law if he continued to meddle with her writing and her writing names. 'I was not the credulous, superimposed young girl any more,' she writes. 'I was a young woman who had been robbed of one name and had made another.[33]

And then came a near miracle. The threats of legal action persuaded Armiger to change his mind and sign an agreement stating the rights for the existing Barcynska works would be split between the two of them, while any new 'Barcynskas' would become Marguerite's sole property. She dared to hope that this would break Armiger's stranglehold. Yet her freedom came at a high price; for all the sixteen Barcynska novels she had written she had signed away fifty per cent of the rights.

The letters from Armiger stopped, but she still held her breath whenever she heard the post land on the mat, wondering if she really had heard the last of him.

Chapter 6
A Dangerous Age

No one would have dreamt she was nearing forty –
the dangerous age for married women of
temperament, if they are foolish enough to fall in
love.
(Oliver Sandys, *Chappy, That's All*)[1]

Marguerite's portrait looks out of place among the debutantes and high commanders' wives. It is 1928 and her dark wavy hair is combed and pressed: a nod to the bob, which was now de rigueur. Her dark skin and square, strong features do not quite fit with the women's page of *The Bystander*. There is something else, too. It is almost impossible to look at this picture without wondering if Marguerite, the daughter of a white colonial family in India, could be of Indian (or part-Indian) origin. Perhaps it is just the lighting or the angle of the camera. Or does it reveal something more than Marguerite had intended?

The biographer Lytton Strachey described Marguerite as 'a vast highly coloured woman in the "Spanish style"'.[2] 'Spanish style' was a coded – and widely recognised – description of a person of part Indian origin, generally known as 'Eurasian'. In British-ruled India, miscegenation was strongly discouraged and those considered to be of mixed race were stigmatised. When that 'bard of empire', Rudyard Kipling, wrote, 'A man should, whatever happens, keep to his own caste, race and breed', he was articulating the received wisdom of his middle-class, middlebrow readership.[3] But scratch the surface of the Raj and a more complex, multi-layered society is revealed. The practice of British men living, and often fathering children, with local women was widespread. Kipling himself wrote a number of stories on the theme, most notably 'Without Benefit of Clergy', a sensitive although ultimately tragic treatment of the love affair between an English civil servant, John Holden, and Almeera, the Indian woman he loves and for whom he has secretly set up a home. Later, when Almeera dies of the plague, propriety demands that the grieving Holden maintain a stiff upper lip and never speak of her again. Marguerite's mixed 'marriage' subplot in her early bestseller *The Pleasure Garden*, where the villain Levett fathers a child with his local 'wife', only to abandon her when his English fiancée turns up, has a similarly tragic ending. Although only spoken of in whispers, it was common knowledge that it was not only white men who took Indian lovers: that lonely *memsahibs* were also known to seek solace in the arms of Indian men.[4] Could Marguerite's mother have been one of them? That is unknowable.

The caption beneath Marguerite's picture reads 'Oliver Sandys', with 'Mrs W. P. Lovell' in brackets: the name she had adopted for the sake of propriety. Marguerite, having finally left Armiger, was still living with retired colonel Walter Preston Lovell. Armiger, now settled in in France, was still refusing to grant her a divorce.

The photograph captures Marguerite at the high-water mark of her career. With a row of successes behind her, her recently published Oliver Sandys novel *Vista the Dancer* was already one of the bestselling books of her career, with a second edition published within a year of its release. Part humorous, part titillating, and with a dash of melodrama and earthy realism combined, *Vista the Dancer* is a fast-paced, entertaining romp that follows the adventures (and misadventures) of Vista, a rich girl who, finding herself penniless following the sudden death of her alcoholic father, takes to earning her living as a scantily clad 'dancing instructress' in a shady nightclub. Twenty years later, its republication as part of the Toucan Novels series was to mark its 104th reprint, with total sales of well over 100,000.

Sales of first-edition rights alone were earning Marguerite more than £1,000 a year[5], while income from second and third serial rights in the UK, the US, Canada, Australia and Brazil (where Portuguese translations of Sandys and Barcynska are still sold today) also came pouring in. Still writing for newspapers and magazines, she was now among Amalgamated Press's highest paid fiction writers, commanding fees of upwards of £500 for a ten-part serial. One of the most versatile authors on the AP list, her stories would appear in everything from the popular *Woman's Weekly* (circulation over half a million) to the much smaller, yet influential, *London Magazine*. Later, Hurst and Blackett would bring out each serial as a novel. Marguerite had turned herself into a one-woman fiction assembly line, with a remarkable ability to write, adapt and rework stories to order.

Another lucrative source of income came from film adaptions. Marguerite's romantic tales, with their glamorous settings and sensationalist plots, were a perfect match for the silent cinema. When the film version of Barcynska's *Tesha*[6] was released, it was the ninth film adaptation of Marguerite's work in less than eight years.

The silent era was a golden age for the female cinemagoer: most films were made with her in mind. Given that an estimated three out of four members of cinema audiences were female – the majority of them young women who worked in shops, offices or domestic service – this was hardly surprising. As 1920s film critic Iris Barry observed, 'Cinema exists for the purpose of pleasing women.'[7] While real-life women might enjoy westerns, comedies, adventures and other films along with their male counterparts, as far as the film industry was concerned women always wanted romance – or 'women's films' as they were known in the trade. This, however, was a far broader genre than the term implied, encompassing everything from Noel Coward's *Easy Virtue*[8] to costume dramas like *Mary Queen of Scots*[9] or *Nell Gwyn*,[10] to social issue films such as the hugely popular *The Constant Nymph*,[11] a controversial tale of a love affair between a fifteen-year-old girl and an older man. Despite their eclecticism, all 'women's films' shared one thing in common: they all had romance at the heart of the story.

The cinema offered rich opportunities for romance authors. Ranked alongside authors like Ethel M. Dell and Margaret Kennedy, it was not unusual for Marguerite's name (or names) to receive a higher billing than even a film's director or stars. Press advertisements for *A Woman in the Night* (the film version of *Tesha*) hailed it as 'the screen version of the world famous novel by Countess Barcynska'. Similarly, billboards for *The Pleasure Garden* made much of its origins as 'the novel by Oliver Sandys',[12] with Alfred Hitchcock's handwritten signature – insisted upon by the film's twenty-five-year-old first-time director – consigned to bottom billing. In later years, Hitchcock was to dismiss this silent melodrama, as he did so much of his oeuvre, as just another 'assignment film'. Nor did Marguerite make much of the film – or indeed, of her involvement with the film industry in general – referring to it only fleetingly as Hitchcock's first film.[13] This is a pity because *The Pleasure Garden* is a tense, emotionally fraught and sometimes witty film that deserves more praise than its author or director were prepared to give it.[14]

As cheques from film companies, publishers and Amalgamated Press poured in, Marguerite might have been expected to keep an eye to the future: anticipating school or university fees for Nicholas, saving for a pension for herself, or simply putting aside some money for the inevitable rainy day. Instead, she spent every penny as quickly as she earned it. 'I was wildly extravagant,' she admits, particularly when it came to buying cars, for which she had a 'mania'. At a time when owning a car was a luxury beyond most people's means, she bought 'a Morris car, then a Vauxhall, then a Daimler, then a Nash, then [another] Vauxhall' in quick succession. Despite this love of motoring, she could not drive and showed little interest in learning, preferring to rely on her uniformed chauffeur.

Indulging her taste for fine jewellery, furs and gowns, Marguerite became a regular at the costumier Jay's of Regent Street, whose customers included royalty and film stars. 'You have no idea how money flies!' declares the fashion-loving Fay in the Oliver Sandys novel *Mr Anthony*. Like Fay, Marguerite was discovering that 'six thousand a year doesn't go very far on clothes, when you must be right up-to-the-minute'.

Perhaps her biggest extravagance of all was an attempt to launch the acting career she had never really begun. In 1925, as *The Pleasure Garden* was being filmed, Marguerite put all her commissions on hold and travelled to Hollywood in the hope of landing a role in its burgeoning film industry. Now approaching her forties and well beyond the age of a Hollywood starlet, she must have appeared deluded.

Later that year, the romantic comedy *Stage Struck* was released. The film's plot of a girl next door who, after losing her boyfriend to an actress, vows to become a star and outshine her love rival, could easily have come from one of Marguerite's novels. Its heroine, Jennie Hagan, was played by one of Hollywood's biggest stars, Gloria Swanson.[15] Hilda Wagner, the pampered daughter of Hagan's employers, who appears alongside Swanson, is played by Marguerite Evans (Marguerite's most recent pseudonym and second stage name). Confounding all expectations, she had landed an acting role[16] – and, moreover, in a high status film with an international star.

It was a remarkable achievement, yet one which Marguerite was uncharacteristically quiet about. In a passing reference to her acting 'alongside Gloria Swanson', she does not reveal the film's name or her role in it.[17] Perhaps she did not want to draw attention to her character, Hilda Wagner, or Hilda 'Fatty' Wagner: the spoilt, lazy and, above all, fat comic character. Perhaps also she did not want to reveal that she had, at least in part, been chosen for her large frame – although this was likely exaggerated by means of a fat suit.

Watching *Stage Struck* today, Swanson's beauty, charm and wit still shine through. Marguerite's performance also has a special quality: one that reveals the same brio, the same flair for comic timing, that permeates her writing. Had she continued in

Hollywood, it is easy to believe that she could have built a career for herself as a character actor. Yet character roles would not have chimed with the image of the glamorous romance author she had so carefully cultivated.

Or perhaps she had discovered that film acting, or Hollywood, or both, were not to her taste. The collaborative medium of film would not have allowed her anything like the autonomy she enjoyed as an author. Or perhaps Arthur Thisone, the actor in the 1940 Sandys novel *Singing Uphill*, reflected her own experiences when he said he 'could not stay any longer' in Hollywood because it had made him feel 'not wanted'.[18]

Whatever the reason, this debut was also to be her last film appearance. She returned to London, apparently now content to jump back on the same writing merry-go-round she had sought to escape. Soon she was back on her old schedule of four novels a year – two Sandys and two Barcynskas – in addition to magazine work. Even by the standards of romance writers of the time, from whom publishers generally expected a high output (higher than that of writers of detective stories, for example), her productivity was astonishing. Although (female) romance writers like Marguerite, or Berta Ruck,[19] or Georgette Heyer – whose 1921 novel, *The Black Moth*, was the first in what was to be a long-running series of swashbuckling Regency romances – earned sizeable profits for their publishers and generous royalties for themselves, they had become the workhorses of the literary world, pressurised by publishers to produce more titles each year. Inevitably, such demands had an effect on the quality of their work, which in turn did nothing to improve the genre's already low status.

To maintain her relentless schedule, Marguerite wrote all day and often through the night: refusing to rest, or even eat, until she had completed her self-imposed daily quota. Her habit of writing while reclining on the sofa, pen in hand (preferring always to write by hand), made it look deceptively relaxed and effortless. Marguerite would insist that hers was an automatic, unconscious act. Yet her study, a bright and airy room that overlooked their rose garden, she barely noticed, let alone enjoyed. The garden, the house, her relationship with Walter, even her son Nicholas, were fading into a vague, shadowy backdrop. Only her work felt real. She worked compulsively, her hand moving as fast as the dancing feet of Karen in Hans Christian Andersen's 'The Red Shoes': compelled by a force beyond her control. Like Gaynor, the heroine of *The Pleasure Garden* and its sequel *Old Roses*, Marguerite would write through the night, stopping only when the book was finished and she would suddenly realise 'how dreadfully tired she was, mentally and physically spent, literally too weary to minister to her own creature comforts'.[20]

She no longer had Armiger standing over her, setting the pace, but she did not feel she had exorcised his presence completely. He was still receiving half the proceeds of her earlier Barcynska novels and, for that reason alone, would not grant her the divorce she wanted. She could not erase her fear that he might strike again, that one of his immaculately written threats might arrive in the post any day. Although they were apart, his presence loomed over her: a threatening cloud that darkened her shining career.

Marguerite, Walter and Nicholas were settled in a newly-built house called Suncrete in Kingsbury, north London.[21] Designed by the eminent architect Sir Reginald Bloomfield in the emerging modernist style, Suncrete was an early experiment in Portland cement.[22] It marked a change of direction for Bloomfield, whose earlier work tended towards the neo-classical. Marguerite writes that the house came with 'the newest labour-saving devices – a special soft water system, special flooring, special asbestos walls, Crittall windows' and the 'geometrically designed rose garden' that her study overlooked.

In her concrete and asbestos palace, Marguerite's life was in tune with the bold spirit of the age. Later, she would claim that she had disliked Suncrete, longing instead for country lanes and quaint old cottages – a longing she satisfied, at least in part, by getting her chauffeur to make an eighty-mile round trip up the Great North

Road for her and Walter 'just to spend an hour or so surrounded by fields and clean fresh air'.[23]

Now retired from the army, Walter made himself useful by acting as her secretary and bookkeeper. With Marguerite immersed in her work, he also spent a lot of time with Nicholas, the two of them becoming inseparable. Whether Walter was the boy's biological father or not, they were as close as any father and son. The nine-year-old Nicholas was being educated at home by a succession of private tutors. Perhaps because he had been starved of the company of other children, Nicholas had developed a fierce temper and was prone to sudden, dramatic mood swings.

Mother and son both leaned heavily on Walter. Patient and kind to a fault, Walter was Marguerite's 'rock' and one 'solid friend'. Yet despite his admirable qualities, Marguerite was growing tired of him. She was particularly frustrated by his lack of interest in books: when she asked him for a critique of a story she was working on, his response was always the same; it was always 'top class'. Marguerite wanted a mentor and critic, something that Walter could never be, but Armiger – warts and all – had been.

If she had socialised with other writers, Walter's different interests and temperament might not have been such an issue. Practical and level-headed, he might even have exerted a healthy, grounding influence over her. But she had cut herself off from literary circles and had no literary friends. Avoiding parties 'or any sort of gatherings where well-knowns or would-be-knowns congregated', she claimed she 'would rather die' than attend a PEN club luncheon or a Society of Authors annual dinner party.[24] Still reeling from her acrimonious legal battle with Armiger, she may have been afraid of running into him at a literary event. Or, more likely, in circles where Armiger would have been known (and where there was even the risk of his making an appearance), her cover of respectability as Mrs W.P. Lovell could easily have been exposed.

She may also have felt reluctant to meet other, more literary, authors for fear that they would look down on her popular brand of writing. Marguerite, who had always prided herself on being a few steps ahead of the latest trends, would have been painfully aware that the show-business romance, her stock-in-trade for the past twenty years, was beginning to feel a little tired.

Despite her phenomenal sales, despite the warm reviews in the popular press, despite even the daily bundle of fan mail from readers, she was plagued by self-doubt. 'Who wants to read brainy books, with sentences left out and asterisks and spaces which is [*sic*] meant for you to fill in because the author can't be bothered to?'[25] When Marguerite put these words into the mouth of the maid in *Old Roses*, she might have been rehearsing a defence of her own, often maligned, work. As her later attempts at a more 'literary' style would testify, Marguerite was harbouring a secret ambition to write some 'brainy books' of her own. While the idea of becoming a 'serious' author appealed, she feared the loss of those luxuries that she had come to adore and which were paid for by her lowbrow bestsellers. So long as women wanted to read her 'light and frothy' romances, she would continue to oblige them.

Now, as she approached her middle years, her work was becoming sidelined by a new generation of writers: women writers in particular. These bright new authors had grown up during the Great War and, in 1918, had watched as women over thirty had won the right to vote. But it was the run-up to 1928, when women finally won the vote on a par with men, that marked their coming of age. This brave new army of short-skirted, bob-haired flappers were unafraid of declaring themselves feminists. To them, Marguerite's tales of good women led astray by bad men were as creaky as the whalebone corsets their mothers still wore.

In the literary pages of the press, the generation gap was all too visible. A 1929 magazine review of Marguerite's latest Sandys novel, *The Champagne Kiss* (about a man who had 'crossed land and water to meet an actress with whose portrait in a newspaper he had fallen in love'), was nudged to the page's outer margins, with column after column given over to a feature on *Halycon, or the Future of*

Monogamy, a utopian pamphlet by the up-and-coming feminist author Vera Brittain. Hailed as 'a brilliant criticism of the relations of the sexes today', *Halcyon* is set in 2050 and framed as a history lecture given by a woman professor who outlines the oppressions endured by women during the twentieth century: in particular, the draconian divorce laws which forced women into dependency and prevented them from 'following the lives they desire'.[26] Brittain's book may have nudged Marguerite's into the shade, but given Armiger's continued refusal to grant her a divorce, she would at least have identified with its premise.

In contrast, reviews of Marguerite's Barcynska offering of that year, *He Married His Parlourmaid*[27] – billed by the publishers Chapman as 'an honest-to-goodness drawing room melodrama' – were as tepid as they were brief. 'It is', said one, 'a much pleasanter and more readable story than the rather sensational title suggests.'[28] Yet to take *He Married His Parlourmaid* seriously (as most critics did) would be to miss the playful irony of its knowingly anachronistic title. Marguerite had no illusions about her role; her business was to create the escapist confections that her loyal female readers could still not get enough of, regardless of the latest trends. She did it with such mastery and such a light touch that she made it look easy, when in reality it was anything but.

In the popular markets, too, her novels were beginning to look a little tired, as women readers turned to stronger stuff. The runaway success of E.M. Hull's 1919 novel *The Sheik*[29] had sent shockwaves throughout popular culture. The smouldering good looks of Rudolph Valentino, who starred as the eponymous sheik in the 1921 film version, increased sales still further, as 'sheik' entered the language as slang for a man with sex appeal. An American bestseller for two years running (sixth in 1921 and second in 1922) and in many ways a forerunner of the twenty-first century's *Fifty Shades of Grey*, *The Sheik* tells the tale of a cold English girl who is kidnapped by an Arab sheik and (it is implied) repeatedly raped until, finally, 'for the first time she surrendered to him wholly, clinging to him passionately and giving him kiss for kiss with an absolute abandonment of all resistance.'[30] Marguerite's stories, once considered sensational, were now rendered tame.

The American import *Gentlemen Prefer Blondes* by Anita Loos,[31] also made waves. Set in New York and a variety of European locations, the 1925 novel follows the escapades and dalliances of a young blonde flapper during the roaring twenties. In contrast, *The Ginger-Jar*,[32] released in 1926, the same year as the British edition of *Gentlemen Prefer Blondes*, reprises Marguerite's earlier tales of chorus girls and the predatory men who lust after them. Although no longer original, it hardly merited the two-page castigation it received from one critic:

> Does anybody seriously ... believe that the only possible way in which any actress can succeed on the modern stage is by forming an illicit liaison with her employer? ... It is a sorry libel on a band of hard-working men, many of whom are among the most conscientious artists to be found in London.[33]

In today's post-#MeToo era, Marguerite's 'sorry libel' seems strikingly prescient, while the views of her critic appear naïve at best or, at worst, complicit.

During the 1920s, the reputation of romance fiction – involving as it did everything from romantic comedy to melodrama, from the 'sex novel' to the problem novel – had hit a low point. Although still loved by its readers, it was sneered at by critics for its sentimentality and implausible plots. Yet authors like Marguerite were not attempting realism; they were in the business of producing escapist fantasies that were as different from real life as possible. Moreover, the women in romance novels had agency, unlike so many women in real life. The romance novel was the only genre where women had control over their lives, where a heroine might enjoy her pick of men, where there was no such thing as the post-war man shortage.

Read mainly by women, most of them working class, the romance novel was doubly castigated. Even its readers shared in the generally low opinion of the genre. Jenny, the young prostitute in Patrick Hamilton's *Twenty Thousand Streets Under the Sky*, knew this all too well: although a great fan of romance novels, she still considered them 'ever so silly ... only written for factory girls really'.[34] Yet, like Jenny, those women who enjoyed them remained loyal, despite their reputation. While critics despised it, romance was far too popular for publishers to ignore.

Like many women writers of romance, Marguerite cut a paradoxical figure. As the critic Elaine Jackson observed, 'Marguerite Jervis (and others like her) were promoting love, marriage and financial dependence on a man, yet – aside from perhaps movie stars – they were the highest earning women of their period.'[35]

Scratch the surface of outward sentimentality and the works reveal an earthier reality. Their heroines would earn their living in one of the few arenas open to them: on the stage, in an office, in domestic service or even, as in *Chicane*, through engaging in criminal activity. Unlike other leading romance writers of her time (including the bestselling phenomenon Barbara Cartland, whose writing career began in 1921), Marguerite was not afraid to break a few moral codes. With Maggy, the chorus-girl heroine of her breakthrough bestseller *The Honey-Pot*, she created a new kind of heroine who, despite being seduced by the hero and later giving birth to his illegitimate child, still has the happiest of endings. Marguerite's novels were unashamed romantic escapism, but they also featured girls who broke the rules and got away with it. Her novels came with their own set of values in which love was prized above all, while hypocrisy, sexual frigidity and marriage for marriage's sake were despised and often punished.

Marguerite's 1927 Sandys novel *The Sorceress*[36] demonstrated her ability to adapt to changing tastes. Marking a departure in style, this light-hearted supernatural romance sees a paranormal femme fatale, a latter-day Circe who bewitches and ultimately destroys men, herself falling in love with one of her victims. Praised for its 'very daring and original theme',[37] *The Sorceress* not only sold well, but, in critical terms at least, restored the author's status as a major figure in the fast-moving romance market.

During this period, most of Marguerite's days were spent lying on the couch in her airy modern study, notepad on lap, writing. She would write almost continuously, anxious to maintain the luxuries that she had come to regard as essential. Even the drives out to the country she had once so enjoyed were now rare events. She began to feel 'restless'. She was beginning to 'tire' of writing stories which had to abide by the strictures of the Amalgamated Press house style, as set out by Winifred Johnson. In particular, she struggled to strip her stories of any humour, in line with Johnson's insistence that contributions should not include any of the breezy, cynical wit which had once been her trademark. Johnson insisted the romance between a man and a woman should be treated seriously, that any humour in a story would lower its moral tone. Nor would she allow anything that could be construed as risqué. Yet Marguerite had learnt her craft writing titillating material for the barely legal *Sievier's Monthly*. The rules ran counter to all her instincts as a writer – they were draining her work of its colour. When later adapting a magazine serial into a novel, she would inevitably inject additional wit and spice into the tale in an attempt to resuscitate it.

Then her publishers phoned. They had received a solicitor's letter on behalf of a Mr Archie Pitt – a well-known music-hall artist and theatrical agent, and the husband and manager of the popular singer Gracie Fields. He was taking out a libel action against her for using his name for the character of a bogus theatre producer in the Barcynska novel *The Curled Hands*. Marguerite insisted it had been just an innocent mistake on her part and Pitt eventually agreed to an out-of-court settlement of £25. Yet the prospect of another legal battle, coming so soon after her protracted legal struggle with Armiger, hit her hard.

Soon afterwards, she also received some terrible news: her

beloved Aunt Tots – the one constant of her unsettled childhood – had died. Her death was as sudden as it was unexpected. Tots had gone away, apparently to recuperate following an illness, and had died without Marguerite or any of her family around her.[38] It was closely followed by another blow. In February 1927, her father died in his sleep following a long illness.

Marguerite's mother felt 'too overcome' to attend the funeral. Her brothers – both working as schoolteachers in nearby Brighton – did not attend either. On the day of his burial, Marguerite and the doctor who had attended during Henry's illness were the only mourners present. It would have made a poignant – although not unusual – ending for a retired officer of the Indian Army. Unlike the working-class men he'd commanded, Jervis was one of those officers whose families had served in the colonies for generations and who returned to his home country to find his family ties loosened, with relatives scattered across Britain and around the world. Marguerite was to dedicate her next novel, *Blinkeyes*[39] to 'Lt. Colonel H.P. Jervis I.M.S. (retd.) (Daddie) with all love'. To the last, Marguerite sought the approval of the father who had called her writing 'trash'.

Then she fell ill with 'nervous exhaustion.'[40] At a time when nervous exhaustion or anything that could be perceived as madness might be treated with alarm or suspicion, it was not surprising she chose to reveal so little. To reveal anything at all, as she did, was in itself a brave and forward-thinking act. She does not say how her illness affected her work. Her books continued to be published at their normal, prolific rate and her stories were also doing the rounds in a number of Amalgamated Press publications, among them the popular literary magazine *T.P.'s Weekly*.

Founded by the larger-than-life Irish nationalist and radical MP T.P. O'Connor, *T.P.'s Weekly*'s mission was 'to bring to many thousands a love of letters'. When Marguerite had submitted an autobiographical feature to the paper, she'd received a letter asking her to call in to discuss it with the assistant editor. Framed as a memoir of her early years in journalism, her real motive behind the article was to refute an earlier article by Armiger, in which he'd revived his claim to have authored *The Honey-Pot*. Anxious that her version of events would be challenged, she was not looking forward to the encounter.[41] She was looking forward to meeting the paper's notoriously volatile assistant editor, Caradoc Evans, even less.

Chapter 7
Marguerite and 'the Man'

*[She] knew he was selfish and probably a little unkind,
possibly bad-tempered, that he would never care for a
woman in the way that women crave to be cared for ... All
the same, she knew that she would get too fond of him.*
(Countess Hélène Barcynska, *The Honey-Pot*)[1]

Marguerite met Caradoc Evans in 1924, although she claimed it was later. It was, she wrote, love at first sight. 'As soon as I saw his shrewd, penetrating, deep-set eyes, I knew this was my hour and my man, whatever was to come afterwards.'[2] Marguerite was thirty-eight, Caradoc forty-five. With his high cheekbones and angular face, his yellow shirt, green silk tie, wide-checked tailored jacket and trademark fedora, the one-time draper's assistant cut a striking figure. Marguerite, her wrist clattering with Indian bangles, bedecked in furs and brightly-coloured chiffons, was that rare woman who could both appreciate and rival this peacock-like man. Sartorially and temperamentally, they were set to become the most colourful of couples.

An eccentric who revelled in his reputation as 'the wild Welshman' of Fleet Street, Caradoc Evans had authored two acclaimed, although controversial, collections of short stories, *My People* (1915) and *Capel Sion* (1916). Their experimental mix of biblical and Welsh modes of speech, combined with excoriating attacks on Welsh rural life, had, outside Wales at least, attracted praise from literary giants such as T.S. Eliot and James Joyce, with some comparing him to Gorky or Swift.

Yet back in his native Wales he was known as a national pariah.

116

His savage attacks on his nation's hallowed rural, chapel-going heartland – involving such grotesqueries as the tale of the poverty-blighted widow forced to live on a diet of boiled rats, or the madwoman whose husband keeps her tethered in the cowshed – had ignited a blaze of hurt and rage. Caradoc's books, deemed 'treacherous' by the Welsh press, were taken off the shelves in most of the nation's bookshops, and their author declared 'the best-hated man in Wales'.[3] His insistence that his stories were based on truths, ones he observed during his childhood in the west Wales village of Rhydlewis, was seen only as further provocation. He did not add that they were, at least in part, sparked by childhood memories of the contempt his 'godly' neighbours had shown towards his widowed mother, a poverty-stricken tenant farmer.

Marguerite's account of 'that day of fate' reads like an early Barcynska romance – one in which she is the heroine of her own story. Caradoc told her how much he admired her writing. Although a conventional enough opening gambit for an editor meeting one of his authors, it had been a long time since she had received this kind of validation. And to get it from someone like Caradoc, who was more than a mere commissioning editor (she already knew how to elicit their praise), and an acclaimed author – and a literary one at that – thrilled her. Better still, he admired her work for the very quality that made others look down on it: its popularity. 'You're a damn successful woman,' he said. 'I'm not a best-seller. I'm a best-talked about.'[4] It was exactly the kind of flattery she had been longing for. That and his 'penetrating eyes', which studied her with undisguised admiration, made her feel every bit as fluttery as any of her fictional heroines.

Caradoc confessed he drank 'a lot of sherries', claiming he was 'the unhappiest man alive'. He also admitted to being married – to a woman who hated him. Even this old cliché could not deter the besotted Marguerite. At the end of their meeting, Caradoc walked her to the lift and they said goodbye. There was no need for further discussion. They had already arranged to meet the next day.

For Marguerite, it was the start of a grand passion. For Caradoc, it was a well-rehearsed routine, with Marguerite only the latest female contributor summoned to his office for him to 'size up'. He was already involved in an affair with another woman journalist, as well as conducting a long-distance liaison with the Derbyshire-based poet Teresa Hooley.[5] An account of meeting Caradoc by Welsh romance author Edith Nepean is strikingly similar to Marguerite's. Still in her twenties and just having sent her first submission to the magazine *Ideas*, Nepean received a message: 'We have a wild Welsh editor chained up, he wants to meet you.' On meeting him, she said, Caradoc lit his pipe, looked through her manuscript, then finally, looking up, offered her £80 for it. Perhaps out of discretion, she makes no claim that he tried to seduce her.

Marguerite, her eyes shut tight, made the most eager of victims. When it came to affairs of the heart, she followed the example of her favourite heroine, Gaynor, who if she fell in love with a man did not hesitate to love him 'too generously',[6] although she was not so naïve as to be unaware of his reputation. As her infatuation turned to obsession, she would check on him every day, anxious he might be seeing another woman. Caradoc's colleague and fellow journalist, Austin Clarke, remembers her as the 'popular novelist in a large fur coat' who made a 'damn nuisance' of herself by constantly calling on Caradoc at work. To Clarke, Marguerite was just the latest in Caradoc's long line of mistresses; to Marguerite, Caradoc was considerably more. Clarke recalls how he would hear Marguerite's raised voice coming from behind Caradoc's door. Once she called when Caradoc was on the phone to one of his other mistresses and snatched the phone out of his hand. Caradoc leapt to his feet, grabbed his editor's scissors and promptly snipped the line.[7]

Despite its tempestuous start, their relationship endured. Caradoc became 'the man'. In turn he returned the compliment by naming her 'the woman'. Five years later, their relationship had matured into what Marguerite described as their 'courtship'.

Caradoc, now a prolific writer of letters to Marguerite, wrote with a voice that was in turn courtly, passionate, manipulative and cruel:

> My lovely one, you hung up on the telephone last night and I do not know what made you or how I have offended you and I cannot rest for thinking and wondering what was wrong with you or me. If you turn your face from me now, or stop coming to see me I shall not be able to stick it ... I am afraid to ring tonight lest you do not answer my call. Then I shall not dare to go home.
> Your Caradoc

The letter ends with a poem, its erotic tone echoing *The Letters of Abelard and Heloise*, which Caradoc had given Marguerite a copy of during their second meeting:

> The stuffing on your bed is my good wishes.
> The down in your pillow is my breath.
> The sleep on your eyelids is my soul.
> Therefor your pillow is too soft for sorry.

In another letter, he reveals both his cruel, sadistic streak and his love of sherry – a combination that was to poison their relationship:

> My darling,
> I am sorry I was late today. I had no business to be late. You know I like to be on time ... I had three sherries only. You ticked me off and I said unkind things to you. I provoked you and went on provoking and could not stop myself. You looked so beautiful. It pleased me to make you cry.[8]

It would have been next to impossible to hide this intense relationship from Walter – if, indeed, Marguerite made any attempt to hide it, which is doubtful. Nor did Caradoc's own infidelities prevent him from feeling jealous of the man she was living with, even accusing Walter of being a gold-digger who only wanted to stay with Marguerite for her money. It was a malicious theory to which Marguerite refused to subscribe.

Although in thrall to Caradoc, she was still fond of Walter and was racked with guilt at the thought of leaving him. Even worse, the prospect of leaving Nicholas tormented her. Now approaching his thirteenth birthday, he was prone to what Marguerite described as 'dark moods' and was already showing signs of becoming a troubled young man. She dreaded the effect her leaving would have on him. There were also the practicalities to consider. Would it be better for Nicholas to go with his mother or to stay with Walter, his main carer? Marguerite was afraid (correctly, as it turned out) that Caradoc and Nicholas would resent each other. Caradoc's 'reassurance' that he would only resent Nicholas if she loved him more than she loved Caradoc only added an element of menace to her dilemma. It may have been Nicholas, or Walter, or both that Caradoc had in mind when he warned Marguerite not to make him jealous. 'Oh, my jealousy can be cruel,' he said. It was a warning that Marguerite did not, or would not, heed.

Then Caradoc asked Marguerite if she would join him in Wales on his annual trip to visit his mother, Mari Evans. She readily agreed. It would make a welcome escape from the tensions at home and provide a chance to spend undiluted time with her lover. Mari still lived in Rhydlewis, the village where Caradoc had spent his childhood and which he had fictionalised as Manteg, the setting for his grotesque tales of Welsh rural life. Marguerite took a more romantic view. Far from finding it grotesque, she found Rhydlewis, and Wales in general, to be a 'land of enchantment and faery'. She also adored Caradoc's mother. Mari, known locally as 'Mari Lanlas' (after her cottage, Lanlas Uchaf), displayed all the humour and quick wit that had earned her the nickname *shortlyd* ('sporty'). Marguerite failed to see any resemblance between Caradoc's mother and his portrayal of her as a poor widow who had been cast out by her community.[9]

Although she had once been expelled from her local chapel when she couldn't afford to pay her membership dues, she had long since returned and appeared to bear no bitterness. Although, as sometimes happens in small communities, Mari's apparently cheerful disposition may have been masking layers of resentment, Marguerite could not find any sign of it. Instead, she was greeted by a lively, smiling old woman who regaled her and Caradoc with local gossip and tales.

It was during her trip to Wales, claims Marguerite, that she made up her mind: she had chosen Caradoc. Walter called her a fool but, in his usual reasonable way, added that she was free to do as she wished. With no marriage vows to bind them together, she was indeed free to leave him. With Nicholas it was not so easy. Just as Marguerite had feared, he took the news badly. To add to his difficulties, Marguerite left him to decide who he wanted to live with: his mother or Walter. It was a choice that no thirteen-year-old should face, especially one as vulnerable as Nicholas. 'It was all very strained and heart-rending for us three,' writes Marguerite. Nicholas, who had taken an instant dislike to Caradoc, decided to stay with Walter. Given that Caradoc still envied his stepson, viewing him as a rival for his lover's affections, this was not so surprising. Considering the unpleasant choice the boy had to face, Walter, with whom he had a close bond, would have been the safer option. It also conveniently fitted in with Caradoc's wishes and Marguerite's desire to avoid any disharmony in their first home together. However, Marguerite does not mention what Walter's feelings were on taking sole charge of his troubled stepson.

Marguerite and Caradoc's new life together came at a time when Caradoc's life was in turmoil. After years of drinking, womanising and treating Fleet Street as his main home, he was finally walking away from his long-suffering wife, Rose. Then came the news that *T.P.'s Weekly* was closing and he was to go with it. The job he loved, and around which he had built his life, was over. He had also lost his comfortable £500 a year salary. The magazine, which had been struggling for some time, finally closed in November 1929. Coming as it did just two weeks before the death of its eighty-one-year-old proprietor, the former radical MP and all-round colourful character T.P. O'Connor,[10] the demise of *T.P.'s* marked the end of an era. It was also the end of an era for its contributors: Dilys Powell, Rebecca West, D.H. Lawrence, and, of course, Marguerite, among them. The end of the magazine noted for paying its writers generously, came as a blow to many, not least Marguerite. Nor were the prospects good for Caradoc. The chances of this eccentric, fifty-year-old literary editor finding another suitable post on Fleet Street during what was a period of mergers, takeovers and redundancies were not good. Caradoc knew that the demise of *T.P.'s* marked the end of his career in journalism – a profession he had burst into through a combination of strength of will and sheer talent. As a young man, he had doggedly attended night classes at Camden Working Men's College, where he mastered his skills in English, his second language, allowing him to eventually escape the drapery trade ('the densest of professions') for the colour and excitement of Fleet Street. Now it had all come to an abrupt halt.

Secretly, Marguerite thought it might be for the best. She had already hatched a scheme for the two of them to go away together to the country, where they could live together in rural bliss and write all day – his bitter, sardonic prose providing the perfect counter to her light and frothy romances. Then in the evening, he would teach her to play Welsh hymns on the piano, or they would sit in front of a log fire and share their day's work with each other. It was as if she wanted to recreate her early days with Armiger at Yew Tree Cottage with its meadows and white-blossomed orchard. Only this time it would not be a literary marriage of convenience, but a grand literary passion. And who knew? Together they might even become a fêted literary couple – a latter-day Mary and Percy Shelley or Elizabeth and Robert Browning. Marguerite felt it was high time for Caradoc to leave Fleet Street – and, more to the point, the drinking habit he had acquired there. Away from temptation, Marguerite told herself, Caradoc would drink less and write more. Without all the responsibilities and distractions of his job, she felt sure his writing would flourish and – who knew? – he might take his place as one of the great literary figures of his age.

Together they left London – 'ran away' as Marguerite put it – to a 'picturesque cottage' in the Cotswolds and quickly settled down to the daily writing routine they had agreed. But it did not last long. Caradoc, who had never liked the country, soon tired of his new surroundings and longed for the excitement of London. Shutting himself away all day to write did not suit his restless, gregarious temperament. Instead of sticking to his writing routine, he would disappear at midday to the village pub, returning hours later in a haze of beer and sherry. Marguerite had underestimated the hold that alcohol had on him. For further amusement, Caradoc took to picking arguments with the gardener, against whom he had developed a grudge. He even took it upon himself to send letters of complaint to the landlord, a tea planter in India, demanding that he sack the gardener for having an affair with the maid. It is not clear if Caradoc's suspicions were well-founded or, indeed, if they were motivated by jealousy. In any case, his reaction seemed excessive and, given his history, plainly hypocritical. Yet Marguerite chose to back him up. She even joined in with his petty cruelties: helping him to collect slugs at night to put on their gardener's lettuce patch and later laughing when Caradoc chastised him for neglecting his crops. Instead of acting as a calming influence, she fuelled his paranoia. Already stormy and unpredictable, the loss of his job and leaving London had destabilised him further. Yet Marguerite was in thrall and could not see that he was becoming increasingly disturbed.

Worst of all were his 'terrifying' moods, when he fell into a 'wild drinking spasm'. Yet she would always forgive him: claiming that she could no more be angry with him than she could 'with a child or a dog that has suffered from an attack of hysteria and snapped and frothed and bitten people'. However violent or abusive he was towards her, Marguerite would always find reasons to excuse his behaviour – in print at least.

To add to her difficulties, she was pining for Nicholas. She recalls how she 'cried and cried in my sleep' and had even considered going back to Walter, just to be with Nicholas. Caradoc's response was to threaten suicide if she left him. A genuine threat or not, it had the effect he must have intended as Marguerite relented and agreed to stay with him. She had rid herself of one controlling man, Armiger, only to fall into the arms of another. The difference this time was that she was a willing victim.

Then Marguerite heard that Walter was leaving London for Devon. Nicholas, now aged sixteen and no longer a child, declared he did not want to go with him. Instead he 'unwillingly, angrily, resentfully' moved in with Marguerite and Caradoc.[11] He had been living apart from his mother for three years. It is not clear what had gone on between Nicholas and Walter, but it appears their relationship ended after Walter went to Devon.

Displaying all the charm that he had employed on Marguerite when she first met him, Caradoc gave his stepson the warmest of welcomes. Greeting him on the doorstep, he ushered Nicholas upstairs to show him his library. Caradoc's library was his pride and his sanctuary – and a temple to his glory days in journalism. Among its treasures was a large collection of books by authors he had at different times commissioned, interviewed or reviewed for *T.P.'s Weekly*. Among the ones that caught Nicholas's eye were *Limehouse Nights*, a collection of earthy short stories by Thomas Burke, and *The Autobiography of a Super-Tramp* by celebrity Welsh poet W.H. Davies, each one containing the author's personal message of thanks to Caradoc. Nicholas took *The Return* off the shelf – a collection of Gothic horror stories by the Welsh author Arthur Machen. When a letter from Machen fell from its pages, addressed to Caradoc as 'a special friend of mine', he was enthralled. Machen had been a member of the Hermetic Order of the Golden Dawn, Caradoc told him, the ritual magic group which had counted W.B. Yeats and Aleister Crowley among its members. The book was to spark Nicholas's lifelong fascination with the occult and the Wiccan craft in particular. In later life, he became a devotee of the cult of Isis, the Egyptian goddess that Nicholas termed his 'god in female form'.[12] In the years that followed, Nicholas and Caradoc's mutual interest in the occult was to form not a bond exactly, but an area of mutual understanding: a kind of no man's land between them and a place they could enter for a temporary respite from hostilities. Theirs would never be an easy relationship. Caradoc's self-confessed envy of his stepson would never leave him. He would goad him about his politics (right-wing to Caradoc's left-wing), his lack of academic success, his lack of income. Marguerite would sometimes try, but always fail, to protect her mentally-fragile son from Caradoc's provocations. Yet when Caradoc's latest rage ended and the dust settled, he and Nicholas would be the best of friends again. Together Marguerite, Caradoc and Nicholas formed a strange, turbulent, complicated trio.

In 1930, Marguerite found out through a newspaper report that Armiger had died in France.[13] He had refused to grant her a divorce to the last. Although now free to remarry, Caradoc was still married to Rose, so rendering her new-found liberty meaningless. She also had more pressing concerns. As complicated in death as he had been in life, Armiger had bequeathed his fifty per cent claim on Countess Barcynska royalties to his mistress in France. Her feeling that she had not heard the last from him now proved well-founded. Even in death, he continued to drain her income. Once again, she sought legal redress.

In the event, the case proved straightforward and Marguerite was relieved to win it easily. After more than twenty years, she owned all her work and was rid of Armiger's shadow at last. Yet her victory came at a cost. The court battle – coming straight on the wings of a turbulent decade – had taken its toll, financially and emotionally.

Chapter 8
Wales, 'The Setting of my Soul'

May the spirit of this company be the spirit of good troupers,
and if we can last until the autumn, I won't look any further.
(Oliver Sandys, *The Happy Mummers*)[1]

Aberystwyth 1933

It was early December and the Christmas baubles were still wrapped up in their boxes. There seemed little to celebrate among the boarded-up shops and down-at-heel guest houses of Aberystwyth. Like the rest of Wales, the town was still reeling from the effects of the Great Depression. It was not a scene which augured well for that evening's launch of Rogues and Vagabonds, the town's first repertory theatre company.

Yet Marguerite could see nothing but a future of full houses and glittering reviews. Why shouldn't she? Still at the height of her writing powers, with over eighty books published – eleven of which had been adapted for film – her achievements were considerable, yet one ambition remained. Now, at forty-seven, she was ready to realise her long-held dream of running her own professional theatre company, even if it did mean pouring all her writing royalties into it.

Marguerite's claim that she and Caradoc 'simply went away quietly to live in Wales'[2] could not have been further from the truth. With her enormous veiled hats, scarlet lips and alabaster-powdered face, she cut a colourful figure in rural west Wales. The Welsh press could not get enough of her exotic glamour and effusive personality.

126

And with a ready supply of attention-grabbing anecdotes, she delighted in obliging them.

Her recent marriage to author and notorious literary *enfant terrible* Caradoc Evans shone an even brighter spotlight upon her. The *Western Mail's* report of Marguerite and Caradoc's 'secret' wedding in Maidenhead, Surrey, included two close-up publicity stills: one of the bride, and another of the groom, both sent in by Marguerite. On the left, a pretty, round-faced Marguerite gazes directly ahead through a pair of large, kohl-lined eyes. On the right, a wide-brimmed fedora looms over Caradoc's high cheekbones and trademark scowl. Caradoc's divorce from Rose had come through earlier that year and they were free to marry at last. The press report quotes the groom's age as fifty-one (he was fifty-four) and the bride's as forty-three (she was forty-six), while the date of their wedding was given as May 1933 (it was 22 March).[3]

Together with Nicholas, now aged sixteen, the couple rented Queen's Square House, a grand Regency town house in an elegant corner of town. Marguerite crammed the spacious drawing room with enormous vases, Russian icons, with a centrepiece consisting of an oversized statue of the Buddha.[4] Her new home delighted her, as did Aberystwyth. With its grey sea and moody sky, its shabby charm and friendly welcome, Marguerite was quick to declare her love for the town. Above all, she saw it as an ideal location for her long-dreamed-of theatre company. During an earlier visit with Caradoc she had already scoured the town for potential venues and had seen a number of empty buildings which – with a splash of paint and lot of imagination – she felt sure could be quickly turned into a theatre. She also noted that, compared to south-east England, the rent was pleasingly cheap.

For Caradoc, the move meant he could see more of his mother, whose health was deteriorating. Now only an hour's drive from Mari's cottage in Rhydlewis, where she was being cared for by her granddaughter (and Caradoc's niece) Lil, Caradoc planned to visit her regularly. He knew he could not expect the warmest of welcomes in his native county of Cardiganshire. He had warned Marguerite he was 'not a safe man to be seen with in Wales', that his fellow nationals had not forgotten or forgiven his grotesque tales of Welsh village life. Marguerite, her mind set on Aberystwyth, dismissed it as Caradoc's usual hyperbole.

Not that Marguerite lacked a reputation of her own. With her readership around the million mark, and commercial successes that Caradoc could only dream of, it was inevitable that a number of local people (most of them women) would have been familiar with her books, even if few owned up to the fact. As Marguerite had once observed, hers were the kind of books that women 'stuff behind their sofa cushions'. Her morally ambiguous reputation – which had always helped her book sales – proved more of a problem when it came to attracting an audience for the all-too-visible medium of theatre, especially in a close-knit, chapel-going town, where theatre itself was viewed as suspect.

Undeterred, Marguerite set about applying her skills as a writer of 'the selling stuff'[5] to create some daring publicity. Rather than simply being the launch of a local repertory company, her opening night must amount to something extraordinary, an event within the event. Enter two of Marguerite's reliable old friends – Intrigue and Mystery.

'A novel written to alleviate the sufferings of a dying woman will be presented as a play', ran the *Western Mail* headline. The paper reported how Marguerite had adapted *Chappy, That's All* from her novel of the same name, a novel written 'for the entertainment of Tots, 'my aunt by relationship and my mother in her heart'.[6] At this point, the report reads as if the journalist handed the pen over to Marguerite. As the novel progressed, the article continued, she would read one chapter at a time to her terminally ill aunt during her visits to the nursing home, with Tots promising her niece that she would not die until Marguerite finished reading her the book. This Scheherazade-like account was, like so many of her 'real-life' stories, as much a product of her imagination as any of her novels. While her aunt had indeed been like a mother to her, the nightly readings of *Chappy, That's All* was a fiction that concealed a painful reality. Tots had died suddenly, without Marguerite or any family member present.

In the *Western Mail* feature, Marguerite adds she is 'absolutely convinced' that her late aunt would be present among the audience on the opening night. 'I am not a spiritualist in the accepted sense,' she says, relating an afterlife experience during a recent visit to a medium 'with a friend'. She explains how the medium surprised her by passing on a message from a woman beyond the grave who was anxious to give her a bouquet of flowers. 'I remembered it was my birthday, on which my aunt invariably presented me with flowers.' In this way, she unleashed a curiosity that could not be put back in the box.

On the opening night, a hatted and coated queue formed outside the Forum Cinema. A cross-section of local life – townspeople, students from the University of Wales, as well as farmers and others who had travelled in from the surrounding hills and villages – were gathered together, all curious to see what the show had in store. As the town's new theatregoers waited for the doors to open, the queue extended down Bath Street then twisted around the corner onto Terrace Road, where icy blasts off the Irish Sea warned them of the early winter storm that was brewing.

Inside the house was full. Imagine the bubbling chatter before the curtain rises: the exchanges of greetings and news and gossip, shifting smoothly from Welsh to English and back again. The audience – many of whom would not have seen a professional theatre production in years, if at all – were piqued by the anticipation of a ghostly apparition.

They would also have wanted a glimpse of the woman who had written those daring novels about dancing girls, female confidence tricksters and morphine addicts. Perhaps some would have been more than a little pleased to witness a humiliating public failure of the flamboyant, attention-loving 'Countess'. There would certainly have been speculation on whether the 'devil' himself, Caradoc Evans, would be present. He was, although the gaunt man in the middle of the third row with his head bent and eyes fixed on the floor might have gone unnoticed by many. Caradoc was keeping a low profile. Even so, his familiar, angular figure would have surely been recognised. Fortunately for Caradoc and Marguerite, that night he was spared the scowls that had followed him since his return to Wales some six months ago. Perhaps it was out of respect for the absent (or arguably present) Aunt Tots, in whose honour seat number thirteen in the front row ('the death number' as Marguerite had helpfully informed the press) had been left empty: empty, that is, except for a bouquet of chrysanthemums. As Marguerite announced in her opening speech that night, chrysanthemums were the favourite flowers of her beloved late aunt.

Although there was no report of any tangible materialisation on the night, the *Western Mail* informed its readers that Marguerite was 'absolutely convinced that my aunt sat in [that seat]'. How much of this was sincerely held belief, and how much show business, is impossible to know.

Perhaps as a distraction for the non-appearance of her dead aunt, Marguerite had another surprise lined up. Reviving her stage name of Olive Bree from her brief theatrical career of some twenty-seven years before, Marguerite made an unannounced cameo appearance in the role of a 'dangerous' vamp. Picture her, in her first theatre role in decades, draped in a feather boa, slinking across the stage, her black satin dress clinging so closely to her hips and legs that from a distance she resembled a mermaid walking on her tail. Her performance would have been intentionally excessive, more Mae West than Jean Harlow: a carnivalesque mix of outrageous costume, self-parody and risqué humour as she worked the audience for all she was worth. Employing her instincts as a writer of popular fiction for hooking an audience, she squeezed out every drop of intrigue and humour from the production, giving a hundred per cent to her precious new theatre company. From this night, she had earned the right to call herself artistic director of a repertory theatre company, as well as a bestselling writer.

Marguerite and Caradoc soon established themselves as a pair of colourful local Bohemians: a couple of exotic birds flown in to add colour to the grey winter months. Marguerite, 'so soignée' and sporting a flurry of furs and satin, her 'pretty, retroussé face' partially obscured by a 'veil of big black spots', exuded a heady mix of glamour and eccentricity, while Caradoc, the ageing Welsh dandy with his distinctly un-Welsh angular features and wide-brimmed fedora, cut a striking figure of a different kind. Arm in arm they took their daily constitutional along the prom, never failing to attract attention. As their friend Berta Ruck later observed, their appearance would 'make strangers look twice, and ask, "Who are they?"'[7] Marguerite, thriving on this attention, delighted in the way shopkeepers would greet her by name and locals would stop her in the street to share news and gossip. It made her feel that at last she had found a home. Since the age of five, when she had been uprooted from India, she had been moving from place to place. Now here was a town where she might put down roots: a place upon which she could project her need to belong. She soon became an enthusiastic public advocate for Wales and Welsh life. Hers was a romantic notion of a mystical Wales, peopled with wizards and 'the fair folk'. With Caradoc as her more than willing accomplice, she established herself as one half of a 'double act': Marguerite the sentimentalist and her dramatic opposite Caradoc, the bitter cynic. As the writer and critic Glyn Jones remarked, 'It was a hell of a combination, the sentimental bestseller and the superb satirist. This was a comic contrast that both of them played up to and clearly enjoyed.'[8]

In the letters page of the *Western Mail*, Marguerite and Caradoc would conduct an open debate with each other. Here Marguerite would lavish praise on Wales for its unaffected simplicity, the hospitality of its people and its traditional values. 'Wales is the setting of my soul,' she declared. 'Here I have found happiness – complete, profound, unspoilable.' 'Incomprehensible,' came Caradoc's reply, 'that I should marry a sentimentalist.' As Ruck observed, 'Caradoc's cynical veneer could barely conceal his pride in her.'[9]

Marguerite, in turn, attempted to orchestrate a reconciliation between Caradoc and his native land, hoping to reverse his reputation as the nation's 'best-hated man' and recast him as a misunderstood genius. He only lambasted Wales, she insisted, because he loved it too much to tolerate its flaws.

Marguerite was not alone in coming to the defence of Wales' prodigal son. Caradoc had recently been discovered by a new generation of Welsh writers, including Gwyn Jones, the founding editor of *The Welsh Review*. Another admirer was the young poet and critic Glyn Jones who, in 1934, on discovering that his literary hero had moved from London to Aberystwyth, drove up from Swansea to meet him. He brought along with him another admirer of Caradoc's work – his friend and fellow young poet Dylan Thomas. When Caradoc's stories later became 'a highbrow success', Thomas claimed it was because of 'my uninterrupted praise of them'.[10] But it was Gwyn Jones, who regularly featured Caradoc in *The Welsh Review*, who had been instrumental in introducing the one-time renegade to a new Welsh audience.

Later, Dylan Thomas recalled the night he and Jones visited Caradoc, claiming that the three of them went carousing in the pubs of Aberystwyth and raised their glasses 'to the eternal damnation of the Almighty and the soon-to-be-hoped for destruction of the tin Bethels'.[11] Yet Glyn Jones makes no mention of the riotous evening, only that Thomas had accidentally burnt a cigarette hole in the bedspread belonging to the hotel where they were staying and spent the next morning frantically rearranging bedclothes to hide the damage. Marguerite, in her biography of Caradoc, recalls Thomas as a shy, polite young man, adding that the two had stayed for tea then left. Later, during the height of the poet's fame, Marguerite embellished her account to include a reference to her 'Miracle Stone', which was imbued with powers to heal and create good fortune, adding the spurious claim that Thomas, having spotted the blue stone in the drawing room, had wished upon it for fame.[12]

While Thomas makes no mention of meeting Marguerite, her exotic appearance made quite an impression on the young chapel-going Jones. She looked like an ex-actress, he noted, 'or what I thought an ex-actress would look like: that is, her face was very much made up, she wore unusual and highly coloured clothing and good deal of conspicuous jewellery, including shoulder-length ear droppers'.[13] He was also struck by her 'extremely cordial' welcome and, in particular, her bohemian taste in décor: the spacious drawing room with its 'splendid antiques of varying periods and styles', the profusion of 'exotic ornaments and large vases of fancy grass, and Buddhas, and icons with scarlet lamps burning under them, and too many damask curtains'.

As acclaim for Caradoc grew, Marguerite could all too easily have disappeared into her husband's literary shadow. Much as she adored Caradoc, she was not willing to be upstaged by any man. Instead of resenting the attention her husband was attracting, she saw it as an opportunity: if Caradoc had once been Wales' 'best-hated man', Marguerite was quick to remind us that she was still 'England's best-loved novelist'.[14] Despite this, snobbery over Marguerite's brand of popular fiction remained stubborn. In Gwyn Jones' later review of Marguerite's biography of Caradoc, his praise for its author is as faint as it is double-edged. 'It would be wrong of me to suggest that the interest of this book is exclusively for admirers of Caradoc. The vastly bigger circle of Oliver Sandys readers will find in it much that is enlightening about her life and her writings.'[15]

While Caradoc delighted in his new-found recognition, he was always aware that sales of his books did not come close to those of Marguerite's. Caradoc admired Marguerite for her ability to turn out 'the selling stuff', an ability he did not possess.[16] As his biographer John Harris notes, he had 'a healthy respect for a novelist selling upwards of 200,000 copies a title'[17] and would boast, to anyone who cared to listen, of his wife's popularity as an author. 'You write like the Angels sing,' he would tell her, 'without effort'.[18]

During these earlier, happier years of their marriage, Caradoc was content to assist Marguerite by bashing out her manuscripts on his typewriter. (While she had still not learnt to type, Caradoc was proficient.) He was stage manager, publicist and, of course, typist, for his wife's theatre company, and, when needed, he would take on a walk-on part. Despite this, he insisted he had 'nothing to do with this venture of sending English plays into rural Wales ... The idea is my wife's, the money is hers, and if there are losses, they will also be hers.'[19] The claim was to protect his wife from being sullied by his reputation.

Marguerite's vision for the company was simple – for the price of a cinema ticket, west Wales audiences would be able to go and see West End plays, performed to West End standards. Marguerite had the money and poured the proceeds of her latest book into the company. The outlay, she felt sure, would be recouped by the end of the first season. Now in her late forties, she wanted to spend her earnings on something more enduring than fur coats and fast cars. For someone of her itinerant background, her choice of name – Rogues and Vagabonds – with its romantic associations with roaming players, had particular resonance.

To promote her new company, she commissioned a series of eye-catching posters with the slogan 'Rogues and Vagabonds are coming'. With Caradoc as her chief billsticker, Marguerite would instruct her chauffeur to drive them around the surrounding countryside where they – or men she had hired for the work – pasted the posters on rocks, gateposts, telegraph poles, derelict cottages, farm outbuildings or any other available space.

Her campaign fell foul of the law, and Marguerite was summonsed to appear before the Magistrates in Tywyn (some thirty miles north of Aberystwyth) to face a charge of exhibiting playbills 'so as to injuriously affect the view of rural scenery' in contravention of local byelaws. Under the eye-catching headline 'Countess Fined', local paper the *Cambrian News* reported that Marguerite immediately handed over three £1 notes to the court to cover her fine, plus the fines of the men she had hired, then 'with a smile to the Bench she left the Court'.[20] Marguerite had performed her age-old trick of breaking the rules and getting away with it. Although she had to pay a fine, it was not before she had saturated the surrounding countryside with advertising that no one could miss.

'It was a venture of love and youth and spring, and we hitched our charabanc and our lorry to a star. The star has smiled upon us. The star has danced,' she enthused to the *Western Mail*.[21] Apparently forgetting its longstanding war of words with her husband, the paper filled column after column with Marguerite's breathless accounts of her talented actors and packed houses. Her charm and ostentatious generosity, displayed at a series of post-show champagne receptions put on for the press, also ensured the journalists were more kindly disposed towards her.

Putting her bestseller-writer's instincts to work, she crammed the first season's programme full of crowd-pleasers – the latest Noel Coward, or a thriller by the likes of Patrick Hamilton. She took care to include liberal helpings of Ivor Novello and Emlyn Williams too: two Welsh playwrights with international careers. Her repertoire of mainstream, middlebrow and much-loved material was devised with both eyes fixed firmly on box-office takings. She also employed the old theatrical trick of flattering an audience. 'My success so far,' she told the *Western Mail* during her first season, 'only bears out what I have always felt about Welsh people – their receptiveness to anything that is new or worthwhile.' In one of her regular letters to the paper thanking her audience for a 'heart-warming reception', she added: 'My players say they have never played to a more receptive audience than the Welsh audience.' Neither was she afraid to resort to that greatest crowd-pleaser of all: adorable pets. 'Does my terrier, Jock, know he is acting? Of course he does.' Jock was starring in the comedy Peg O' My Heart, with Peke, her Pekingese, in a minor role. 'Jock adores the theatre,' she continued. 'He loves his part so much that [when] his services were no longer required, he got into the company char-a-banc and stowed away.' Warming to this narrative, Marguerite added, 'As a matter of fact, he is the offspring of a circus dog, so he can truly be said to have professionalism in his blood.'

One reviewer observed that a member of the audience got so excited she rushed up during the curtain call and presented Jock and Peke with two bones wrapped in blue ribbon.[22]

Spurred on by early successes, Marguerite began searching for a permanent venue. Seizing upon a long-empty council-owned hall as a potential prospect, she offered to hire it; however, the negotiations were protracted and eventually fell through. While Marguerite told the *Western Mail* she had decided to walk away, saying her patience gave up 'when they asked me if repertory meant dirty plays', more likely it was because the council had refused to let it to her at a peppercorn rent, as she had requested. Her search for a venue big enough to house an audience of at least three hundred (the number she needed to turn a profit) was proving next to impossible.

Bruised but determined, she resumed her search. When she heard a recently-closed garage had come onto the market, she was desperate enough to consider even this most unlikely of venues. Set in the shadow of the monolithic Queen's Hotel, with the scarred cliff face of an abandoned quarry looming above, it was undeniably ugly. Yet once inside and finding it bigger than she thought, she decided it had potential. Marguerite's imagination did not stop at storytelling; putting to work the talent for creating exotic interiors she had displayed to such effect on her house in Queen's Square, she wasted no time in transforming it. Deciding on a yellow and gold colour scheme, she had a proscenium arch fitted then decorated with a mural of a Welsh mountain and crowned with the motto 'The Best for Wales'.[23] Aware of the local power of Welsh branding, she enthused to the press that her décor represented 'a symphony in the Welsh colours ... green and yellow [with] the Welsh dragon conspicuous on the sign'. She was also aware of the importance of making an audience comfortable, so in place of hard benches and chairs, she acquired a set of comfortable tip-up seating from London's Steinway Hall, which thirty years earlier had been the venue of her less than remarkable stage debut.

The Quarry Theatre opened its doors in November 1935, the

disused garage transformed into a dazzling hall of colours. As the audience gathered in its foyer, they could examine the display of greetings telegrams on the wall, sent by the likes of Noel Coward, Edith Evans, Ivor Novello and other illustrious well-wishers. The *Western Mail* was similarly supportive; its reporter, enthused by the romantic qualities of the new Quarry Theatre, commented that while it looked 'like a garage set in the foot of a cliff, within it might easily be a theatre at Cannes or Nice'. In just one month, the garage had been transformed into a romantic oasis.

With its stated aim to bring English drama, performed by professional actors, to rural mid-Wales, the company continued to put on shows by such members of the theatre aristocracy as Noel Coward, J.B. Priestley, Patrick Hamilton and, of course, those talented Welshmen, Ivor Novello and Emlyn Williams. With the Quarry as its base, the troupe embarked on a gruelling twice-weekly touring regime. Travelling in the Rogues and Vagabonds charabanc, it staged shows in any possible venue within a fifty-mile radius, from the fashionable resort of Aberdyfi in the north to the spa town of Llandrindod Wells to the east.[24]

One of the Quarry Theatre's early productions was an original play by Marguerite called *Hell Freezes*.[25] Billed as a satire on the English 'county set' who loved nothing more than hunting foxes, it took aim at a subject close to Marguerite's animal-loving and blood sports-loathing heart. While many of the surrounding rural community would not have agreed with her anti-hunting stance, the significance of the wife of Wales' most notorious satirist now satirising her own English upper-class society would not have been lost.

In another production, Marguerite revived the 1921 hit play *A Bill of Divorcement* by the novelist, playwright, painter and screenwriter Clemence Dane (the pen name of Winifred Ashton). The play centres on a woman desperate to divorce her husband and to marry the man she loves, but whose husband (recently released from an asylum after twenty years) refuses to give his consent. (The parallels between this and Marguerite's experience of being refused a divorce by her first husband Armiger, are all too plain.) Once again, she had chosen a theme close to her heart.

During its original London run (and following the release of the 1923 film adaptation), *A Bill of Divorcement* not only whipped up a stir but fuelled the growing demand for reform of the divorce laws that ultimately led to the 1923 Matrimonial Causes Act. For the first time women could petition the court for a divorce on the grounds of adultery, regardless of whether the man consented. Alas, this legislation did not conclude the matter. Around the time *A Bill of Divorcement* was being performed in Aberystwyth, divorce had emerged again as a hotly contested topic. Pressure was mounting for more reform, eventually leading to further revision of the divorce laws in 1937, when cruelty, desertion and incurable insanity were added as grounds for divorce.

During the summer of 1936, Marguerite sought to take advantage of the town's seasonal visitors by putting on a string of plays by the ever-popular Noel Coward and Ivor Novello. Among them was Novello's *A Symphony in Two Flats*, a musical comedy with the unlikely comic scenario of a blind composer who is deceived by his wife and her lover into believing he has won a major award for his work.[26]

The repertoire that summer also included Rodney Ackland's *After October*. Marguerite would have instantly identified with its hero, the eternally optimistic playwright Clive Monkham, and his perpetual hope that his next play will be the commercial success needed to rescue his family of impoverished bohemians. Like Monkham, Marguerite was sustained by her eternal optimism. Now balancing her creative life with supporting a husband and son who relied on her income, she had to be optimistic. Acquiring the play was also something of a coup for Marguerite, who had managed to secure the rights immediately following its West End run. The *Cambrian News* duly promoted it. In a puff piece that reads like Marguerite's verbatim account (which it probably was), the newspaper announced that 'theatrical history is being made in Wales when Countess Barcynska makes it possible to see in Aberystwyth a London play in a two-and-fourpenny stall at the Quarry Theatre'.[27]

The *Western Mail* were equally obliging with their gushing reports on after-show parties where the likes of the Hon. Mrs Shelley (whose father Lord Atkin had fined Marguerite for unauthorised bill posting just two weeks earlier), the women golfers 'Mrs. Rieben and Miss Rieben', or 'Lady Spilsbury, Lord and Lady Ratendone and Lady Ratendone's mother' were all in attendance.[28] Rogues and Vagabonds also attracted visiting London journalists to its shows, possibly one-time associates from Marguerite's or Caradoc's Fleet Street days. One London journalist, on seeing the company's production of Emlyn Williams's translated French comedy *The Late Christopher Bean*, judged it 'point for point' every bit as good as its West End production.[29] The anonymous *Western Mail* gossip columnist who went under the name of the 'Lady of St. James' was less complimentary. Her praise for the 'great service' the 'Countess' was providing to local audiences came heavily seasoned with irony:

She has brought romance and glamour into their workaday lives. It is grand to think of young men getting back from the cornfields, changing into their Sunday best, and setting forth for the village hall to enjoy the witty epigrams of Noel Coward or the cynical remarks of Mr. Somerset Maugham.

The author, academic and playwright Idwal Jones also lavished ironic 'praise' on Marguerite for her 'salutary attempt' to educate 'the benighted people of Aberporth and other Welsh villages' with plays by Noel Coward and others 'portraying, as they do, life in the more erotic [*sic*] circles of the West End of London'.[30]

It's easy to see how a theatre company, with a 'countess' as a proprietor, performing West End plays (in the English language) in such a deeply Welsh rural area, might make itself the softest of targets for satirists. It was also a huge financial gamble. Even by the variable standards of repertory, Rogues and Vagabonds was a risky enterprise. Yet this was more than just a vanity project for Marguerite; under her shrewd commercial eye, shows would regularly sell out during the company's first summer season, so much so that they were turning people away each night. By the end of the season, the company had even turned over a modest profit of £150. For a theatre in a small, out-of-the-way resort, where a combination of mountains, sea and a westerly wind made for a short summer season, it could hardly have got off to a more promising start. The 'venture of love and youth and spring', that first season at least, was paying its own way.

Although she had recruited the core of her cast from London, Marguerite also opened her doors to some local talent. One of her young stars, Cicely Bowen, a cattle dealer's daughter from Newtown, had read about Rogues and Vagabonds in the *Western Mail*. In a correspondence that lasted two years, she begged Marguerite to give her a chance, saying that she 'had dreamed of going to RADA, but it was impossible for her'. Eventually, Marguerite agreed to take her on as a 'free pupil'. 'I shall make it my special duty to help this little Welsh girl in the career she has chosen with such earnest determination,' said Marguerite, adding that if there were any more girls like Cicely Bowen, 'I shall be glad to meet them.' Another of Marguerite's discoveries, Sally Latimer, also discovered the company in the pages of the *Western Mail*. Unlike Cicely, Latimer was no aspiring schoolgirl but had joined the company straight out of RADA. Marguerite enthused about her protégée to the press, apparently promoting her as something of a stage siren. 'She is an incredibly slim wisp of a girl,' she states. 'She sea-bathes, swims, and hikes, and even when she goes to bed late at night, she looks as fresh as a rose.' There was more to Latimer than looks and versatile athleticism and she later went on to become the joint proprietor (together with the playwright Caryl Jenner) of the Amersham Playhouse. Her experience at Rogues and Vagabonds would have prepared her for the theatre's inevitable spells of financial uncertainty. After the war, the Playhouse received a grant from the recently formed Arts Council, which allowed the company to carry on until 1949, when Latimer and Jenner sold it as a going concern.

In addition to its actors, Rogues and Vagabonds also employed carpenters, painters, electricians, handymen, box-office clerks, usherettes, bookkeepers and cleaners, all of them from the local area. During the difficult depression years of the 1930s, the jobs that Marguerite created were a distinct boon for the town. Her glowing reference for a Mr Fred Mower, who had worked for the company over the summer season as an electrician and stage carpenter, reveals the versatility of her stagehands. 'He is a most efficient electrician and extremely thorough,' she wrote. 'He is also an excellent poster writer with some very artistic ideas.' The letterhead reads, in gold-embossed copperplate script, 'Countess Marguerite Hélène Barcynska'.[31] Marguerite had her stationery printed in the style of the letter she had received as a teenager from theatrical doyen Ellen Terry, warning the young Marguerite about the perils of a career in theatre – a warning she never heeded.

Perhaps remembering the hardships she had endured during her chorus girl days, Marguerite took pains to act as a model employer. As well as paying her actors generously, she insisted that they could not perform on an empty stomach and would lay on a generous spread of pork pies, sandwiches, cakes and drinks before each show.[32] 'Running a repertory company is like tending a garden,' she enthused. 'A good gardener keeps his eye on his tenderest buds and plants, and in due season an exquisite flower or fruit will be his reward.'[33] Her employees, in turn, seemed to appreciate her generosity. Following one of her early productions, the cast and crew presented her with a gold Indian necklace, lavishly decorated with garnets: a thoughtful addition to Marguerite's collection of Indian jewellery.[34]

At last she found herself the object of gratitude and admiration from those who needed and depended on her. Removed from her self-imposed isolation, when she had shut herself away for month after month to write, she now surrounded herself with people who adored her. It was the long-overdue homecoming she had been yearning for, a return to a time when she had reigned over her world and her retinue of nursery servants in India. Now she was queen of her company of actors and stagehands, just as, when a child, she had graciously bestowed riches to her Indian servants on behalf of her father:

> Once a week my father used to pour a stream of rupees from a bag and count them out into piles. It was my great delight to distribute the money as the servants came up for their wages on to the veranda. Before they appeared, father always impressed upon me that this was money he had made and worked hard for, but I hoped the servants would think it was my money, and I bestowed it queenily.[35]

With Rogues and Vagabonds, she could be Daisy Baba again, her actors and crew replacing her adoring *ayah* and household servants and indulging her every childlike whim. This regal role extended to Nicholas, her prince and heir. Marguerite used the theatre to establish her son in his chosen career of acting and Nicholas became one of the company's permanent fixtures. Although tall and striking, his awkward manner made him unsuited to playing the male lead. Instead, specialising in shifty or unstable characters, he tended to play the villain – a role he relished. In Marguerite's 1933 adaptation of her novel *Chappy, That's All*, the seventeen-year-old Nicholas was cast in a walk-on part as a thief. In *Hell Freezes* he played a jealous, insecure husband. In their 1936 production of Patrick Hamilton's *Rope*, he was cast as the weaker of the two young murderers. Later that year, he played his tour de force: the lead in *Dracula*, a part which, the *Western Mail* reported, 'suits his style of acting and he does it most convincingly'. It was a role that Nicholas would make his own offstage as well as on. Returning to live in Aberystwyth in the early 1980s, Nicholas could often be spotted around town: a tall, gaunt figure in a black cape with red satin lining. On dark nights, with his cape flapping disconcertingly in the breeze, he could unnerve those who weren't familiar with him and didn't know him as the harmless eccentric he was.

In his angrier moments, Caradoc would accuse Marguerite of setting up the company solely for the benefit of her son's theatrical ambitions. Although secretly admiring Nicholas's talent as an actor, he could not resist goading this already insecure young man. In one diary entry, he reveals the toxic mix of envy and sexual jealousy that lay behind his taunts:

> Nick put up some fine performances this season ... I told him he didn't bring a bob into the box-office, this was untrue. He believed me ... The woman has no sense of humour where Nick is concerned. Little girls wait at the stage-door for his autograph. Actors' autographs are not scarce.[36]

Although Marguerite would vehemently deny it, Caradoc was becoming an increasingly troublesome presence in her life. While her husband's literary reputation was being reassessed, many in Wales still branded him a traitor and saw Marguerite as guilty by association. The letters page of the *Western Mail*, which had initially given free rein to Marguerite and Caradoc's self-publicity, was now running angry letters from their detractors. 'Why does a man, now so ready to defend "his people" now apparently so repentant for any damage he has done in the past allow his wife to misrepresent his country?' fumed one (anonymous) correspondent.[37] While giving no example of Marguerite's apparent misrepresentation of Wales, the author's patriarchal logic that Caradoc was responsible for his wife's actions is perhaps more telling. Although she had taken care to distance herself and her company from her husband and his reputation, the 'curse' of Caradoc still haunted her. Whatever her achievements, many viewed her as Caradoc's wife above all else. A similar sentiment was expressed by the reviewer of the Rogues and Vagabonds production of Noel Coward's *The Marquise* in Newquay, who barely mentions the play but writes at length about Marguerite's infamous husband. 'The people of Wales are still angry with Mr. Caradoc Evans,' the review says, 'because he chose to unburden the bitterness of his soul by creating hideous caricatures of his fellow countrymen.' Marguerite only receives a brief mention at the end of the review – and, even then, it is only in relation to Caradoc:

> Countess Barcynska hastens to assure [her audience] that her husband is in no way responsible for the production. That in itself has saved a great deal of criticism, but it has not saved Caradoc himself from many looks of open antipathy from the audience.[38]

As she was beginning to realise, Caradoc's warning that he was not a safe person to be seen with in Wales was no joke. As she and Caradoc went about their daily business in town, they were often on the receiving end of hostile glances. Caradoc's reputation as Wales's 'best-hated man', easy to laugh off in London, did not seem so amusing in Wales. Yet he relished the attention. In Fleet Street, he had been a well-known figure: a prominent literary editor. While he was not universally liked, he was well respected by his peers, as well as by those authors in search of commissions who would gladly pay court to him. After leaving, he found it difficult to settle into obscurity. At least in Wales he could take his place as a well-known figure. Loathed by many and defended by few, at least there he was noticed.

Marguerite's attempts to orchestrate a reconciliation between her husband and his country were not going well. Caradoc's caustic satire had caused too much offence. The hurt it caused ran deep and could not be easily healed. Even today, when Caradoc is generally lauded as a formative influence on Welsh writing in English, there are many in Wales who still consider him a pariah. On the centenary of the publication of his first book of short stories *My People*, in 2015, the Welsh author Huw Lawrence wrote, 'I still will not forgive him.' In Wales, he added, 'the only place he is remembered', his name will always be associated with the old Welsh proverb, 'Cas gŵr na charo'r wlad a'i maco' (Hateful the man who does not love the land that bred him).[39]

Marguerite attempted to defuse the hostility by dealing with Caradoc's reputation head-on with a production of his controversial *Taffy*. Billed as 'a play of Welsh village life', it came with all the comic grotesques and satirical mistranslations of the Welsh that had made Caradoc a legion of enemies. *Taffy* also brought its own particular controversy; its 1926 production had made theatre history when a rowdy group of London Welsh protestors invaded the theatre, forcing the curtains to close before the third act.

Marguerite insisted the disruption would not be repeated, feeling certain that, in Wales itself, the audience would behave quite differently. 'The Welshman in his own country is a gentleman,' she said, while in London he may 'be infected with the spirit of Cockney hooliganism'. Not satisfied with showing the play in relatively liberal-minded Aberystwyth, she also took it on tour around the Welsh-speaking, chapel-going rural heartlands. Her decision seemed counter-intuitive in the extreme. Caradoc thought no good would come of it, but knew he could not talk her out of it.

Marguerite proved him wrong. To Caradoc's surprise, *Taffy* was well received by audiences and critics alike, even enjoying an extended run in Aberystwyth. This Marguerite credits to the subtlety of her production and its emphasis on the 'poetry of the language'. She had ramped up the love interest, too, and dampened down the satire until it was barely evident. There was little danger this tamed-down adaptation would incite another riot.

Having pulled off the seemingly impossible with *Taffy*, Marguerite expanded her theatrical ambitions. Now setting her sights beyond west Wales, she voiced her intention to lead an emergent national theatre of Wales. Although there was already a self-styled Welsh national theatre at Plas Newydd in Llangollen, led by the aristocratic patron of the arts Baron Howard de Walden, Marguerite felt it did not 'represent the spirit of the people'.[40] To express such outspoken disapproval of de Walden, a vaunted figure in Welsh cultural life, was unwise. She was overreaching herself. Her cut-glass colonial English, her ostentatious clothes and her tenuous title (the 'countess' which she used so freely when conducting her theatre business) did nothing to contradict this impression. The more anxious she became to impress the public and win them over with charm and flattery, the more patronising she began to sound. 'Aberystwyth audiences are extremely intelligent,' she insisted:

> People warned me at first ... that I was just throwing my money away [but] I think I have the proper estimate of the intelligence of the Welsh people ... They are quite as subtle as Noel Coward and the audiences are as quick on the uptake as a West End audience ... I have found that the Welsh are intensely dramatic. They are born actors.[41]

Despite proclamations that she had been 'received with such warmth and kindness', the full houses of the earlier productions had been partly stimulated by curiosity, as one report of a 1935 production in New Quay implies: 'I talked to several members of the audience [who] admitted that curiosity more than an actual desire to see the play had brought them there.'[42]

Once the shine of novelty began to fade, audiences started drifting away. Back at the Quarry, Marguerite was facing attacks of a different kind. A combination of stormy weather, a leaking roof, competition from local dances and whist drives, the offerings of three local cinemas, plus the 1935 general election, conspired against her. As takings fell, Marguerite's press interviews began to sound an increasingly urgent tone.[43] Her mission to entertain seemingly forgotten, she claimed an 'improving' role for live theatre in general (and hers in particular). 'The extraordinary thing to me is the number of clergymen who have come to see my company,' she writes, valuing as they do 'the educational value of English plays.'[44] Warming to her self-appointed pedagogical role, Marguerite issues an open invitation to 'any amateur Welsh producer to come and see how presentation and lighting are done by experts. I am sure they would learn a great deal.'

As the money dried up, so did the champagne that had once flowed at press receptions. The reviews were beginning to lose their earlier sparkle too. Some, such as the 1935 review of *Outward Bound* in Machynlleth, adopted a condescending 'between the lines' tone that was usually reserved for amateur productions, offering only the weakest of praise by noting that there was 'not a moment of hesitation throughout'. Another review, by leading Welsh-language playwright and critic Kitchener Davies, is equally lukewarm. While crediting the Countess Barcynska for setting up the only surviving repertory theatre in Wales (following the demise of a Cardiff company a few years earlier), Kitchener was less than impressed with the production itself, describing it as 'meritorious considering the limitations of the available stages, costume and scenic designs'.[45] Despite this, the Quarry Theatre had its loyal band of supporters, among them the Aberystwyth resident and theatre-lover who wrote to the *Cambrian News* in October 1936 to praise the company, while also anticipating its demise:

> The plays are well produced, the acting is easily up to the best repertory standard; the seating is very comfortable, the hall is warm and the prices are reasonable. All that is missing is a crowd of steady supporters. It would be a lasting reproach if we lost the only repertory theatre in Wales.[46]

Through it all, Marguerite stuck rigidly to the relentless writing regime that had been instilled in her by Armiger. Notebook on lap in her usual style, she continued to write, throughout all the company's ups and downs, 'an Oliver Sandys and then a Countess' as usual. In place of her old practice of working behind a closed door, she wrote backstage during rehearsals, no longer isolated but surrounded by a lively cast and crew and distracted by constant comings and goings. Despite this, she was still averaging an astonishing four novels a year, most of them light romantic comedies featuring, not surprisingly, an ailing repertory theatre in a small Welsh town. At first, they reflected the initially cheerful – and some would say blind – optimism she felt for her company. *The Happy Mummers*, for instance, is a light-hearted account of the struggles of a hopeful new company as it tours remote Welsh villages in the face of obstinate landlords, temperamental stars and even a fire (a setback from which they ultimately recover).[47] In a similar vein, *The Show Must Go On* follows the ups and downs of a theatre company in a small Welsh town with an eccentric proprietor.[48] *Hollywood Honeymoon* follows the fortunes of its star-struck heroine, Gwyneth Jones, as she is discovered by a talent scout and is forced to choose between her dream of Hollywood glamour and a simple, happy life as part of a cheerful band of repertory players in Wales.[49] *Hollywood Honeymoon* attracted mostly lukewarm reviews. 'Once again Oliver Sandys makes real appeal to her admirers,' wrote the *Daily Mirror*. Perhaps mindful of her status as one of its readers' favourite authors, the paper conceded, 'She has a style peculiarly her own which is rated high in the world of fiction writers.'[50] Her Barcynska novel *Pick up and Smile* was written in 1936, when the company's cracks were beginning to show. Marking a return to her earlier melodramatic style, and receiving a warmer reception than the more upbeat novels that preceded it, it featured as the *Daily Mirror*'s romance book of the month in June that year. Praised by the *Mirror* for its 'incident, drama and romance', *Pick up and Smile*'s cheerful title did nothing to prepare the reader for its torrid storyline.[51]

The *Daily Mirror* also devoted a page to an excerpt from the novel, together with a short biographical piece on its author, listing her likes, dislikes, hobbies and other details. Admitting that she was 'extravagant', she lists her 'loves' as 'feminine fashions – and her husband'. Her 'Countess' title, she claimed, had been acquired through her marriage 'before the age of twenty' to her first husband 'Count Armiger Barcynska' [*sic*]. Marguerite's insistence that she had been married to a count was, among her theatre company and Aberystwyth locals alike, becoming a running joke.[52] Yet she persisted, perhaps in the belief that 'Countess Barcynska' would bring a certain aristocratic cachet to her theatre company.

In *Pick up and Smile*, her fiction and her life (or her romanticised version of it) coalesce yet again, as the 'tormented half-devil' Dai Bushville carries its heroine, Peggy Packer, off to his mountain home in Wales. The parallels between Bushville, the 'savage genius' prone to 'terrifying moods', and Caradoc, with whom she 'ran away' to his native Wales, are as clear as its thinly disguised erotic subtext.

From the beginning, Marguerite had always drawn her fiction from her own life. Perhaps viewing it as an opportunity to increase sales, she had recently begun to capitalise on this by using it to market her books. When a *Western Mail* journalist asked her if *The Show Must Go On* was based on her experiences with Rogues and Vagabonds, Marguerite replied with an ambiguous, 'Not entirely, but if people search for any resemblance to themselves they are sure to find something in practically every novel.' Although in a later interview, she cheerfully contradicts this with her claim that the book 'is more or less the story of my Rogues and Vagabonds'.[53]

Propelled by the conveyor-belt demands of popular fiction, and romance in particular, she had acquired an exceptional talent for recycling themes and stories and, increasingly, episodes from her own life. She had been astute at staying on the right side of that thin line between pleasurable familiarity and simple repetition. Now some of her plots and settings were beginning to look as hastily assembled as the scenery of a touring pantomime. Despite her insistence that she could manage her writing career while running the theatre, the fault line was starting to shift.

More than ever before, Marguerite's exhausting writing schedule was driven by financial necessity. During the ailing second season of Rogues and Vagabonds, ticket sales fell to the point where she could no longer cover her costs, as each production lost her more and more money. 'I was losing very badly,' she writes. The greater her losses, the more frantically she would write to try and cover her costs. Anxious to keep the company afloat, she decided to double their repertoire by putting on two plays a week. Instead of recouping some of the losses, as she hoped, this only made matters worse. Still Marguerite continued to burrow into her savings to pay the salaries of the players and crew, the rent and maintenance costs of the Quarry Theatre, and for the costumes, props, scenery, touring costs, hall hire and cost of printing tickets until her finances began to haemorrhage. The scene in *Hollywood Honeymoon*, where theatre proprietor Dudley Beresford frets over his balance sheet, more than hints at the perilous state of the company's (and Marguerite's) accounts:

"Oh, Lord, what am I to do?"

In the manager's office of the Queen's Hall Theatre Mr. Dudley Beresford Wing stared at his own awful statement of figures and the more he stared the more awful it looked.

On one side of the statement ran:

	£	s.	d.
Rent for one week...........................	24	0	0
Electric light...............................	10	12	6
Heating....................................	5	0	0
Stage staff (electrician and 2 men)	7	0	0
Printing...................................	4	3	2
(advertising, billing and programmes)			
Advance fees on plays.......................	9	0	0
Box-office attendant........................	1	10	0
2 Usherettes................................	1	10	0
Cleaner.	1	0	0
Milk (for theatre cat)		6	
	63	16	2

The other side ran:

	£	s.	d.
Net receipts up to Thursday.................	8	0	6
(including programme and chocs)[54]			

As their productions multiplied, Marguerite's troupe began to buckle under the strain of constant touring. Inevitably, the quality of their productions suffered and, in an increasingly downhill spiral, box-office takings shrank further. Marguerite's predictions that their next production would break even were starting to sound optimistic to the point of being delusional. But still she kept trying. 'I would not admit even to myself that I was very tired,' she writes. 'I just went on and on.'[55]

Haunted by memories of his poverty-blighted childhood, Caradoc was disturbed to see his wife pouring her savings into a venture that was now in freefall. He would fume that her employees were taking advantage of her largesse and were spending her money extravagantly. He complained that Bry Ferguson, the stage manager, spent £5 a week on props – an excessive amount, according to Caradoc. Ferguson was a 'realist', he writes, who 'provided real eggs, real bacon, real haddock, real everything for stage food [all of it] at the woman's expense'. Caradoc was not alone. Berta Ruck thought Marguerite 'Confiding and trustful to the verge of gullibility', with a personality that 'fairly asked to be exploited'.[56]

For Marguerite, the venture was more emotional than financial. Even the threat of bankruptcy was not enough to make her break up her little troupe and return to her previous solitary daily routine. 'I had got so fond of my artists,' she writes, 'that I could not bear to part from them or the little world of theatre I had created in the town.'[57]

It took a nervous breakdown to sever the bond. It forced her to retreat to bed and miss the rehearsals and performances of *Cinderella*, the 1936 Christmas pantomime. She'd left the production in Caradoc's hands and it had gone well, he assured her. His account of the illuminated stagecoach and the performers' antics even cheered her up a little. She was beginning to feel a little better: well enough to feel sorry she had missed it. Then he broke the news. The notices had gone up; he had closed the Quarry Theatre. The luxurious gold seating that Marguerite had been so proud of was sold off to the local cinema. All that could not be sold

– the curtains, scenery, props, lighting – remained until, finally, the Great Storm of 1938 swept it all out into the Irish Sea.

Marguerite was too weak and exhausted to be angry at Caradoc for closing the theatre without her consent – too weak even to consider Nicholas, who had lost the company that Marguerite had promised would be his. During her time away from the Quarry Theatre, she had also come to realise her company was reaching the end of its life and she needed to find the least painful way to leave it behind. Caradoc, 'the craggy rock between her and exploitation,'[58] had provided it.

In June 1937, when Marguerite felt stronger, she and Caradoc put their plan to leave town into action, fleeing 'under the cover of darkness' as local gossip claimed. Caradoc was being pursued by the courts for maintenance payments to his ex-wife Rose. Too proud to accept Marguerite's offer to pay the £72 that he owed (a negligible amount compared with her estimated loss of £1,300 on the theatre), he chose to run away – supposedly to give him time to raise the money to pay off his debt.

They fled to Ruislip on the outskirts of London: an apparent compromise between Marguerite's love of the rural and Caradoc's hankering after London. For Marguerite, an added attraction was the village's proximity to London's theatres. She was still harbouring hopes that Nicholas might land an acting role in the West End, or that she and Caradoc might have one of their plays produced in a prestigious London theatre. Not long after, they would be on the move again – to another seaside resort: the larger, wealthier (and very English) Broadstairs, on the Kentish coast.

Chapter 9
Broadstairs and Ruislip –
Brief Theatrical Interludes

I often wonder on a very fine morning what it'll be like
... for night to come. And I never can. And yet it's got to.
(Emlyn Williams, *Night Must Fall*)[1]

Broadstairs today. A fibreglass giraffe peers over a high shingle wall.
A gold Rupert Bear, head on hand, reclines on a giant pink clam
shell. Bleak House, the clifftop folly named in honour of its spell as
the summer home of an elderly Charles Dickens, looms above the
bay. In 1915, when John Buchan spent summer in the town
recuperating from a long illness, he discovered a series of rickety
wooden steps that zigzagged down to the bay.[2] They were to be the
point of departure for his novel *The 39 Steps*. In 1935, three years
before Marguerite chose the resort for her home and the new
location for Rogues and Vagabonds, Buchan's 'shocker' had found
new life in the hugely popular film version, starring matinee idol
Robert Donat.[3] It was made nine years after the director had
debuted with his adaptation of Marguerite's *The Pleasure Garden*.[4]
But that was another age. Since then, Hitchcock's career had been
on a steady ascent towards Hollywood fame, while Marguerite's had
taken a downward turn. As the 'talkie' reigned, silent films like *The
Pleasure Garden* (along with the other nine silent adaptations of
Marguerite's novels) were all but forgotten.

Although Marguerite had claimed that she and Caradoc 'gave
our hearts to Wales', as she confessed to her friend Evelyn Lewes, it
was easier for her to feel at home in 'awfully nice' Broadstairs.[5] A

favoured resort among London's middle classes, bankers and bohemians, surgeons and shopkeepers alike – their maids, nannies, cooks and chauffeurs in tow – would occupy villas, cottages or hotel suites for the summer season.[6]

Yet Broadstairs had not been Marguerite's first port of call. After their hasty exit from Wales, she, Caradoc and Nicholas had retreated to Ruislip in Surrey, where they'd spent an eventful, often vexatious, ten months. They'd rented (or rather, Marguerite, who was still paying all the bills, had rented) a large house on King's End Avenue. To Marguerite – whose childhood after leaving India had been a merry-go-round of moving around the Home Counties and south coast – this very English, very Home Counties, town was the closest she could get to coming home.

Around this period, a court report shines a light on their domestic situation. 'COOK LOST HER TEMPER – Refused a Month's Wages' ran the headline of a story that would not have been out of place in a music-hall comedy routine. Marguerite's cook had returned at midnight to find her mistress waiting up for her, accusing her of returning in a drunken, 'disreputable state' and of not having cleaned the kitchen taps before she left. Marguerite testified that the cook had told her to go to hell and clean the taps herself, for which she was sacked on the spot, her mistress refusing her a month's wages in lieu of notice.

Caradoc, backing up his wife, testified that Miss Bennet had been insolent and, on one occasion, when he had asked her to do a job, had replied, 'Why don't you do it yourself? All you do is scribble all day. Scribble, scribble, scribble.' This time, the law was on the couple's side. As was usual in disputes between employer and servant, the judgement came down in favour of the employer, although, in a concessionary gesture, Marguerite waived the costs made against the cook.[7]

Putting the dispute behind her, Marguerite now turned her attention to something more pleasurable. For some time, she had been hatching a plan to produce plays on the West End stage.

Encouraged by her well-received production of Caradoc's controversial play *Taffy* in Wales, she decided (in February 1938) to put it on at the Grafton Theatre in Tottenham Court Road. Described by the celebrity journalist Hannen Swaffer as a 'toned down' version of the play,[8] Marguerite had indeed glossed over the satire, had applied the same formula that had proved so successful in her earlier production in Wales. Neither could the romantic novelist in her resist ramping up the love interest, an innovation which had also gone down well with its Welsh audience. As Marguerite would have known, there was no reason to assume a play's success in west Wales would be repeated in the West End; the London run failed to turn over the profit that she and Caradoc had been hoping for. Marguerite put this down to the Grafton's limited seating capacity, claiming the theatre was so small that even a full house was barely enough to cover expenses. This assertation was likely an excuse for poor ticket sales: the theatre had 280 seats rather than the 150 she claimed. She would have wanted to protect Caradoc's pride. But, despite the poor returns, Marguerite claimed Caradoc 'was rather pleased about it, for it took his mind off his immediate worries',[9] not least, she could have added, those outstanding maintenance payments owed to his first wife Rose.

'CARADOC EVANS TOLD JUDGE – "I LIVE OFF MY WIFE"' ran the headline in the *Daily Herald*. Caradoc's maintenance arrears had finally caught up with him and he was appearing before the judge at Uxbridge County Court to face a summons for the £287 he now owed Rose. The case laid bare his impecunity and the extent to which he depended on Marguerite. He never made more than 'a few hundred' from a book, he told the judge, before adding – perhaps more out of a sense of wounded pride than genuine expectation – that the novel he had just completed 'might make £5,000 or £10,000'.[10]

'While you have been writing one novel, in two years,' the judge asked, 'can you say how many novels your wife has written?' If it had been the judge's intention to humiliate Caradoc, he had surely hit the mark. As a young boy, Caradoc had witnessed the very public humiliation of his father, William Evans, who was tied to a wooden frame then paraded around the village to be pelted and insulted: one of the last enactments of the traditional Welsh punishment known as the *ceffyl pren* (or wooden horse) and a punishment for Evans's alleged adultery. Caradoc's biographer, John Harris, interviewed an eyewitness, Annie Rees (née Owen), who claimed that the shock of her husband's punishment had caused the heavily pregnant Mari to collapse. There was a local rumour her baby Josi had been born an 'imbecile' as a result.[11]

Caradoc's mix of shame and rage never left him and was to become the source of his excoriating wit, his weapon against further humiliation. Now, in the face of the judge's contemptuous verdict, his barbed tongue was silent. No, he replied, he didn't know how many books a year his wife wrote. When the judge ordered he pay £10 a week to his ex-wife, 'or more, if the book was a success', he could only listen in sullen silence.[12] Marguerite claimed she had offered to pay Caradoc's maintenance costs, but he would not hear of it. As he did not breach his maintenance order again, however (and never earned anything like the £5,000 to £10,000 rights he quoted in court), it's likely she did cover his costs.

Despite the disappointing returns for *Taffy*, Marguerite was putting on another play at the Grafton Theatre. This was to be the adaptation of her popular comedy romance *Chappy, That's All* – the play she had chosen as her theatrical debut in Aberystwyth.[13] Although Marguerite does not refer to the production in any of her biographical writings, it received more critical acclaim (and quite likely, given her popularity as an author, better box-office takings too) than *Taffy*. It was later listed in *The Stage* as one the plays of the year in 1938. To have been credited among the plays of the year in her London debut as a playwright was a major achievement – one she should have been proud of. Yet there is no record of her ever alluding to it. No doubt the fact that *Taffy*, produced the same year, did not make the list, had something to do with this. Even if

Caradoc had been more secure in his achievements, it would not have been easy to see his precious play, and one-time cause célèbre, upstaged. With the judge's thinly-veiled mockery still ringing in his ears, his famous wife, whose books outsold his own a thousand times over, had outshone him in the theatre too. Marguerite remained silent to protect his wounded pride.

His wife's ability to turn out novel after novel, seemingly effortlessly, was fast becoming a source of envy as well as pride for Caradoc. Her successes, which he had once delighted in, began to torment him. The more he lived in Marguerite's shadow, the more he pined for his old life on Fleet Street. At least in Wales he had found some consolation in his status as a public figure, albeit as a renegade. He had revelled in the attention he'd been getting from the new generation of Welsh writers and critics, including the young Dylan Thomas, on whose work Caradoc's wickedly playful 'Anglo-Welsh' style had been a major influence. Renegade or revered, it made little difference to him, so long as he was the centre of attention.

He took to making frequent trips to London, to revisit his old Fleet Street haunts in search of colleagues who could remember him from his *T.P.'s Weekly* glory years. But they had all gone, many of them pushed out, as he had been, by a merger or closure. Ye Olde Cock Tavern and Ye Olde Cheshire Cheese – pubs he had relished for their gloomy corners and bright gossip – were now frequented by more youthful faces. Caradoc had become one of the ghosts of Fleet Street, haunting the bars in search of someone who might listen to his anecdotes. He must have felt, as surely as if he had drunk H.G. Wells' secret formula, that he had become invisible.

In Ruislip, Marguerite was entertaining hopes of relaunching her theatre in an empty medieval barn on the Ruislip Manor Farm estate and had written to its owners, Surrey County Council, claiming it would make a marvellous cultural facility for the entire town. The council's committee were not so convinced, replying that the need for dressing rooms and other facilities would spoil the character of the historic building.[14] Instead of seeing this as a cue for further negotiations, Marguerite took it to heart, viewing it as evidence that she had 'never fitted into Ruislip'. The Home Counties of her childhood had changed, she complained; a 'rash' of mock-Tudor housing had destroyed its old rural character and turned it into a London dormitory.[15]

Still smarting from the rejection, she decided to set up her theatre elsewhere: in a seaside resort, perhaps – one bigger and more prosperous than Aberystwyth. Broadstairs, with its summer show and thousands of seasonal visitors, made an appealing choice. During the summer months, the town was a magnet for entertainers of all kinds, there in search of sea and fresh air, but also in the hope of landing a role in a play, or a turn in variety, or, for young women, a stint on the chorus line of a summer show. Perched on the nose of the Kentish coast, Broadstairs had the added advantage of being far enough from London to put Caradoc's old watering holes out of reach: or certainly too far for a day trip on the train.

Marguerite secured a flat in a large converted Edwardian villa. In the 1938 edition of *Kelly's Directory for the Isle of Thanet*, the name Countess Barcynska appears as the sole tenant of 12a Western Esplanade, Broadstairs. Soon, she had also found a home for her theatre. The Playhouse, on West Cliff Avenue and just a few hundred yards from Marguerite's new home, had been lying empty for five years. A 'drabbish, black-and-white corrugated iron structure',[16] teetering on the brink of hopeless dilapidation, it did not make an instantly appealing prospect. Caradoc tried to talk her out of it. There was a war coming, he said, and her money would be 'safer in your purse than in the theatre'.[17] But Marguerite would not heed his advice. Recalling how she had transformed the derelict garage in Aberystwyth into something resembling 'a theatre at Cannes or Nice', she was certain she could work the same magic a second time around.

She was not the first hopeful theatrical to have taken out a lease on The Playhouse. Since the early 1920s, when the brother-and-sister-run Grant Anderson Theatre Company presented a frenetic repertoire of up to three plays a week during the season, it had seen (and seen out) a succession of hopeful proprietors, each of them lured there by a combination of cheap rent, the hope of the summer season and a dose of blind optimism. As company after company moved in, each would follow a similar routine of redecorating, holding auditions, then begging, borrowing, making and (as a last resort) buying scenery, props and costumes. There followed the daily grind of rehearsals, plus a round of promoting the next production with notices and features for the local press, and finally (to spare the journalists the effort of having to see the show for themselves), their own glowing 'reviews'. Attempts to recoup losses by putting on more productions simply led to more debts. Companies would limp on until late September, when the season ended and their lease expired, and – if they were not put off repertory altogether – they would move to a livelier, more promising location. But Marguerite was resolute. Even the theatre's location – so out of the way that its publicity had to reassure readers that it was only 'five minutes from the Grand Hotel' with trams from Ramsgate and Margate passing the door – did not deter her. The Playhouse, she decided, would be a perfect new home for her 'venture of love and youth and spring', or as Caradoc might have put it, another of the woman's foolhardy notions.

Despite his scepticism, Caradoc threw himself into decorating and scenery-making with all the vigour he had put into the Quarry Theatre, working tirelessly to get the derelict building ready in time for the 1939 summer season. 'He became more normal in his behaviour,' wrote Marguerite, 'though not nearly normal all the same.' With the temptation of easy access to London now gone, Marguerite was relieved to find Caradoc curbing his drinking.

Yet Caradoc was far from content. His output now slowing alarmingly, he found he could barely manage more than a couple of hundred words a day: words that were rarely his best. His most recent novel, 'Kitty Shore's Magic Cake', had been rejected by his publishers, Rich & Cowan, as too 'dangerous and obscene' for publication.[18] While it contained a rich mix of unsavoury material – murder, prostitution, masochism, violent circumcision, incest and some frankly odious antisemitism – it was not pornographic, as the publishers had implied. While Rich & Cowan did not mention the quality of the copy they received, or that the work was rambling and at times incoherent, they could have done so with some justification. While Marguerite characteristically defended it, claiming that it had been rejected for fear its scurrilous content might prompt a libel suit, it was more likely to have been a commercial decision on the part of the publishers, following disappointing sales of his novel *This Way to Heaven* earlier in 1934.[19]

Caradoc was also becoming increasingly anxious over the looming threat of war. As the prospects of war in Europe drew closer, he became an obsessive scourer of newspapers and a devourer of news bulletins on the wireless. 'The war scare had him taut and on a string,' said Marguerite.[20] The journalist in him could interpret every nuance of a news report and would follow the press's shifting position as the war grew closer: from *The Times*, *The Daily Telegraph* and the *Daily Mail* (lukewarm support for Hitler, then cooling during the late thirties as the war shifted closer to Britain), to the *Daily Express* (ambivalent at first, then avowedly anti-Nazi later), and the paper Caradoc had once worked on as subeditor, the *Daily Mirror* (an early flirtation with Hitler, now an outspoken opponent).

The location of Broadstairs also troubled him. Less than forty miles across the channel from France, its location made the threat of invasion all the more immediate. Then there had been the home-grown threat of Oswald Mosley's British Union of Fascists, better known as the Blackshirts, who had chosen Broadstairs as the somewhat unlikely setting for their headquarters. They had closed their office in 1937 (the year before Marguerite and Caradoc's arrival in the town), leaving behind them a heap of final demands and summonses for unpaid rates. Yet the memory of Broadstairs resident and prominent Blackshirt William Joyce (the notorious

'Lord Haw-Haw', later hanged for treason),[21] whose charismatic oratory would draw hundreds to hear him speak at St Peter's Catholic Hall, was as sharp as the easterly breeze off the harbour.

The wind was changing. In 1938, as a group of German and Austrian refugees – most of them Jewish – were being housed in a converted army camp in nearby Richborough, another charismatic politician was addressing a full house in Broadstairs. Aneurin Bevan, the backbench Labour MP and future founder of the NHS, railed against Prime Minister Neville Chamberlain for his appeasement of Nazi Germany and for allowing 'the fabric of peace to be destroyed by the gangster methods of Hitler and Mussolini'.[22]

As Caradoc grew increasingly agitated, Marguerite tried to ignore politics altogether. War or not, as far as Marguerite was concerned, the show must go on. It *had* to go on. It was not the threat of war that kept her awake at night, but the prospect of her company failing again. In Aberystwyth, Rogues and Vagabonds had consumed much of her savings. Now she was pouring what remained into resuscitating the company and, more to the point, Nicholas's sluggish career. This time she hoped it would be a joint mother-and-son enterprise and put Nicholas's name on the lease alongside hers.

Marguerite had been cheered by his recent debut as a playwright. *The Jade Claw*, a horror billed as 'a weird story in which the mysterious East comes to a quiet alley in Wales', was produced as a BBC radio broadcast in 1938.[23] Now, with an offer by Margate Theatre Royal to produce it with Nicholas in the lead role of the Indian prince, he was understandably ambitious to write more. Though he was now joint proprietor of the theatre company – something Marguerite hoped would spur him on – his behaviour was becoming more erratic and resentful. Prone to long bouts of depression and despondency, he would struggle to sustain a project. *The Jade Claw*, 'his first solid attempt at writing'[24], was destined to be his only completed play.

The Playhouse opened its doors on 26 June 1939 with a sure-fire crowd-pleaser in Gerald Savory's comedy *George and Margaret*. 'The most sparkling and wittiest comedy of the past 25 years,' went a puff piece in the *Thanet Advertiser*, which had almost certainly been written by Marguerite. 'The lady in the partnership is the novelist who writes under the pen name of Oliver Sandys (pronounced Sands),' it adds helpfully, 'and she is described as "the most beloved of living novelists".' As with the early reviews of Rogues and Vagabonds in Wales, it ends with a list that reads like a roll call of theatrical luminaries – Ivor Novello, Edith Evans, Robert Donat, Irene Vanburgh and others – all of whom were said to have 'sent personal greetings to Countess Barcynska wishing the venture success.'[25]

A glowing review also appeared under the 'Provinces' section of *The Stage*. 'No expense has been spared in bringing the Playhouse up to date,' it read. 'It has been entirely redecorated in a colour scheme of duck-egg green and silver, new seating accommodation has been provided and the stage has been fitted with the latest system of lighting.' It goes on to praise the performers, with a special mention for 'the handsome, bearded' Nicholas Sandys for his 'natural performance' in the leading role of Roger, the stranger who captures the heart of the play's heroine.[26] We can only imagine how confusing Nicholas must have found this kind of praise, knowing that his well-meaning mother, the 'Countess', was behind it all.

The review also commends the company's veteran actor–producer James Hart, who had worked with Marguerite in Aberystwyth before rejoining her company in Broadstairs. Throughout Nicholas's increasingly frequent disappearances, or when Marguerite was distracted by her latest Sandys or Barcynska, the sixty-five-year-old Hart would steer the company through the tightest of schedules. He even won that most difficult badge of approval, Caradoc's admiration. 'James Hart, producer, is no jackal,' he wrote in his diaries. 'I like him ... [H]e is not afraid to take off his coat and sweat changing scenes with me to help him while the jackals look on.'[27] James Hart's career was to continue well into his seventies, when, after the war, he emigrated to the United States with his wife, Elizabeth Hart, where he worked as a radio producer for NBC's Colgate Theater.

Hart decided to give Nicholas's *The Jade Claw* another outing in Broadstairs, with Nicholas again in the lead role as an Indian prince. His choice of play and casting may have been an attempt to entice an apathetic Nicholas into engaging more with the company. The review that followed (again almost certainly by Marguerite), bestowed only faint praise on Nicholas with a passing mention of his 'realistic performance'. Perhaps Marguerite, realising the need to balance her son's ego with those of the rest of the company, was being careful not to lavish too much praise on him.

Thanks to the long, kind summers of the Kentish coast, the season at Broadstairs was a thriving affair that stretched well into September. Rogues and Vagabonds capitalised on this four-month gold rush by cramming in a dizzying round of shows, putting on play after play, with as many performances as it could accommodate. Even by the relentless standards of repertory theatre, the schedule bordered on the unachievable. As the newest attraction, Marguerite's little out-of-the-way theatre had to work hard to be noticed; this she understood. It was especially true in the face of dazzling competition from the likes of The Pavilion, 'the garden above the sands' where visitors would flock to see Uncle Mack's minstrel show.[28] Competition also came in the form of the enticingly named Broadstairs Bohemia, with its mixed programme of variety and repertory, including Cally Lambert's *Peep Show* of 1939, billed as 'an ideal summer entertainment'. (Children were half price and, for 6d, cars could be garaged during the performance.) Unlike The Playhouse, both The Pavilion and the Bohemia occupied prime locations frequented by holidaymakers and day trippers, and their gaudy exteriors would daily catch the eye of thousands of passers-by. The cinema – now in its golden heyday – was also thriving: visitors to Broadstairs had a choice of three picture houses, all showing twice-daily double bills featuring stars like James Cagney, Katherine Hepburn, Cary Grant and Bette Davis. In the face of such competition, it was easy for anyone, other than the most dedicated theatregoer, to miss a little repertory theatre hidden away at the quiet end of town.

All too aware of the competition, Marguerite and her company went into battle. Applying the formula she had perfected in Aberystwyth, she put on a varied, popular and constantly changing repertoire of farces, drawing-room comedies, whodunnits and 'shockers', all of them advertised by a parade of exuberant, eye-catching notices in the local papers. Each show would then be followed by a favourable review (penned by Marguerite) praising its 'well-chosen cast' and its 'light and confident touch', abiding by the unspoken rule of repertory that even if only two people turned up, the audience was always 'good'.

On 17 August, the Rogues and Vagabonds production of another comedy, *Third Time Lucky*, failed to live up to its name. It received only the briefest mention in the listings section of *The Stage*, on a page which was dominated by the likes of Exmouth Pavilion's *Would You Believe It?*, a variety show that featured acts such as 'Elroy, the armless artist', compère Jack Joyce who 'dances well on his one leg', Lemo the lioness, Eliza the educated pig, 'burlesque juggling' and the acrobatic Bonita Sisters.

Marguerite, beginning to tire of theatre, threw herself back into her old punishing writing regime. In contrast to her life in Aberystwyth, she was increasingly shutting herself off, keeping the theatre on the boil only for her son's sake and making little effort to meet people in Broadstairs. *A Kentish Lad*, a childhood memoir by the scriptwriter, comedian and raconteur Frank Muir, offers up a rare account – beyond Marguerite's self-generated publicity for the local press – of her Broadstairs years. Muir recalls the 'Polish Countess Barcynska' as the 'famous romantic novelist' and as 'a sad old lady with rouged cheeks and a floppy hat'. She would have been fifty-four years old at the time: an age that would no doubt have qualified as 'old' to a child. It is not clear why he describes her as 'sad', although anxiety over her theatre, as well as Caradoc and Nicholas, may well have told on her face.[29]

Broadstairs must have inspired Marguerite. There, for the first time in her long career, she produced a Barcynska novel that was more reflective, less formulaic and more literary in style. *Writing Man*, her most serious and psychologically complex work, is set in the small Kentish seaside town of Chalkliff (a thinly disguised Broadstairs).[30] Centring on Dick, a frustrated estate agent who longs to be a serious writer, the novel charts his agonising choice between the security of his nine-to-five job (and the loss of creative confidence it entails) and the perilous life of a full-time writer. Along the way, he meets Daisy Bell, a middle-aged author and yet another fictionalised version of Marguerite (recalling her family's pet name for her in childhood), who acts as his guide to the writing life. Despite its fashionable 'social issue' realism, and the tragedy of the death of Dick's wife and baby, the novel ends on a hopeful note with Dick, inspired by his wife's 'presence', beginning to write another book. The author Daisy Bell echoes Marguerite's feelings when she says: 'It's very consoling to make one's characters happy at the end of one's books and it makes people who read them happy too – especially the ones who are sad.' *Writing Man* was also an exploration of Marguerite's own writing dilemma. Tired of the incessant demands of commercial writing, which were hobbling her creativity, she decided to experiment with a more literary style and increase her repertoire beyond the constraints of romance fiction. Her publishers, Hurst and Blackett, went along with her proposal. It was the least they could do for one of their most prolific and enduring authors.

Writing Man was well received, with one critic even comparing it to A.J. Cronin's acclaimed novel *The Citadel*. Yet critical acclaim did nothing to boost sales – quite the opposite. Moving away from the light romances that had made her so well loved was a commercially risky strategy. She began to fear that her new style, if pursued, could alienate her loyal readers while failing to attract a new following. She knew all too well, from Caradoc's tales of the gifted authors he had met as a literary editor, as well as her husband's own experience, that critical acclaim bore no relation to sales. Through Caradoc she had learnt of the struggles of the Welsh poet and tramp W.H. Davies, and the Shropshire novelist Mary Webb, to scrape a living. (Although both eventually achieved commercial success, it was not before they had endured decades of poverty.) With Caradoc and Nicholas to support, she knew she could not afford any more forays into literary fiction but would have to stick to the old Sandys and Barcynska styles.

She was also still bankrolling Rogues and Vagabonds, the company now beset by debts and low morale. Her anxieties were not helped by Nicholas, who had failed to take over the reins as Marguerite had hoped and appeared to be growing increasingly apathetic. With these pressures in mind, Marguerite decided to play it safe with her next novel and return to one of her old favourite themes: a light romance set in a provincial repertory theatre company. *Calm Waters*, dedicated to 'all my troupers in the wish that in calm waters we shall meet again', was set in another fictionalised Broadstairs (this time, the seaside town of Dumpton).[31] In this unequivocally biographical novel, a theatre company run by the eminent author Maggie Alban (a familiar theme) sets about restoring a derelict theatre and proceeds to dazzle the town with its lively repertoire. The ups and downs of the struggling company (and the foibles of its incorrigibly optimistic manager and its kindly, carefree players) were already familiar Marguerite territory.[32] This time, the good-natured comedy is set against a darker backdrop as war looms. Published in 1940, the novel's timely tone – and sensitive handling of people struggling to maintain some kind of everyday life amid terrifying world events – was well received. 'This is an intensely human story, so handled as to be definitely uplifting,' said one critic, while another praised it for its skilful handling of 'not only the great upheaval caused by the war, but its great levelling effects as well'.[33]

Praised by the *Daily Mirror* as one of the first novels to deal 'with the immediate effect of this war on the lives of ... ordinary people',[34] *Calm Waters* captures the nation's anxiety through the lightest of touches. In contrast to her earlier apparent denial of the approaching war, Marguerite now tackles the subject head-on. Instead of 'squandering' her anxiety by fretting over radio bulletins and newspaper reports, as Caradoc did, she poured it straight into her writing.

While *Calm Waters* was praised for its realism, for Nicholas it may have been too realistic for comfort. Lewis Morris, the Caradoc figure, directs the full force of his invective at his stepson, Jon, whom he resents for living off his mother. 'He has been worshipped from the cradle', he fumes, 'and he can't understand why I don't worship him.' Morris also directs his spleen at the spendthrift habits of both mother and son and their penchant for the season's Bond Street fashions. Above all, he rails at his wife for squandering her money on her theatre company, just to provide a stage for her aspiring actor son to strut upon. Maggie's son Jon, now approaching his thirties and still dependent on his overworked, high-achieving mother and the theatre company she has set up for his benefit, made a painfully accurate portrayal of Marguerite's diffident, directionless son.

In the Barcynska domestic drama *Sweetbriar Lane*, the Marguerite and Caradoc figures are the bestselling author Florence Bree (a mix of her second given name, Florence, and her one-time stage name Olive Bree) and her hard-drinking ex-journalist husband Hector Fleet (so named after his tendency to go 'careering in Fleet Street like a mad dog').[35] They are, she writes, 'two utterly unbalanced and incredible opposites who could not exist without each other'. Florence's hapless son Heron is also a thinly disguised Nicholas. In a portrayal that is both poignant and, for its ruthless assessment of her son's character, chilling, the book describes Heron as a 'bewildered youth without father to confide in or mother who understood, [who] experienced a loneliness that adolescence could not put into words.'[36] With the writer's 'splinter of ice' lodged firmly in her heart, nothing was out of bounds, least of all her family. Perhaps she was wielding a writer's revenge on both husband and son. Since it fell to her to write in order to support the indigent men in her life, she quite possibly reasoned they had no right to complain if they recognised themselves, with all their faults laid bare, in her books.

Caradoc played by the same rules. In turn, Marguerite refused to be offended, no matter how personal and cruel his fictional portraits. His then still-to-be-published 'Kitty Shore's Magic Cake' centres on the relationship between Kitty and her son Peter, who was 'incapable of earning a living'. Kitty is warned not to spoil her son so much as 'Spoilt children grow up into monsters as often as not.' That Kitty and Peter are a thinly veiled Marguerite and Nicholas would have been all too obvious to anyone who knew them and, of course, to Marguerite and Nicholas themselves. The novel also features a theatre company, which is, of course, a proxy for Rogues and Vagabonds. Here Caradoc lets rip with his contempt for its actors, who, 'as worthless as the cigarette ends which encircled their feet at the bar', laugh at Peter and his mother as soon as their backs are turned. 'Where there are actors there is treachery,' he concludes.[37]

If Marguerite was hurt by her husband's sardonic portraits, she kept her feelings to herself, at least in print. When 'Kitty Shore's Magic Cake' was finally published as *Mother's Marvel* in 1949, four years after Caradoc's death, Marguerite was its most passionate advocate in the face of a hostile reception, insisting it was 'as fine a piece of writing as anything he ever did'.[38] It was as if they had entered into an unholy writers' pact, agreeing that everything they held dear, including those closest to them – *especially* those closest to them – could be used as raw material. It was a game of words that left Nicholas, who did not have their outlet of fiction, a shuttlecock to be tossed around between them.

The war came at a particularly bad time for Nicholas, as he had yet to establish his career. As Marguerite was beginning to realise, her son showed little of the drive and dedication (and none of the self-confidence) needed to shine in the theatre. For Marguerite, the war was another opportunity to bail out. Having taken on three properties and a new car, and still supporting her husband and son, she confessed she was 'not frightfully rich at present'.[39] As Caradoc had predicted, her latest theatre venture was proving as financially ill-advised and as profligate as the first one. Although Marguerite claimed the company was beginning to turn over a small profit, the summer season was almost over and they faced the prospect of covering The Playhouse's rent with no significant box office takings except for a possible Christmas show.

As money worries put pressure on an already strained marriage, Caradoc resumed his old destructive ways. He began to drink more heavily than ever. His rages had also returned, and he railed against his wife's 'stupidity' for throwing away what was left of her savings on a theatre company. 'In those days he wasn't my Caradoc at all,' writes Marguerite. 'He was a mad dog. Half the time he didn't know what he was doing or saying. I had to get him away ...'

Caradoc had almost fallen out with most of the cast and crew, accusing them of taking advantage of his wife's generosity, as he had done in Aberystwyth. These 'mad dog' moods inevitably disrupted Marguerite's precious writing routine, just when she needed to produce more in order to compensate for her theatre losses. Caradoc's furies could not have come at a worse time. 'She says I lost her a book a year,' wrote Caradoc. 'Maybe.'[40]

On 3 September 1939, the much-feared and anticipated war with Germany was declared. Marguerite, who no longer attended rehearsals routinely, had been present that day. The company was rehearsing for the third night of the season's final show: a popular Emlyn Williams thriller which had been brought there straight from a sell-out West End run. The first two nights had gone well. (What better than a tense, psychological murder thriller to take people's minds off world events?) The prophetically named *Night Must Fall* would be their finest production yet, Marguerite told the company. Perhaps she had known, or at least sensed, that it would also be their last. Later that day, The Playhouse was closed down under air raid precautions orders. Its curtains did not go up again.

Nicholas loaded up his mother's car, helped by Jack Berrangé, the company's juvenile lead whom Marguerite – refusing to accept that she could no longer afford such luxuries – also employed as her chauffeur. She had not told Caradoc she was leaving. As Marguerite, Nicholas and Jack headed west, Caradoc came home from the pub to find 'the Woman's' note on the kitchen table. It did not say where she was going.

Chapter 10
Hill of Tempests

Take me where the daisies
Cover the country lanes.
We'll make hay while the sun shines,
We'll make love while it rains.
(Nacio Herb Brown and Arthur Freed,
'We'll Make Hay While the Sun Shines')[1]

The Edwardian villa sits in the middle of the hamlet of New Cross: brick-built and bay-fronted, it stands out from its more traditional stone neighbours. This is Brynawelon, where Marguerite spent most of her war years. The hedge of rowan, beech and white-blossomed hawthorn, once tended by Marguerite and Caradoc, now lies beneath a jumble of rhododendrons, their seeds blown in from the gardens of Nanteos Mansion. Next door is Horeb Chapel, where Marguerite and Caradoc would attend services as the mood took them: today it is deconsecrated and a cheerful-looking family home. In other ways, New Cross – five miles south of Aberystwyth with a pub, chapel, garage and one hundred inhabitants – is changed little from when Marguerite, Caradoc and Nicholas lived there.

As anyone who knew Marguerite might have predicted, her attempt to leave Caradoc in Broadstairs was short-lived. Reunited the next day, the couple decided to return to Wales, to Aberystwyth, where they had spent four relatively happy years together following their marriage. West Wales – far away from the Kentish coast and the ever-present risk of enemy invasion – would make a safe and peaceful wartime haven. Indeed, others with the same idea had got there before them and had snatched all the best properties in town. By the time Marguerite and Caradoc arrived, they had to take their search out of town and into the surrounding countryside. Eventually, four miles south of Aberystwyth, they found a few rooms for rent at Aber-mad farm.

The accommodation was basic: without electricity, indoor toilet or a bath, its sole supply of water a nearby well. For Caradoc, the farm was a return to the spartan conditions of his childhood, which made him both miserable and grimly stoical.

With many of the local young women gone to take up more lucrative jobs in the munitions factories or in the Land Army, domestic help was also hard to come by. As a result, Marguerite took on much of the cooking and cleaning herself. (It would never have occurred to her to ask Caradoc or Nicholas to help, any more than it would have occurred to either man to offer – although Caradoc was useful at outdoor tasks that involved digging or cutting.)

Almost as soon as they arrived, the freezing winter of 1939–40 followed, making conditions more difficult still. Yet in the face of hardship, Marguerite adopted a determinedly cheerful disposition, even surprising Caradoc when she uncomplainingly learned how to light the stove. She draws on this experience in *Meadowsweet*,[2] a morale-boosting comedy romance in which a variety star gives up a life of glamour to work on a wartime farm. Despite the back-breaking work, harsh weather and primitive conditions, the heroine remains resolutely cheerful through all the setbacks that come her way.

As spring approached, Brynawelon, a Nanteos Estate property some three miles from Aber-mad, became available. When Marguerite saw it she declared herself immediately enchanted. It was not the house which captured her heart – although, in terms of comfort, it made a huge improvement on the farm – but the uninterrupted views across the valley and the mountains beyond. The landscape reminded her of India, she said, claiming even the Welsh language spoken by her neighbours resembled 'the speech of India and the speech of myself with my early playmates'.

Shortly after moving in, Marguerite began work on her autobiography. Unlike her fiction, it was a book she had been planning (and postponing) for some time. Eventually published in 1941 as *Full and Frank: The Private Life of a Woman Novelist*, Brynawelon – or her version of it – takes centre stage. Featuring Caradoc as the male lead (whom she refers to only as 'the man'), they become a pair of romantic bohemians who have escaped the city for a simple rural life. Like the couple in the popular song 'We'll Make Hay While the Sun Shines', she and 'the man' find themselves 'in a little cottage sitting pretty', their life together one long country honeymoon. She enthuses about the daily walks they take together, when they would wander down 'Fairy Lane' to the stream below. 'From earliest spring till mid-winter,' she writes, the lane is brimming 'with primroses, violets white and blue, ragged robin, starry aconite, the lesser and greater celandine, eyebright, orchids, wild strawberry, harebells ... on as frail a stem that when you pick them you can hear them ringing.' No longer bad-tempered or prone to bouts of heavy drinking, Caradoc is cast as her courtly lover. One morning, she writes, on coming down to breakfast, Caradoc had left a surprise for her:

> In front of my chair on the breakfast table a sight that fills me with joy. He has been gathering gold for me. Flung down in a jumble, feathery bits of grass and pinches of moss clinging to them, lighting all the candles in my heart – a plate of primroses – a plate of first primroses.[3]

Their neighbours are given walk-on parts as charming rustics whose cottage doors are constantly open and who are always eager to invite the couple inside for stories and gossip. Also introduced is 'Old Griff', the local *dyn hysbys* (part healer, part wizard), whom local farmers would seek out for help with everything from curing sick cattle to lifting witches' curses. The couple's semi-feral but adorable dogs make cameo appearances: Timber, the sheepdog puppy they rescued from a cow-house: Jock, their 'elderly but not sedate fox-terrier', and Marguerite's much-loved adopted part-Sealyham mongrel Taffy.

While its evocative description of Brynawelon provided a romantic escape from the stresses and anxieties of war, *Full and Frank* also gallops through Marguerite's various careers on the stage, in film and on Fleet Street; her life as a bestselling author of risqué romantic fiction; her string of volatile real-life romances; and her passions for fast cars and fine clothes. Described by *The Times Literary Supplement* as 'a strange, rather painful story that should serve as an antidote to romantic fiction', it gives away little of its author's inner life.

Full and Frank touches on, then brushes past, Marguerite's lonely early childhood in India. Her absentee mother and stern and distant father are there, although only just, and painted with the lightest of touches. Marguerite was a master at rousing the reader's interest and sympathy, heightening each revelation with deft brushstrokes of sentiment: the stock-in-trade of the much-loved author Oliver Sandys who is always cheerful, always the reader's friend. Despite its title, the book is far from full and frank, with Marguerite retreating behind her various masks – in turn humorous, sentimental and worldly.

In Marguerite's effusions about her life at Brynawelon, there is one notable absence: her son Nicholas. Now in his mid-twenties, his relocation to rural Wales from the thriving resort of Broadstairs had cast him adrift. Although his life had not been perfect in Broadstairs, he had at least had an emerging, although sluggish, theatre career to occupy him. Now uprooted and lacking direction, Nicholas's state of mind worried Marguerite.

In a letter to her friend, Nell Dunbar, she writes of her fears that Nicholas's 'old self will never be completely restored'. Blaming his unhappiness on the war, she adds, 'He is such a peace-loving person the whole idea of war and killing revolts him.' Yet the 'peace-loving' Nicholas had tried to sign up to the Royal Navy Volunteer Reserve, only to be told, 'So far no vacancies.' Marguerite admits to doing all she can to keep Nicholas at home. 'If my son is snatched from me I could never live,' she confesses to Dunbar. 'I cannot see anything good can ever come out of the shedding of blood.' She was hatching a scheme to acquire 'some small holding [sic.] and start off with a few sheep and chickens' in the hope that it would give him land-worker status and so exempt him from military service. In the event, she managed to obtain thirty ewes from a local farmer.[4] While the sheep may not have granted Nicholas exemption from active service, his fragile mental health may have been reason enough. Either way, Marguerite got her way and Nicholas was not called up, regardless of his wishes.

The reality of life at Brynawelon fell far short of Marguerite's sentimental accounts. Caradoc's unflinching description (in contrast to Marguerite's) hints at another, darker side to the rural idyll of his wife's imagination:

> There is an unproductive garden (on a rock) and an acre field on a slope ... Next to the cottage comes the chapel house. Next to the chapel house the Chapel Horeb. Back of it is the schoolhouse and playground and back of that stretches the burial ground. It looks as if we are here for the duration.[5]

It is as if the burial ground perched above Brynawelon – a view that Marguerite omits in her accounts – is waiting for them. Nor was Marguerite as besotted with Brynawelon as she claimed to be. 'I do not like this house – It's infested with rats!' she wrote to Margaret Powell, her landlord and dowager of Nanteos, with a request that 'another house on the estate' be made available.[6] It could have been a result of the difficulties of finding rented accommodation during wartime, but Marguerite's wish would not be granted. They were to remain there, as Caradoc had predicted, 'for the duration'.

Trapped in the very Welsh countryside he thought he had escaped, Caradoc's moods turned blacker. Marguerite, in turn, grew more fearful, constantly tiptoeing around him, trying not to provoke him. Writing after Caradoc's death, she recalls how, when one of his dark moods took hold, he would behave like 'a daemon drove him', turning on her 'like a mad dog'.[7] It must have been difficult for Marguerite – the self-confessed sentimentalist – to expose this side of her marriage to her readers. Perversely, she did it out of a sense of duty, feeling certain that Caradoc would have wished it; claiming he had told her, 'If I die before you and you write about me, don't canonise me: don't whitewash me.'[8]

Their fiery relationship was well known in New Cross. Caradoc's biographer John Harris interviewed surviving neighbours who could still remember the raised voices and sounds of breaking crockery coming from Brynawelon. Most saw it as nothing more than clashes between two temperamental characters.

While it is not known if Caradoc ever raised his hand to Marguerite, he was cruel in myriad other ways – not least in the perverse pleasure he got from taking Marguerite's possessions and giving them to other women. Once, when a barmaid admired her hat, she recalls how Caradoc had snatched it off her head and given it to the astonished woman. Marguerite, struggling to save face, insisted that she keep it. When her dog Taffy began to suffer fits, Caradoc took him to be 'properly done in' at Aberystwyth Police Station without her knowledge. Later, he taunted a shocked Marguerite by telling her it had all been her fault – that Taffy's fits had been caused by her forgetting to buy his worming pills during her trips to town. 'I am sorry I said this,' he wrote in his diary, 'for I am not sure it was worms at all ... I have since told her this but ... she continues to reproach herself.' In common with many abusive men, Caradoc would later regret his behaviour and promise it would not happen again. As with other abusive relationships, his promises were soon broken.

Gwyn Jones, a regular visitor at Brynawelon, felt that 'Caradoc treated her abominably'. Yet he lays most of the blame on Marguerite's 'blood-sucking devotion', which had made Caradoc 'like a dog on a chain'. While conceding that 'Marguerite's nature was warm and loving', he thought 'she did her menfolk no good'.[9] An academic and editor of *The Welsh Review*, Jones was among the most perceptive of observers. Yet his analysis of a relationship that in retrospect, can only be described as abusive, reveals a blind spot. Although writing in 1978, almost forty years after the events he describes, his pragmatic approach to domestic abuse, particularly when the abuse was psychological rather than physical, echoed the received wisdom of his time.

Marguerite found more understanding in the form of her fellow bestselling romance author Berta Ruck. Berta was married to the popular Welsh author Oliver Onions, who also had a violent temper. As two leading ladies of their genre, Marguerite and Ruck had been aware of each other's work for decades. Yet they only met after Ruck had read *Full and Frank* and, struck by the similarities between them, felt compelled to write to Marguerite. Both were born into British military families in India, both had struggled with emotionally distant fathers, and both had begun their careers on Fleet Street.[10] Most notably, they had both achieved outstanding success in the field of romantic fiction. Yet for all their successes, each woman was in thrall to a cruel husband.

Caradoc's moods darkened the atmosphere at Brynawelon. The tension even affected their dogs, especially Jock, whom Jones described as 'that hysterical, lynx-coated, easily hated but much to be pitied dog of theirs'. Even the relatively mild-tempered Timber had turned on Caradoc, biting his owner so badly that he had to seek medical attention. (Caradoc blamed himself for coming between the dog and his bone.)[11] The couple's preference for letting their dogs run free also made them unpopular with their farming neighbours. When 'two awful farmers' called round with guns, threatening to shoot them, they reluctantly decided to keep them tied up all day. 'It seems hardly worth being alive for the poor things,' Marguerite complained.[12]

Despite this oppressive atmosphere, Marguerite's Brynawelon

years were among the most productive of her career. Driven by the need to write more books to stay afloat, she completed a remarkable seventeen novels during the four years she lived there. Yet it was her autobiography, *Full and Frank*, that was far the biggest commercial success of that period, with a first reprint appearing only months after publication. War made Marguerite more prolific, infusing her writing with renewed focus and sense of purpose. Thanks to directives from the Ministry of Information, which insisted that all literature and film should aim to support the war effort and lift morale, Marguerite knew exactly what was expected of her. During this period she dutifully – and seemingly effortlessly – produced the propaganda-centred novels the Ministry of Information required. In particular, she invented a number of creative variations on the theme of a hero who is reluctant to fight, but who later changes his mind, putting his country before himself. It was a formula that Marguerite would embellish with a rich, colourful palette – entirely her own – of characters and settings drawn from her new rustic surroundings.

In *Jack Be Nimble*[13], the reluctant hero is a 'rascal gypsy' who does his best to avoid getting called up, but later sacrifices his life for a fellow soldier at Dunkirk, while in *Swell Fellows*[14] the hero is an author who turns down the offer of a comfortable job writing propaganda to go and fight in Libya. *Wellington Wendy*,[15] 'A BOOK FOR THE BLITZ!',[16] has a hero who is reluctantly convalescing following an attack of blackwater fever. As his frustrations bubble over, he steals a German plane and uses it to destroy a German bomber, while the eponymous 'Wellington Wendy' (a land girl named after her footwear) unearths a Nazi fifth-columnist spy masquerading as a Welsh rural squire.

The 1944 Barcynska novel *Astrologer* offers a more complex variation of the wartime sacrifice theme.[17] Evan Evans, the illegitimate son of Welsh gypsies, is brought up as a member of an old Welsh county family upon whose woodland estates the same gypsies still camp. Running away to seek his fortune, he is seduced by the decadent side of London society during the Blitz until, disgusted with his aimless life, he joins the RAF. Later, blinded in action, he returns home to Wales, where he finds the long-lost gypsy love of his youth. (The parallels between this and Marguerite's journey from the decadence of London to her simpler life in the Welsh countryside are all too clear.)

In *Black-Out Symphony* Marguerite reveals a more personal, ambivalent, view of war.[18] Centring on Brian Hereford, a young musician who, despite his 'dangerously sensitive mentality', is called to active service, *Black-Out Symphony* is more complex than the earlier 'do right by your country' narratives. Although Hereford survives the war, the trauma has rendered him so psychologically damaged that he is drained of all creativity and can no longer compose music. While fiercely patriotic, emotionally Marguerite was still a pacifist. For her the war was a struggle between her innate patriotism and her deeply held hatred of violence of any kind. This conflict would at times find expression in her impassioned arguments for peace. Caradoc recalls, with a mixture of affection and amusement, Marguerite's Lysistrata-like insistence that women should refuse to sleep with men until the war was over. 'When she gets going she is priceless and totally without logic,' he wrote.[19]

Marguerite must have had Nicholas in mind when writing *Black-Out Symphony*: like its hero Hereford (and indeed, like Marguerite herself), her son was increasingly prone to debilitating bouts of depression. Marguerite feared that even if Nicholas survived the war without any physical injuries, like Hereford, he would not recover from its emotional scars. It is not clear what exactly, but there must have been something in the experiences of this daughter of a one-time proud military family that made her sympathetic to pacifism. Perhaps she felt that the all the injuries and deaths her military surgeon father had witnessed had left him psychologically scarred.

Even in her quiet corner of the country, seemingly far away from the war, Marguerite could not escape its realities. In 1941, she received news from Brighton that her mother had died just weeks after her home was destroyed by a bomb. She was sixty-nine. Although her mother had not been injured in the blast, Marguerite was convinced that she had later died of shock. Marguerite, who had never been close to her – had never, it seems, really known her – did not attend the funeral. While she put this down to the wartime rationing of petrol, not showing up to relatives' funerals appears to have been something of a Jervis family custom.

She found some spiritual consolation, however, in the form of a vision she describes as a 'bird of heaven', which she felt certain was her mother returning to her after death. Soon afterwards she wrote of how another vision – that of her late Aunt Tots with flowers in her hair which were not 'the earth's flowers' – appeared to her in a 'waking dream'.

While Marguerite's belief in spiritualism was sincere, she would have also been aware it was a subject that aroused considerable interest among her readers – believers and sceptics alike. This would have been especially true during World War Two, when, for many of the bereaved, spiritualism emerged as a very real source of comfort. This was brought into sharp relief in 1944, when the sensational Helen Duncan case gripped the nation. One of Britain's best-known mediums, rumoured to number Winston Churchill and George VI among her clients, Duncan had alarmed the authorities by revealing classified information during a séance. When she disclosed the news that two battleships had been sunk, her information was not only accurate but included details which had been suppressed in the interests of public morale. In a bid to stop her revealing further state secrets, an Act of Parliament dating back to 1735 was invoked and, in a controversial decision, Duncan was found guilty of witchcraft and sentenced to nine months in Holloway Prison.[20]

Caradoc, himself a dabbler in spiritualism, was experiencing a spiritual awakening of a different kind. Despite his infamous satirical accounts of Welsh chapel communities, he was now attending services at Horeb, the Calvinistic Methodist chapel next door to

Brynawelon. It is not clear if this was a change of heart on his part, or if he was just on the lookout for new material for his writing. Perhaps his attendance was prompted by feelings of boredom and rural ennui at a time when petrol rationing limited even the ten-mile round trip to Aberystwyth to no more than once a week. Marguerite began joining him and – although unable to understand a word of the Welsh sermons – became an enthusiastic attender. Together she and Caradoc would sit in the front pew, with Caradoc leaning forward to catch every word. Eleanor M. Beynon, wife of the minister Rev. Tom Beynon, remembered how, as her husband addressed the congregation, Marguerite would study Caradoc's face intently, sometimes hissing, 'What does he say now, Caradoc?', prompting her 'avidly listening' husband to translate for her.

In *Full and Frank*, Marguerite claims to have experienced an epiphany at Horeb: 'Here, then, in this Welsh Calvinistic Methodist chapel I drew nearer to God than I had ever been, so near that I felt that my sins were forgiven me and whatever happened to me at whatever hour I should not be afraid.' Stopping short of naming these 'sins', Marguerite alluded to the feelings of guilt that had haunted her since the age of five, when she first remembered her father calling her the 'devil's child'.

Despite her problems with Nicholas and Caradoc, despite her frenetic pace of writing, Marguerite found time in those early years to welcome visitors. With her usual flair and charm, she opened her doors to an array of people, transforming her isolated rural home into an unlikely setting for a literary and artistic salon. When Marguerite threw one of her soirées, everyone from artists and authors, priests and nuns, farmers and academics – all apparently undeterred by petrol rationing – would travel miles to attend. Among their chief attractions were the generous spreads – almost certainly packed with black-market foods – and entertainment consisting of music or recitations.

While everyone thought Marguerite the most charming and welcoming of hosts, even Caradoc would rise to the occasion and make himself surprisingly amenable. The poet and critic Glyn Jones, one of the regulars at Brynawelon, recalled Caradoc as 'a great encourager, a concentrated and smiling listener, an enthusiastic nodder and agree-er'.[21] Other visitors included the *Sunday People* astrologer, Edward Lyndoe and his wife Kristi Hague, the psychologist John Carl Flügel and his wife Ingeborg, and the University of Wales historian, Dr Frank Lewis. George Green, lecturer and organiser of the Aberystwyth Peace Pageant, made another regular figure. Green was a favourite of Marguerite's, who had once quipped 'he was as large as his brain and his heart'.[22] Another regular was a university student, Anita Jones, who would entertain the guests at the piano with her repertoire of traditional Welsh songs. Anita recalled how glamorous Brynawelon had seemed to her: how it was crammed full of antiques, Buddhas and Russian icons of the Madonna. She was also charmed by the sign on the gate inviting tramps to go round the back to get their pipes filled. But it was Marguerite – with her heavy make-up, 'lipstick all over the place', and generosity as a host – that made the strongest impression of all.[23]

While Marguerite took great care in preparing these evenings, it was her maid, Pauline Block, who bore the burden of her mistress's love for entertaining. To the overworked Pauline, a German Jewish refugee, these gatherings would mean even more labour than usual. Aged thirty-seven, with no pre-war experience of domestic service, Pauline had to single-handedly carry out a daily round of onerous duties. Rising at 6.15 a.m. to light the fire and cook their breakfast (of black-market bacon and eggs),[24] the rest of her day would consist of cleaning, lighting and tending fires, darning and mending, polishing their extensive collection of brass – 'the foremost obsession in this household' – then cooking the evening meal 'on the miserable Calor gas stove'. Later she would wash the dinner dishes, scrub the kitchen floor 'to the endless music of the rattling old typewriter next door', then fall into bed at 9.30 p.m. Pauline was also put in charge of feeding the dogs, for whom she had to boil sheep heads in large, heavy pans, as well as deal alone with the unsavoury business of deworming them, accompanied as it was by 'an obnoxious scene in smell and sight'.[25]

Pauline's is a deeply disturbing account of Brynawelon. Made almost thirty years later, in 1969, it was prompted by an article on Caradoc Evans in *The Times Literary Supplement*. Pauline, then a retired psychiatric nurse living in Warwick, wrote to its author Trevor Williams offering her perspective on Caradoc 'as a once "intimate" and often injured witness of this weird and grotesque household'.

In her account, Brynawelon is revealed as a theatre of cruelty: a 'grey and joyless ... place' where Caradoc's tyranny reigned supreme and where Marguerite, 'painfully writhing under [Caradoc's] oral lashes', would respond with 'hysterical outbursts'.

Pauline arrived at the house in 1942, when she was hired or 'kidnapped as a Maid or Servant in the true sense of the word' by 'this bizarre looking family of three'. Uprooted from her country and vulnerable, Pauline fell victim to the 'warped mentality and sinister traits' of Caradoc:

> In my whipped up emotions – through his evil allusions and contemptible treatment of me I saw him then as 'Devil Incarnate' who spent his foul words and mad accusations (on me) – who had no protection from either friends or knowledge of the fair English Law ... or sufficient courage through lack of English language to defend myself.

In a series of letters to Williams, Pauline describes Caradoc's bizarre and psychologically cruel treatment: how he would secretly open her letters and hide her suitcases to stop her running away; how once, when she was serving breakfast, he announced that all Germans 'should hang or be shot without exception', and would make bizarre accusations that she had worked as a prostitute in Germany; how one night he dragged the terrified Pauline out of her bed, demanding to know why she had left a tray cloth in the garage. As his paranoia spiralled out of control, Caradoc denounced her to the authorities as a German spy. As a result, Pauline had to make a 130-mile round trip alone to appear before a political tribunal in Brecon. The case was dismissed, but, already struggling on her wages to pay her son's boarding school fees, the cost of the journey had left her penniless. It was an episode that left her close to suicidal.

Pauline likened Caradoc to Krespel in *Tales of Hoffmann*, 'who actively wanted to conjure up feelings of hatred toward him'. She might equally have cast Marguerite, or Nicholas, or herself, in the role of Krespel's daughter Antonia, the victim of his tyrannous sorcery.[26] Brynawelon could also be likened to a Welsh Wuthering Heights, with Caradoc the ageing Heathcliff: the hero turned vindictive tyrant who had established a reign of terror over his household.

Together, Pauline, Marguerite and Nicholas formed a web of unstable, shifting allegiances: a complex and toxic alliance of fear in the face of Caradoc's terrifying moods. Marguerite was in turn Pauline's ally and Pauline's tormentor: an unstable mother figure who called on her maid for support against Caradoc before betraying her by reverting to the role of imperious, demanding mistress. As with all relationships at Brynawelon, Pauline found it cruel, confusing and bizarre.

Even at the best of times, Marguerite's relationships with her maids could be complex and fraught. With the necessity of keeping up her daily word count, she dreaded becoming suddenly burdened with domestic responsibilities. If no maid was available, it was a given that the tasks of cooking, cleaning and lighting fires would be done by Marguerite, in addition to being the family breadwinner. The prospect of finding herself buried in domestic chores instead of writing created such anxiety within her she was willing to take extreme measures to find and keep a servant. Once, when a maid from the village (who was sometimes called to help out) was called up for essential war work, Marguerite felt sufficiently put out to write to her MP asking him to intervene on her behalf. But this fixation on finding a maid, combined with the emotional as well as domestic demands she would make on her staff, went beyond practical necessity. It was a need that went back, once more, to her early childhood in India when she reigned over her *ayah* and retinue of devoted servants. Her longing to return to that golden pedestal was doomed to disappointment, the more she demanded of her servants, the sooner she drove them away.

These were the emotional complexities which Pauline, a traumatised refugee, was forced to negotiate. It is striking how, in their different ways, both Caradoc and Marguerite were indifferent to Pauline's feelings. In his better moods, Pauline would hear Caradoc recount 'stories full of indulgence in his poor upbringing and childhood restrictions', his narcissism allowing no empathy for his maid, the one person in the household who needed the greatest indulgence of all. Nor can the couple's apparent callousness be explained away by their ignorance of the horrors that Pauline had endured. One entry in Caradoc's diary records Pauline's account of witnessing the torture of members of her family at the hands of the SS: 'The German Jew woman servant in this house saw her father-in-law thrown in Lake Constance. When he came out he was thrown back again. Thus for about twenty times. Then he was put in a cellar and beaten.'[27] This account by the socialist-leaning and avowedly anti-Nazi Caradoc is remarkably devoid of emotion. Marguerite's descriptions of Pauline show a similar lack of empathy; in *Full and Frank* she even casts 'Paula' (as she calls her) as a comedy stooge:

> She has a coloured handkerchief over her head and a musical comedy apron falling from her waist ... She walks like a little circus pony. When she is happy she sings, when she is upset she weeps buckets ... Sometimes it is very difficult to be patient with her.[28]

The narrative continues in a similar vein for over three and a half pages, with Marguerite mocking her maid's 'incompetence' and

184

itemising her domestic shortcomings: her ineptitude at lighting fires, her lack of familiarity with English cookery, and her lack of fluency in the English language. Even her habit of 'lingering too long' in Marguerite's bedroom after serving the morning tea is mocked. Pauline, her dignity stripped by the Nazis, is now publicly humiliated by her mistress.

Pauline had arrived in Britain following a period of separation from her son, who had arrived some nine months previously as one of the German Jewish child refugees brought to safety on the Kindertransport. Yet Marguerite, the doting mother, gives an account that is sanguine to the point of flippancy:

> Seeing how things were going with the Jews in Germany she sent her son to a school in England a year before the outbreak of war. She followed him in nine months. She says she landed in this country with seventeen shillings. In Germany she was fairly well-to-do.[29]

In 1945, when *Full and Frank* was in its second edition, film footage of the horrors of Auschwitz and Dachau were shown in cinemas across Britain. As the full extent of the persecution of the Jews was revealed, Marguerite's lampooning of her refugee maid was jarringly out of step with the public mood. The novelist, who had once possessed an almost uncanny instinct for what her readers were thinking and feeling, was now sounding increasingly reactionary and out of touch.[30]

This sorry episode comes with a more cheerful postscript. For Pauline, her correspondence with Trevor Williams was an opportunity to recall those disturbing memories from a safe distance of decades. Like many refugees, her achievements in learning English and finding a profession (as a psychiatric nurse) were evidence of her resilience and her determination not to be paralysed by past traumas.

Marguerite's dissatisfaction with Pauline served to distract her (and her readers) from the root cause of her frustration: her abusive husband, Caradoc.

Some months after Pauline's departure, Marguerite wrote to her, adopting a tone that was in marked contrast to her exasperated mistress routine in *Full and Frank*:

> Now do you remember when you were here we were going to a solicitor about my husband's dreadful unkindness to me, but of course I was weak and didn't and after that when you were going you said that if ever I needed your testimony you would give it, well I think I have truly made up my mind it must end or I shall be in my grave and it not [sic.] fair on Nick.[31]

Having heard that Caradoc was 'seen with this Welsh girl', Marguerite resolved to sue him for divorce. Now she was telling (rather than requesting) Pauline to write a letter, 'a truthful letter that I may, if necessary, give to the solicitor'. She told her one-time maid to say that, despite 'Mr Evans's bullying', she never saw her mistress 'get cross or angry with him in spite of the dreadful things he would say to you and the wicked way he would talk to your son'. It was more than could be said of Marguerite's behaviour towards Pauline. Not wishing to get tangled up in a dispute between two former employers, especially two who had made her life so unpleasant, Pauline did not reply.

On another occasion, following a furious row between Caradoc and Nicholas, Marguerite fired off an emotionally charged letter to 'George' (possibly her friend George Green):

> If anything happens to me tonight – I mean if I were to die in my sleep – I feel so ill, so tired, so spent. Nick would be terribly upset naturally. After all that has happened today, God knows in his sorrow he would blame one person.[32]

The argument had begun, as their arguments often did, as a political debate. Caradoc the socialist took pleasure in goading Nicholas for his right-wing views and Nicholas would fall for the bait. Yet it was not a fair fight. Caradoc's erudition and dry wit would have been enough in themselves to ensure he ran rings around the undereducated Nicholas. But Caradoc went further, apparently not satisfied until he had reduced Nicholas to a state of tearful, impotent rage. Their relationship had always been fraught; as Caradoc had once confessed to Marguerite, he was jealous of Nicholas and feared that she might love her son more than him. Yet for reasons that Marguerite could not fathom, but were possibly rooted in undiagnosed depression, Nicholas lacked the confidence to leave.

Marguerite's hopes for Nicholas were raised when he developed a friendship with Anita, the pianist and student at Aberystwyth. But their relationship ended abruptly when Nicholas sent her a heart-shaped card containing a proposal of marriage. Underneath he had written the words 'Yes' and 'No', inviting her to choose one. Perhaps Nicholas had hoped that she would find his ploy charming, that it would disarm her and make a 'yes' more likely. It had the opposite effect. Such a binary choice, combined with his reluctance to propose to her in person, made her 'No' reply all too easy. Perhaps Anita had just been being kind, or simply polite to the son of her host. Although Nicholas would go on to have other relationships with women, they would all of them be fragile and short-lived. He could not shake off his burden of awkward shyness, or the aloofness that tended to drive people away.

As her son approached his mid-twenties, Marguerite began to worry how he would cope without her. In a letter to her friend and one-time theatre producer James Hart, and another to a Major Brian Watson (sent care of the Milkmaid Snack Bar in Hereford), she begs that if anything should happen to her that they would become 'a friend to Nick'.[33]

While her behaviour could be dismissed as histrionic, Marguerite was indeed living in fear of Caradoc and, to judge by her letters, sometimes feared for her life. As Pauline had observed, Caradoc was a 'complex-burdened unhappy man' experiencing 'total frustration as an artist and a writer'. While the power of his earlier stories, with their vivid and grotesque characters, still resonated, it was as if his writing had lost its magic. The more he tried to call up his old powers of scathing observation and pithy storytelling, the more he began to sound like a parody of his former self. With the critical acclaim, or even the modestly healthy sales, of his early career eluding him, any hopes of his writing another *My People* or *Capel Sion* were waning. The more he struggled, the more envious he grew of his wife's ability to keep on writing what he used to admiringly call 'the selling stuff'. He was also becoming increasingly frustrated at his financial dependence on his wife.

Marguerite in turn was struggling under the burden of supporting both Caradoc and the still-dependent Nicholas. The National Government's directive to cut authors' fees during the war by half had also hit her hard. Although reluctant to admit it, the woman who could once command an array of cars, furs and Regent Street clothes now had to count the pennies. In *Full and Frank*, she touches on the truth only obliquely. In a convoluted explanation for her relatively modest home of Brynawelon, she claimed that, during wartime, because no one wanted to live in them, mansions were cheaper than smaller houses. Yet Marguerite would have secretly adored the county mansion which was now above her means. 'I wanted a big house,' she writes. 'I wanted luxury cars. I wanted to run a theatre, I wanted furs and jewellery and lovely clothes. I worked for them and they were mine.'[34] Yet less than a year after these words appeared in 1941, all of those luxuries were beyond her reach.

Cuts in the publishing industry were not the only cause of Marguerite's drop in income. After almost three decades of bestselling popularity, her fiction was beginning to date and her sales to slide. The 1942 Beveridge Report, which served as the blueprint for the welfare state, had grown out of a groundswell of support which would eventually lead to the post-war Labour election landslide. Along with these changing social attitudes, public taste

188

was changing too. Social realism was in the ascent, as embodied in films like *Millions Like Us* (1943) and *A Canterbury Tale* (1944). Public taste was turning away from romantic escapism, favouring instead more realistic portrayals of people's lives. In the publishing world, the hugely popular *Mrs Miniver*,[35] along with imports of hard-boiled American detective fiction by the likes of Raymond Chandler and James M. Cain, were topping the bestseller and library loans lists. In recent years, Marguerite's novels had lost the tough, worldly optimism of her earlier works, as her struggling chorus girls and breezy, tough-edged comedy was replaced by gentler tales with quaint Welsh settings and even quainter Welsh characters. The names Oliver Sandys and Countess Barcynska were also becoming associated with a pre-war brand of sentimentality and a set of assumptions about British society that had suddenly fallen out of step with popular taste.

While her novels were still being read and enjoyed by her loyal (mostly older) readers, their failure to reach new audiences were causing sales to spiral slowly downwards. If it had not been for *Full and Frank*, which had achieved sales approaching those at the height of her career, it would have been worse still for her.

Despite this change in fortune, Marguerite struggled to curb her taste for luxury. In February 1940, she received a summons for an unpaid bill of £11, 6s, 8d owed to the National Fur Company. (The newspaper report states that she did not attend the hearing.)[36] Now her spending habits were being decided for her. Her name blackened by a summons, her suppliers would no longer give her credit. While hoping her book sales would pick up in peacetime, she took to draping her new, relatively modest, lifestyle in the flag of patriotic austerity. As her satins and silks faded, she could at least blame it on the war. Caradoc, the one-time dandy, had to make economies of his own. To Berta Ruck he now appeared a 'lanky, loose-limbed figure' in 'tramp's clothes' topped off with 'a scarecrow hat'.[37] No longer able to afford his tailor, he began to resemble the elderly down-at-heel eccentric he had become.

Having once revelled in the freedom money had bought her, Marguerite was now trapped by the lack of it. Unable to afford clothes, furs or a car, let alone the prohibitive cost of a divorce, she was stuck 'for the duration' on her cold 'Hill of Breezes'. It made for an uncomfortable reality, one she endured only through writing and retreating further into the mystical.

Chapter 11
After Caradoc – The 'Unbroken Thread'

Life, from birth to grave and After, is an unbroken thread.
(Oliver Sandys, *Unbroken Thread*)[1]

On 11 January 1945, Caradoc died following a short illness. His death came suddenly, less than two weeks after his sixty-sixth birthday and four months after he and Marguerite had moved back from Brynawelon to Aberystwyth. Even if he had planned it in advance, he could not have arranged it better. It was as if he wanted to make it as easy as possible on Marguerite: there had been just enough time for the two of them to unpack and settle into their new flat in town. Whatever his faults, he knew that Marguerite's writing could not bear too much disruption.

They had been ready to leave Brynawelon: even during the summer months the cold and dampness was unforgiving. Marguerite was also convinced that the house was to blame for Caradoc's 'brassy' cough, although he dismissed her concerns. The couple missed the convenience and sociability of living in town, made worse by the petrol rationing, which limited their trips into Aberystwyth to once a week. The final straw came when Pauline, their long-suffering maid, finally walked out on them. Once again, the lack of domestic help was most keenly felt by Marguerite: faced with the prospect of doing all the cooking and cleaning herself, she traded in the 'mountain views' she adored and 'fairy lanes' for the practicalities of town.

They found a flat in the heart of Aberystwyth, on the second floor of 36 North Parade. Nicholas moved into separate accommodation in town (which Marguerite would almost certainly have paid for) and was, for the first time in his adult life, living apart from his mother. Marguerite appreciated being back in 'Aber' again: she enjoyed the freedom of strolling through the streets and visiting shops, pubs and cafes, as the mood took her. She and Caradoc also appreciated the proximity of friends like Gwyn Jones, editor of *The Welsh Review*, and his wife Alice, even calling on them unannounced on Christmas Day, ostensibly to drop off an article of Caradoc's.[2]

After Christmas, the weather turned wet and stormy and Marguerite did not venture from her flat. Yet no amount of bad weather could deter Caradoc from his habit of taking a long daily walk. Anxious about his cough, Marguerite would plead with him to wait until the weather was better, but he would have none of it. On New Year's Day, the sky turned pewter and stayed that colour. Throughout the day, the little town was lashed by blasts of rain and wind from the Irish Sea. It was the kind of day when anyone who could would choose to stay at home – anyone, that is, but Caradoc. He insisted on ignoring the weather and taking his constitutional as usual. Soon afterwards, his brassy cough developed into pneumonia.

Although too weak to go out, Caradoc still refused to stay in bed. It would only be pushing his gravestone a little further away, he insisted. Consumed by anxiety over the progress of the war, he would heave himself out of bed, leave his bedroom with its warm fire (the only heating fuel rationing allowed for) and head to the cold room where the wireless was kept. There he would sit, leaning forward in his chair, straining to catch every word of each news bulletin as he followed the Red Army's advance on Poland or the retaking of Burma by British troops. He was so engrossed by the progress of the war's final stages that he appeared not to notice his condition was worsening. Then, one day, Marguerite found him struggling to breathe and too weak even to sit in his chair. He was rushed to hospital.[3]

Even in his hospital bed, he would sit up, writing letters to Marguerite, mostly of a practical nature. In one he asks her to send him a copy of *Droll*, the collection of Rabelaisian short stories by Balzac, one of his favourite authors. To the end he remained true to his taste for brutal satire, refusing anything that was moralistic or philosophical or, heaven forbid, sentimental. In another letter to Marguerite, he leaves precise instructions on how to find some papers that he wanted to work on in hospital. 'There is some completed work in the drawer,' he writes. 'Do not bring it. The stuff I want is loose.' In his last letter to Marguerite, dated 6 January, he makes no mention of books or his work. Instead, he turns his attention to arranging his funeral. 'When I die,' it begins, 'I would like you to arrange to rest beside me.' Five days later, he had a heart attack and within three hours had died.[4]

The press reported Caradoc's death a few days later. The news that dominated the papers that day, of the Russian Army's advance on Budapest, would have delighted him. Seven months later, the war that had so consumed his emotions would all be over. Marguerite, feeling certain she had heard Caradoc's voice telling her to 'New Cross' him, decided to bury him there, in the small hillside graveyard in the grounds of Horeb Chapel and just above Brynawelon. His gravestone – featuring engravings of a closed book, a quill and an inkwell – was chosen by Marguerite. She had also selected the epitaph, 'Bury me lightly so that the small rain may reach my face and the fluttering of the butterfly shall not escape my heart'. These words, she claimed, had been written by Caradoc some years previously.[5] Yet the highly charged, romantic style – a world away from Caradoc's terse prose – would suggest Marguerite as its true author.

'Mountainside grave for Caradoc Evans', went the *Western Mail* headline, followed by a lyrical report in which any reference to Caradoc's notoriety is tactfully omitted:

To the summit of the steep, sloping, hummock-strewn cemetery at Horeb, New Cross, from where can be seen a broad picture of Welsh countryside, including Cader Idris and Snowdonia, the body of Caradoc Evans, the Welsh novelist, was taken on Tuesday afternoon by a group of farmers and farm-hands with whom he had formed firm friendship while living at Brynawelon, New Cross.[6]

The 'handful' of mourners present included 'a nun, a Presbyterian elder, a college lecturer, an educationalist, a doctor, a Fleet-Street journalist and a tradesman, representing his diverse interests'. Marguerite, as one of the chief mourners, was listed as 'Mrs. Caradoc Evans (widow)', along with 'Mr. Nicholas Sandys (stepson), and nephews and nieces from Tresaith and Rhydlewis'.[7] Marguerite was not present at the burial. This could have been in accordance with the old Welsh tradition of men only attending the graveside or, more likely, because she was too distressed to attend. Over the coming weeks, as news of Caradoc's death was reported in the national and local press, messages of condolence to Marguerite began to pour in, many of them elegantly expressed, most of them moving and empathetic, the war having seemingly turned condolence into an art form. Among the correspondence was a telegram from Marguerite's publishers Hurst and Blackett, another, with an offer of help, from her friend and fellow romance writer Berta Ruck,[8] and a letter from Margaret Powell, the dowager of the Nanteos Estate and Brynawelon's landlord.

Letters also arrived from former members of Rogues and Vagabonds, including James Hart, their stage manager (and one of the few members of the company who Caradoc had seemed to like), who had followed the company from Aberystwyth to Broadstairs, and the actor Violet Lamb, whose career had begun with the company. But it was the message she received from the company's one-time cashier and theatre attendant Diana Swain (née Jones), which urges Marguerite to 'look forward to the day when you both will be joined together again', that perhaps offered her the greatest consolation.

Marguerite's oldest friend, Monica Dunbar, expressed a similar sentiment. 'You have, no doubt,' she writes, 'already felt him near and trying to comfort you.' In a similar vein, Sarnicol, the epigrammatist and a friend of Caradoc's, offered consolation in the form of a poem – his translation of a Welsh verse – which includes the lines:

Rest here, along with our fathers,
When they arise, do thou likewise.

In contrast, the letters from her brother Eddie (Edmund), now teaching in a private school in Yorkshire, were curiously detached and stilted, one of them urging Marguerite to 'Cheer up, old girl'. Her other brother, Charlie, also teaching and about to take up a new post in a private school in Birmingham, wrote: 'I have been thinking a lot of you dear. It is a comfort for me to know you have sympathetic people around you to help.' This sentiment, however, is marred by his request that Marguerite pays the bill for his wreath. 'So would you mind doing it for me?' he writes, adding that, in his 'bustle', he 'forgot to settle up'.

Marguerite replied to everyone by means of a specially printed card. 'Thank you so much,' it read. 'The song and the shout and the tempest have gone out of life for me and I do not like the calm.' She signed it Oliver Sandys, the first pen name that had been entirely hers, with her married name, Marguerite Evans, in brackets.

During the months that followed, Marguerite carried on in the only way she could, by soldiering on with her work. Around this time, she also embarked on compiling a biography of her late husband: a project that brought her a great deal of solace. Later, it also gave her respite from her money worries when her publishers offered a substantial advance of £500. Titled simply *Caradoc Evans*, it was released in September 1946. Gwyn Jones, reviewing it in *The Times Literary Supplement*, called it 'an unusual, and in many ways a remarkably successful, experiment in biography ... intimate, revealing and tenderly drawn [but] not the definitive work'. Austin Clarke of *The Irish Times* was less flattering, dismissing it as a 'sugared confection' which 'dramatizes her husband as if he were the hero-villain of one of her novelettes'. Despite the mixed reviews, the sales seem to have held up well. Figures are not available, but a reprint two years after first publication suggests it achieved some success, albeit relatively modest.

As the second imprint was published, Marguerite brought out another book about her late husband. *Unbroken Thread: An intimate journey of the daily life in the Welsh countryside of England's best-loved woman novelist* is a peculiar, idiosyncratic spiritualist memoir, in which Caradoc 'returns' and communicates with Marguerite from the 'Other Side'. The voice of her late husband is, she claims:

> [S]omething like the Whispering Voice I used to hear telling me stories as a child when I had a fever in India, only the Whispering Voice was mysterious, remote, impersonal. This voice is distinguishable – belonging to one only. Caradoc's voice.[9]

Published by Rider and Company, specialists in books on spiritualism and the supernatural,[10] *Unbroken Thread* comes with an effusive introduction by the charismatic journalist and self-styled authority on spiritualism (and old drinking companion of Caradoc's) Hannen Swaffer. The book, he says, is 'remarkable', not only for its 'brilliant' literary style, but for the 'proof' it offers that, 'in a home where there is psychic mediumship that is used naturally, death cannot separate'. Swaffer goes on to claim that Marguerite was a natural medium whose powers first displayed themselves in childhood and had been rediscovered during her bereavement 'as a source of comfort and guidance'. Such words, written in the late 1940s, would have offered consolation to the many readers who had suffered a wartime bereavement.

Caradoc and Marguerite had shared more than a passing interest in spiritualism. During the early 1930s, Caradoc had attended seances by the celebrity American medium George Valiantine, whose repertoire involved bells, tambourines and even a miniature jazz band. Caradoc – one of the writers, editors, artists, doctors, scientists and other influential people invited to attend – recalled how in one seance a child spirit had sat on his knee and kissed him 'with moist lips'. In another, he heard the voice of his father addressing him in Welsh.[11]

Marguerite claimed Caradoc had also attended the mass spiritualist spectacles that were held in the Albert Hall during the late 1920s and early 1930s. She does not say if she went with him, or if either of them had been present at the most famous event of all: the sensationalist seance which attempted to contact the recently deceased Sir Arthur Conan Doyle, who was almost as famous for his spiritualist beliefs as he was for his authorship of Sherlock Holmes. The seance was conducted in front of an audience of 10,000 with celebrity medium Estelle Roberts. To her right sat Conan Doyle's widow, Jean Leckie, herself a devout spiritualist, who waited to receive messages from her late husband on the other side. As seances so often did, the event ended inconclusively, with believers insisting that contact had been made as sceptics demanded to see some evidence for the claims.[12]

Ultimately, Caradoc came down on the side of the sceptics, claiming that he had only attended seances out of curiosity. Marguerite held firmly to her beliefs, but it was only after his death that she turned to spiritualism for hope and consolation. Now she recalled the promise her husband had made, namely that, if he went first, 'and I am anywhere around ... I'll prove it to you three times and you'll know it's me'.

Even the book's title, *Unbroken Thread*, was claimed by Marguerite to have been dictated by her late husband.[13] Its full title, *Unbroken Thread: An intimate journal of the daily life in the Welsh countryside of England's best-loved woman novelist*, establishes the excessively self-promoting tone of much of her later work. As anxiety over sales turned to desperation, there was no gimmick she would not consider if it might improve sales. While advances for her novels were in steady decline, her non-fiction at least was still proving lucrative. As sincere as she was in her belief in spiritualism, she also saw it as a new route to commercial success.

Partly written as a long conversation between the author and her late husband, *Unbroken Thread* begins as 'Caradoc', now on the other side, instructs Marguerite on how to communicate with him. 'Every time you want to talk with me,' he says, 'write it down and I'll come to you somehow.' (His words are written in italic.)

As a study of grief and loneliness, written in the depths of what Marguerite calls 'the dark lake of my loss', the book is at times an uncomfortable read. As a very public account of private grief, it feels a little too raw in places – as if it was rushed off before its author had time to heal and reflect. Yet sharing her feelings so directly with her readers (and the letters that would have undoubtedly followed) must have offered her some consolation.

In the book, she turns to 'Caradoc' not so much for spiritual advice but for practical instruction. She has received a proposal of marriage, she tells him, from one 'R.Y.', a judge working in India, and wonders if she should accept. ('Caradoc' urges her to seriously consider it for the sake of her financial security – advice she ignores.) Perhaps inevitably, her old recurring problem of not being able to find any domestic help comes up. This time, due to the post-war labour shortage, her search is more difficult than ever. 'The Labour Exchange tells me that they have not a maid on their register,' she complains, 'and that if girls do come in, priority must be given to laundries, hostels and hospitals. No priority whatsoever for a novelist woman who has a contract with her publishers to write so many novels a year – and an even deeper obligation to her public.'[14]

Lost in grief and self-pity, she is unable to view her need for domestic help in the context of the nation's urgent need for health and housing. Although central to her, it was a problem that few of her readers would have identified with. Marguerite, it seems, was forgetting the old Fleet Street maxim that the writer should be, first and foremost, the 'reader's friend'.

Through her daily difficulties, 'Caradoc' was there to comfort her. When her beloved Jock, 'as perfect as a dog could be', died, 'Caradoc' cheered her up with a reassurance that there are dogs in the afterlife, 'but no lamp-posts'. When she was ill, 'Caradoc' advised her to, 'Go and lie down my love. Take an aspirin. Take two and pull the eiderdown right over your head as I used to put it over you.' Even after death, Caradoc's words of comfort still carried an unsettling sadistic edge.

Marguerite consulted her late husband on literary matters too, turning to him for advice when she was feeling blocked. The hero of her latest Sandys novel, Milwyn Roberts, she told him, was 'you – at the age of about thirty-six. I'll make him talk and behave and look like you.' Caradoc, she told her readers, also gave her its title, *Learn to Laugh Again*: a lesson Marguerite felt she desperately needed.[15] She noted how Caradoc's advice had 'put wings on her pen' and that afterwards she had been able to write effortlessly once again.

When a journalist from *Reynold's* (the paper which published Caradoc's first short story) approached her about a possible serialisation of her *Caradoc Evans* biography, 'Caradoc' warned her not to let them 'hack' her work about without her approval. As an afterthought, he also wondered if the newspaper's politics would chime with her own Tory tendencies.[16]

It was 'Caradoc' too, she claimed, who told her to move house and directed her towards an auctioneer's window. There she found the bill advertising a 'white and long and low' bungalow 'with a high double hedge' in Penrhyn-coch, a village some six miles north of Aberystwyth that stretches along the base of a steep valley. It was the scenery that first drew her to it, with its 'great forests of hills and mountains'. Like New Cross, the view reminded her of the cool Himalayan mountain resort where her mother had taken her to escape the heat and dangers of the monsoon. Even the yellow marigolds in the garden reminded her of the ones that grew around her bungalow in India.[17] 'Caradoc', as practical in death as he had been in life, instructed her to knock down a wall and build a new staircase to her writing room, even relayed to her the new colour scheme.

The name of her new home delighted her. *Heddle*, meaning 'peaceful place', made a fitting name after a war: one that resonated with her pacifist beliefs. She had its name printed – in Welsh, with the English translation underneath – on her stationery. She decided it would be a peaceful place for 'Caradoc' too: a place where they could still be together, only in a different way.[18] Death had mellowed him. The 'Caradoc' who returned to her from the other side was a kinder, gentler version of the man she had loved. He was no longer the 'mad dog' whose rages terrified her, but the gentler, tamer Caradoc she had always longed for.

There are people from Penrhyn-coch today who can still remember Marguerite living there, on and off, between 1946 and 1952. They recall her bright pink rouge, scarlet lipstick and penchant for hats that sported startling collections of waxed fruit. Her vivid style of dress was enough to turn heads wherever she went, let alone in a quiet village on a Welsh mountainside. The Aberystwyth-born magician and author David Conway remembers her as a friend of his mother's (who knew Marguerite by her married name of Mrs Evans). 'She did not so much wear clothes,' he writes, 'as envelop herself in yards of taffeta and silk, over which hung diaphanous layers of pastel coloured chiffon.' With rings on every finger, bracelets up her arms and rows of beads around her neck, she 'brought to mind some gaudy tropical bird blown off course by the wind and dumped on us dowdy sparrows'.[19]

Today Marguerite's bungalow is still there, now called *Dolwen*, or 'white meadow' in English. The box hedge at the front, which would have screened Marguerite from the gaze of curious passers-by, is gone. In its place stands a freshly-pointed stone wall with cultivated shrubs and a column topped by a stone griffin. Penrhyn-coch, neat and well-scrubbed, is now a dormitory village for Aberystwyth. Yet, on certain days, when the mist creeps down from the mountains and wraps itself around the houses and fields, it still feels like a place set apart from the world below.

A short walk from Marguerite's old home will take you to the

Portrait of Marguerite by Evan Walters (circa 1930).

Nicholas Sandys, actor's publicity photograph.

DRACULA

Adapted from Bram Stoker's novel by Hamilton Deane and John L. Balderston

Characters :

DR. SEWARD	...	Hector Andrews
JONATHAN HARKER	...	Reginald Cornish
MAID	...	Louise Smith
COUNT DRACULA	...	Nick Sandys
PROFESSOR VAN HELSING	...	James C. Laurier
MINA HARKER	...	Monica Stutfield
LORD GODALMING	...	Philip Yorke
MISS MORRIS	...	Violet Lamb
WARDER	...	Eric Andrews
RENFIELD	...	John Gill

Directed by James Hart
Scenery by David Lambert and F. Mower

Telephone kindly lent by The Postmaster General
Lamps and Shades by A. W. Miller, Pier Street, Aberystwyth

ACT ONE
Jonathan Harker's house at Hampstead Heath.   Evening in mid-Autumn

ACT TWO
Mrs. Harker's boudoir.   Same evening

ACT THREE
Same as Act One.   Three days later

Business Manager : Eric Andrews	Art Director : David Lambert
Stage Director : Bry Ferguson	Electrician : F. Mower

Among future plays are : "WHITE CARGO," "THE OUTSIDER," "MURDER ON THE SECOND FLOOR," "AFTER OCTOBER," "DUSTY ERMINE," "CHILDREN TO BLESS YOU"

Quarry Theatre programme for Dracula.

Poster for Rogues and Vagabonds, Broadstairs Playhouse. War was declared less than one month later.

Detail of woman in 'Fairground' by Evan Davies, almost certainly based on Marguerite.

The portrait hangs in the South Reading Room of the National Library or Wales.

Brynawelon, Marguerite's 'Hill of Breezes'.

The Show Must Go On (1936), cover sleeve of reprint.

Tesha (1923), cover sleeve.

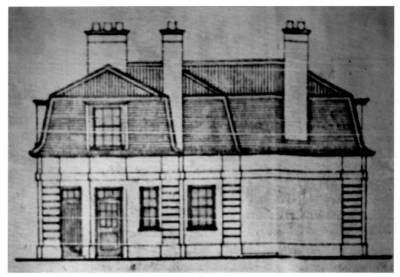

Architect's drawing of Suncrete, Kingsbury.

Publicity Baby (1935),
cover sleeve.

Shining Failure (1950), cover sleeve.

Marguerite with Timber at Heddle, Penrhyncoch, Christmas 1946.

Marguerite, late 1930s/early 1940s.

Marguerite circa 1956. Publicity shot for the 'Happiness Stone', Panteidal, near Aberdyfi.

war memorial; carved from a hulk of rough crystal quartz, it looks as if it has just been hauled down from the mountains. On top of it is a roughly-hewn granite cross and at its base four slate plaques, each one etched with the names of the fallen (one for World War Two and the remaining three for World War One). This is the spot where Marguerite and Nicholas (now moved in again with his mother) attended a thanksgiving service where one of the hymns was sung in English for their benefit, as the only residents who did not speak Welsh. The villagers were 'so welcoming and courteous to the stranger,' she writes, 'the Englishwoman who has come into their midst.' Yet she also worried she was fast becoming 'an eccentric recluse and a hermit', so lonely she had 'befriended' the spider that lived in her bathroom.

Marguerite spent her first Christmas without Caradoc at an Aberystwyth hotel. Nicholas went with her. As the weather turned bitterly cold, they discovered the fireplaces of their bedrooms had been boarded up. The reception they received from the hotel proprietors, complained Marguerite, was just as icy. It was the unhappiest of Christmases, she writes: one 'without holly, without laughter, without mirth, without comfort, without warmth, without joy, without love' – and without Caradoc. The only bright moment came when one of the guests, a 'business woman' from Birmingham on holiday with her husband, was thrilled to discover that Marguerite was not only Oliver Sandys but Countess Barcynska as well – two authors who had given her so much pleasure. She asked Marguerite for her autograph, saying she would 'treasure it forever'. 'How extraordinary,' Marguerite declared, with obvious pleasure.

In January, she was joined at Heddle by her younger brother Charlie. He had left his job of thirty years as a master at a prep school and had suffered a nervous breakdown. 'He won't admit it,' writes Marguerite, 'but that is what it amounts to ... Fifty is an age when thirty years of schoolmastering in prep schools begins to tell.' Apart from at Caradoc's funeral, which Charlie had attended, she had not seen him for over twenty-five years. 'It is a little difficult at first to bridge the gulf of years,' she writes, seeing the young man she had remembered looking 'gaunt, thin, hollow-cheeked'. She also found it difficult to cope with his moods. 'He gets very cross and impatient,' she writes, but 'that is all due to his nerves, for normally he is a sweet-tempered person. Then I, forgetting it is his nerves, flare up and snap back at him.' In an attempt to avoid the growing tension, she arranged for him to stay in the village, 'at little Miss Jenkins' cottage'. 'Caradoc' was quick to admonish her for failing to carry out her filial responsibilities. She had taken on the job of looking after Charlie, he told her, now she should give up work for a few weeks to concentrate on taking care of him.[20] While once she would not have dared ignore an instruction from her husband, now he was dead she brushed it aside.

As she listened to Charlie's experiences, an idea for her next novel formed. She would write a story set in a prep school. 'Hugh Walpole covered the ground in *Mr. Perrin and Mr. Traill*, and so did Alec Waugh in *The Loom of Youth*.' The 1947 BBC radio adaptation of Terrence Rattigan's *The Browning Version*, with its moving portrayal of the tragic prematurely-retired classics teacher Andrew Crocker-Harris, was also broadcast around that time and was likely to have been an influence.

When Charlie recovered, he went off to take up a job as a private tutor at a farm near Cardiff and left Marguerite in peace to write this next novel, *We Lost Our Way*.[21] Marguerite had ambitions for it to be more than simply another piece of what Caradoc would have called 'the selling stuff', aiming to create a social issue novel that might 'materially improve the lot of schoolmasters in prep'. Despite this noble aspiration, after a couple of compelling opening chapters *We Lost Our Way* loses its own way. Although it does draw attention to the poor pay, poor food and derisory conditions in boarding schools, these are quickly passed over en route to the novel's main focus, a romance between the school's young, put-upon schoolmaster and the equally put-upon matron. This love affair is

202

also given the unlikeliest of *deus ex machina* happy endings. The lovers, whose rock-bottom wages had left them too poor to marry, unexpectedly inherit the school, leaving them free both to marry and to run the school together along the lines of their educational ideals. Possibly through pressure from the publishers, or perhaps due to her own limitations, the novel does not deviate far from Marguerite's usual comforting formula.

Around this time, Marguerite also met the charismatic bestselling writer and dog expert Clifford 'Doggie' Hubbard, who lived some eight miles away in the village of Ponterwyd.[22] They embarked on a friendship that was conducted mostly by mail: full of promises and hopes of meetings, at least on Marguerite's side. Her early letters are effusive and filled with praise for the author of the bestselling *Dogs in Britain*. 'Dear Mr Hubbard, What a book!' she enthused, a 'work of art as well as interest'. This was in a letter to congratulate him on his latest publication, a study of the traditional English longbow. As with almost all of Marguerite's letters to Hubbard, it ended with an invitation to visit. 'Come over with bow for a whole day ... I think we've all so much to talk about, too. You see, you're human and the rest of mankind is only practically human.' It appears that Hubbard did not reciprocate in the way Marguerite had hoped as in her letter dated 18 April 1949 the tone turns accusatory. 'You didn't ring up', she begins. 'Possibly you didn't go to Aber. Anyway, we couldn't have made it as Nick was in bed and is still groggy though better as soon as he is fit and about again.'

In June, she writes to Hubbard again, with the news that she is recovering from a broken right arm, complaining this had kept her from writing 'with any sort of facility'. Marguerite, no friend of the recently elected Labour government or its newly established NHS, complained of a two-hour wait to see a specialist 'under the new scheme with my number-card amongst all the other casualties sitting on a narrow wooden plank'.

Following Caradoc's death, Marguerite's political views had shifted sharply to the right. Always a Tory at heart, as Caradoc's wife she had tolerated, or even expressed some sympathy with, his left-leaning views. She may have moved further to the right as she got older, as people often do, or perhaps it was because without Caradoc she was free to express her opinions more openly. Her new outspoken brand of conservatism could have been part of an attempt to ingratiate herself with Clifford, who was – as a letter sent to him from W.H. Smith & Son reveals – a hater of all things socialist. Responding to a letter of complaint from Hubbard about their not stocking his books, the company's reply is scathing:

Dear Sir

We are rather surprised at the tone of your letter of June 3rd, a tone which we hardly think is necessary. We are only asking you to conform to regulations which apply to all publishers who travel our branches and we are sure that on reflection you will appreciate that with an organisation of our size we must have a system of this sort [...] As regards your paragraph referring to the 'Daily Worker' perhaps the least said about that the better, but you must bear in mind that we are in business to render a service to the general public, irrespective of their political creeds, etc.

Yours faithfully, W.H. Smith & Son Ltd.

Book Department.[22]

In another letter to Hubbard, Marguerite writes of her despair at the 'new regime', adding that Nicholas – who shared her loathing for the new Labour government – is particularly anxious to leave 'this miserable country'. She wonders if he should advertise in *The Times*, offering his services as 'a journalist collaborator to big-game hunter or zoologist – go anywhere'. It does not seem to occur to her that, without experience of either journalism or big-game hunting, Nicholas's chances of finding employment in either field would have been slim. Ever hopeful that Nicholas would eventually be able to make his own way in the world, she funded 'business' trips to Cornwall, London and Paris.[23]

'He is dreadfully lonely,' she confided, 'because he doesn't make friends, not being sufficiently interested in people for themselves for them to be interested in him.'[24] Overshadowed by his talented mother and chronically low in confidence, Nicholas had even been passing off his mother's work as his own. In 1946, a notice in *The Stage* listed a play, co-starring Nicholas Sandys, with the Harry Hanson Court Players at the Leeds Royal Theatre: 'Nicholas Sandys, who is the son of Oliver Sandys, the novelist, and stepson of the late Caradoc Evans, has written a three-act comedy extravaganza, shortly to be tried out, entitled "Hell Freezes".'[25] Yet *Hell Freezes* was his mother's work: written and produced by her during the 1930s, when it was shown at Aberystwyth's Quarry Theatre. Either without or with his mother's blessing – or perhaps at her instigation – Nicholas had been reduced to claiming her work as his own.

For her son's sake, Marguerite had sunk far more of her savings than she could afford into a second attempt to resurrect their old theatre company, Rogues and Vagabonds, appointing Nicholas its sole proprietor Lacking any of the gung-ho enthusiasm of its two earlier incarnations, run on a shoestring and without a director, designer, stage manager or administrator, it half-heartedly limped through a short-lived season in 1946 as a touring company without a dedicated theatre before closing down for the final time. Nicholas's whirlwind romance and engagement that summer to one of the company's female leads, Barbara Miller, had a similarly short run, lasting as it did only until the end of the summer season.[26] Given the happy couple's lavish photographic spread in the *Cambrian News* – which tied in perfectly with the launch of their show – their engagement may have been little more than a publicity stunt.

After the demise of Rogues and Vagabonds, Nicholas's moods turned darker, as his mother grew increasingly anxious. 'Nick only thinks I want him to remain in the isolation of Penrhyncoch which I truly do not,' she tells Clifford. 'It must be a hell of a life for him sans wife or ties and hating everything to do with the regime!' (The hated 'regime' of the Labour government had by now become a proxy for all her troubles.)

She was further troubled by strange goings-on with Heddle's water supply, which appeared to be mysteriously drying up. At times, when she turned her tap on, the pipes would splutter and no water would come out, while at other times the water ran as usual. It was not until months later that the mystery was explained. Some of her neighbours, she claimed, had been deliberately letting the village standpipe run so that the water would drain before reaching Marguerite's house. Marguerite was puzzled over why anyone would want to do this to her. A neighbour explained that it was because her house had so many basins that they feared she would use up all their water. Another claimed the water did not belong to her. When one neighbour saw Marguerite turn the offending standpipe off, she responded by turning it back on, insisting that the water belonged to the villagers, not to Marguerite. Later, Marguerite accepted the explanation given by yet another of her neighbours: that they were doing it 'because you have got a bit of money'.

Outnumbered and defeated, there was no option but to connect her bungalow to the mains, but the work was never carried out. Maybe she just couldn't afford it – with her savings fast disappearing, she was not as wealthy as her neighbours imagined, despite her reputation and exotic appearance. Besides, connecting to the water mains could not have repaired Marguerite's hurt feelings. To find herself made so unwelcome by her neighbours – many of whom had greeted her warmly when she had first arrived – made a brutal rejection. 'It took me a long time to tumble to it, or even to believe that a bunch of Welsh people could show such pettiness and poor spirit for nothing at all.' Her peaceful place had gone – and her sentimental vision of Wales along with it. Yet she refused to be disillusioned with Wales altogether, insisting that New Cross, with its doors 'always wide' with a 'Come in and sit down', was nothing like Penrhyn-coch,[27] where, with only a few exceptions, the doors stayed firmly shut.[28]

206

With her sentimental vision of Wales in shreds, her 'intimate journal of the daily life in the Welsh countryside' begins to sound more like one of Caradoc's acerbic attacks on his native Cardiganshire. She also felt 'Caradoc' was leaving her. It had been three years since his death, and now the voice that had been her constant companion was beginning to fade. It was Marguerite, not Caradoc, who decided she did not fit in with the 'closed peasantry' and no longer felt at home among the 'mountain people' of Penrhyn-coch. In the turn of a tap, Wales had become a darker, more hostile place. It was as if Caradoc, as his parting shot, was nudging her and saying, 'See, woman, I told you so.'

Chapter 12
A 'Miraculous' Ending

Everyone in the world imagines at some time or
other a happy valley, a Shangri-la of peace and rest,
of wishes fulfilled, of tranquil happiness.
(Oliver Sandys, *The Miracle Stone of Wales*[1])

Panteidal, Aberdyfi

High above the Dyfi estuary you can see the patterns on the water
made by the ebb and flow of its currents. Higher still, the hills are
chequered with freshly-felled trees. The timber is still being
harvested today, as it was in Marguerite's time. Her Swiss chalet-
style lodge is gone and in its place are twenty pristine holiday chalets
arranged around an immaculate lawn. Escapes. Boltholes. With its
sweeping views and clear, invigorating air, the spot provides a
tranquil retreat from modern life.

For a woman in her mid-sixties who hated walking, who
preferred high heels and a fur stole to wellingtons and a mackintosh,
The Lodge in Panteidal made a wildly impractical home. But
Marguerite was too taken with its views – and with the man she
shared them with – to concern herself with such practicalities. She
had moved there to be with Captain Gordon Hewitt, her 'Kenya
Gordon', with whom she was enjoying a late-flowering romance.

She had met Gordon in 1950, after five years with scant company
except her increasingly unstable son and the 'voice' of her late
husband, Caradoc. Gordon, with his 'soldier's bearing' and his grey
Savile Row suit 'of a cut dating back about twenty years', provided

the companionship she had been longing for. With her captain by her side, she was no longer lonely and did not have to face any battles alone. Despite his white hair and beard, Marguerite felt he was 'not old', but a man with 'no age'. He was in fact sixty-three: a year younger than Marguerite. He was also married.

Gordon had remained in Kenya for some time after leaving the army to set up a tea plantation. Now he and his wife were settled in Minton, a hamlet near Stretton in Shropshire. Marguerite claims she met him in Aberystwyth, at the house of a mutual friend. Gordon, she writes, had entranced her with his tales of Kenya. Closer to home, he also charmed her with his description of the delightful hideaway he was planning to buy – a chalet with panoramic views of the Dyfi estuary, some twenty-five miles north of Aberystwyth. He drove Marguerite along the winding, narrow road to Aberdyfi, to the spot where the estuary runs into the sea. Gordon called the promontory 'Bishop's Island', claiming the Bishop of Bangor had a holiday home there. He had fallen in love with the beauty of the area while working there towards the end of the war.

When he discovered The Lodge – the former lodge of the now deserted Panteidal Estate – it was little more than a wreck. Teetering precariously on a rocky bank high above the road, it had been lying empty for so many years that its current owner, a local forester and timber merchant known as Timber Davies, had all but forgotten it existed. Marguerite writes that Davies was surprised that anyone wanted to live in the chalet. Not only was it badly run-down, but it lacked electricity and running water.[2] But the businessman in him agreed to let Gordon take out a lease. There was no accounting for taste, after all, especially when it meant an unexpected new stream of income. For Gordon, whose army pension did not run to mod cons, the rock-bottom rent he negotiated was more necessity than bargain.

Marguerite was unsure at first. Having converted two abandoned buildings into theatres, she had already experienced enough dereliction. Nor was Marguerite, a lover of bright colours, impressed by its faded 'dull yellow and brown' paintwork. But Gordon persevered, assuring her that he would transform it into 'a little palace'. True to his word, he set about digging into the side of the hill and, a few months later, had carved out a veranda – complete with rambler roses, vines and heart-stopping views of the estuary – to the front of the chalet. Gordon, whose work along the Dyfi estuary had involved digging a drainage scheme for the Ministry of Agriculture, knew how to tame the rocky soil of the locality. His determination won over Marguerite. Newly converted, she set about choosing the chalet's colour scheme, deciding on pale pink and powder blue, which she thought would give it a 'continental charm'.

When the work was complete, the once reluctant Marguerite was every bit as enthusiastic as Gordon. Delighted with its transformation, she called it their 'fairy palace' and its surroundings their 'Happiness Island', even comparing it to 'the famed Port Meirion, designed and made so beautiful by the distinguished architect Clough Ellis'.[3]

She moved in with Gordon in 1953. She had not come straight from her home in Penrhyn-coch, as she claimed. In recent years, she had been spending most of her time in Shropshire, where she owned a flat in Church Stretton. It had been her refuge from the tensions between her and some of her Penrhyn-coch neighbours. Most of all, it was her refuge from Nicholas. Now in his thirties and showing no signs of settling into a career, he was still leaning heavily on his mother – both financially and emotionally.

When Nicholas won a publishing deal in America for his novel *Starset and Sunrise*, Marguerite seized upon it as a hopeful sign that he had finally found his vocation.[4] Yet with a plot described by one reviewer as 'a farcical romp about a girl from a Catholic approved school who ends up as a movie star', it sounded suspiciously like a novel his mother might have written. Whether Nicholas was its true author or not, his mental distress (arguably undiagnosed depression) made concentration difficult. Only able to write sporadically at best, he appeared incapable of committing to a regular routine. Marguerite, who had consistently followed the strictest of regimes, was at a loss to understand why her son could not do the same. 'He just starts & never finishes,' she complained to her friend Monica Dunbar.[5]

Nicholas's behaviour grew increasingly unstable until, in 1951, tensions between him and his mother came to a head. Marguerite made an emergency call to her local police station; Nicholas had got hold of a gun and was threatening to shoot them both.[6] That year, for the first time in her career, she found herself unable to complete a single book. Desperate for an escape and ready for a fresh start, Gordon offered her the passport to both.

The black-and-white photograph is dominated by its backdrop: a pair of wind-blasted pine trees against a silver-sheened Dyfi estuary and the round foothills of Snowdonia. In the foreground sit an elderly couple in deckchairs either side of a small table covered in a white cloth: Marguerite and Gordon, on the veranda outside Panteidal. Marguerite is on the left, her face in semi-profile, wearing a thick fur (possibly mink, her favourite) winter coat. It is the mid-1950s and her white hair, waved and lacquered against the breeze, is carefully styled in the fashion of the day. Even from a distance, her face looks pale with powder, the monochrome print turning her blood-red lipstick black. She is looking at Gordon opposite her. Her expression, possibly intended as an enigmatic smile, looks frozen – literally. Her entire being looks cold and huddled, as if she is longing to rush inside to warm herself by a blazing log fire. Sitting in shadow, most of his body turned against the camera, Gordon leaves few clues to his identity other than his receding hair and white, well-trimmed beard.

The photograph is in Marguerite's mystical memoir *The Miracle Stone of Wales*. Published in 1957, the book gives a highly embellished version of her life with Gordon in Panteidal and – as the title suggests – a stone that holds miraculous powers. (Perhaps because he is still married to someone else, she refers to her companion only as 'Gordon' or 'Kenya Gordon'.) The translucent blue stone, resembling a piece of 'roughly hewn glass or quartz', had been in her possession for some twelve years. But only recently, she claims, had she discovered the full extent of the powers of her 'Happiness Stone'. It was the colour that first caught her eye. 'I had never seen any stone of such a colour before. Green of the sea in the depths of it mingled with the predominant sapphire blue.' Weighing around fifteen or sixteen pounds, 'about the shape and size of a sheep's head', it had a flat bottom (convenient for resting on Marguerite's shelf) 'where it appeared to have been cut from a larger rock'. *The Miracle Stone of Wales*, published by Rider (specialists in the occult who had also published Marguerite's spiritualist memoir *Unbroken Thread*), contains a full account of the stone's powers – powers that she does 'not pretend to understand, but which I do truly believe'. It had been bequeathed to her, she claims, by Old Griff (Evan Griffiths), 'the grand old shepherd of the Hills', who was reputed to be a wise man or *dyn hysbys* descended from a long line of healers. When the cattle fell ill, local farmers would turn to him for help, asking him to lift the 'bad spells' of ill-wishers. Tales of Griffiths abounded. He was never known to refuse his services and would travel for miles on his pony, in all weathers, to offer his help. Marguerite had been introduced to Griffiths by Caradoc when she was suffering from a rare attack of writer's block. Part sceptic, part believer in magic, Caradoc took her to Griffiths' cottage at the foot of the Pumlumon mountains. There the old man had first examined Marguerite's hands, then instructed her to go home and sleep. The next morning her block would be gone, he told her, and she would be able to write again. Just as Griffiths had predicted, Marguerite's block disappeared overnight.

Marguerite and Caradoc soon became regular visitors at Old Griff's cottage. She claimed it was there where Griffiths presented her with the translucent blue stone that he kept at the foot of his fireplace, which Marguerite had often admired. Insisting she keep it, he told her that one day she would know why. (This was a claim that Griffiths' sons dismissed, saying that their father had only kept

212

the stone as a doorstop and had never thought it possessed any magical powers.) Days later, when Griffiths died, Marguerite felt certain that she had been given the stone for a reason. Although not yet clear what it was, she was sure it would be revealed to her one day. In the meantime, she displayed it to full advantage on top of her antique French cabinet and just below a painting of the Madonna and child,[7] the display she called her shrine. Ten years later, as Marguerite emerged from the hermit-like state in which she had been mired since Caradoc's death, she looked at the stone anew. Despite the comfort she had found in her belief that Caradoc was still with her, his voice had grown fainter over time, leaving her feeling 'rudderless' and lost.

Now, with Kenya Gordon as her aide, the lodge and the Dyfi estuary as her backdrop, and Griffiths' stone (now rebranded the 'Miracle Stone') as her prop, Marguerite was ready to enter the public arena again. And what an entrance it was. She made her debut with the 'Stone' (always with a capital 'S') in the 1955 Cardiff-made BBC television documentary *The Secret Arts*.[8] Hosted by Dr Glyn Daniel, the programme, which purported to be a serious investigation into Welsh folklore and the occult, was, according to one critic, marred by cheap special effects and 'atmospheric' music. Marguerite sat alongside her fellow guest, the Archdruid of Wales, his accounts of lake maidens impressing her as a 'dramatically put-over performance'. The *Western Mail* was less impressed, with one critic describing it as 'a swirling cloud of half-truths, hearsay and mumbo jumbo',[9] while another wrote that he did not believe 'the programme did Wales much good in putting a searchlight on us as superstition-ridden people'.[10]

Despite the bad reviews, some viewers – from England as well as Wales – were moved to write to the BBC asking if they could visit the Stone. Soon afterwards, a succession of pilgrims made their way to Panteidal in search of its curative properties. While Old Griff was concerned with curing sick animals and the lifting of witches' curses, Marguerite turned her attention to 'those who carry deep in their hearts a wish or a need unfilled'. Never one for understatement, she soon branded Panteidal as 'the Lourdes of Wales', claiming it as a centre of pilgrimage for people of all classes and backgrounds: 'Some are poor, some are young, some old, some cultured and educated, well-born, low-born.'[11] A cynic might add they were also gullible or desperate, or both. Among her detractors was the publisher Keidrych Rhys, [12] who ridiculed the 'poor countess' for having been reduced to 'finally running a Lucky Stone touch in Aberdovey'.[13]

Undeterred, Marguerite would personally escort each visitor to the Stone, instructing them to look at it, then 'place your fingers on it', and then, when they felt ready, to 'wish deeply as if you are saying a prayer and meaning it – believing and hoping'.[14] She would also encourage visitors to spend as long as they liked with the Stone, 'until they felt sure that it had worked its magic and they could go home feeling at peace'. Her Miracle Stone soon become a minor visitor attraction.

Her claims for the Stone's powers were as extravagant as they were unfounded. It had cured an elderly woman crippled with arthritis. A young woman who had been bed-bound for years with a 'prolonged nervous debility' was able to get up and lead a normal life. A man's drink problem was cured and a blind man's sight restored. Marguerite also recalls a visit from a young couple who longed to get married but couldn't afford it. Their wish was apparently answered when – in a change of fortune that would have been at home in an Oliver Sandys novel – the young woman's father won a thousand pounds on a newspaper crossword.[15] While such far-fetched tales made an easy target for mockery from the likes of Rhys, others would travel – often some distance – in search of a miracle. Among them was a woman whose husband had recently committed suicide. She had travelled from Holyhead in Anglesey on a series of rattling rural buses followed by a six-mile walk in the rain to touch the stone. Later, claimed Marguerite, she received a letter from the grieving woman in which she described her new-found 'deep and satisfying conviction' that her husband was with her, urging her to be 'brave enough to carry on'.[16] The Stone had seemingly worked its magic once again.

Marguerite's theatre days had taught her the value of celebrity endorsement. Yet despite what we can safely assume were Marguerite's best efforts, no celebrity had turned up at Panteidal. Undeterred, she embellished her earlier account of a visit by the young Dylan Thomas, who during the early 1930s had visited Caradoc at Queen's Square, Aberystwyth. The visit was enough for her to claim the poet as one of the Stone's 'most famous visitors', adding that he had wished upon it 'for wealth and fame when he was completely unknown'.[17] This spurious claim is repeated on a promotional postcard for 'The Miracle Stone of Wales', along with a black-and-white photograph of an unremarkable-looking stone and directions for prospective visitors: 'The Miracle Stone of Wales is at Panteidal Lodge, near Aberdovey'.[18] Dylan Thomas's untimely death in New York City, three years before the book's publication, meant he was not around to dispute his association with Marguerite or her Stone.

The Stone was as much a source of comfort and consolation for Marguerite as it was for her visitors: its first 'miracle' was to bestow on its owner – a lonely, grieving widow – a new life as part sorceress and part salon hostess. With it, she transformed herself into the self-styled Wise Woman of Aberdyfi, healer of the grieving, the sad, the lonely and the frustrated. It was a role she played with aplomb. Thanks to its 'magic' – and her belief that it had been given to her 'for a higher purpose' – she was no longer isolated, but once again the queen of her own domain. The gratitude and attention she received as a result were as welcome to her as a burst of warm sunshine in November.

She would have also welcomed any payment she received for her services. The decline in sales of her books, which had begun during the war, had left her with only her older (although fiercely loyal) fans. Yet apart from the £5 she received for her appearance on *The*

Secret Arts, she tactfully avoids any mention of receiving payment from the Stone's visitors in her book on the topic.

It was Nicholas – now living in London where he was making another attempt to break into theatre or film – who was the biggest drain on her resources. Fearing that he would not be able to cope in the big city and haunted by visions of him lost and alone in some seedy Bayswater hotel, she continued to bankroll him, paying him around £600 to £700 a year even though her own income had fallen to less than £1,000. 'I would give my life & soul to make things right for him if I could,' she confided in a letter to Monica Dunbar. 'If he had any job ... he would feel there was some pattern in life.'[19] Perhaps hoping to galvanise him into finding work, she would intermittently warn him she would not be able to afford to go on supporting him. Nicholas would respond by threatening suicide – a threat to which his anxious mother would always relent. Unable to make sense of this complicated, co-dependent relationship, Monica was infuriated by Nicholas's inability to support himself. In a similar vein, the critic Gwyn Jones, who'd known Nicholas as a young man, later recalled how he 'rarely spent much time in his company without wanting to cry: "'Get away from here! Get a job, anywhere. Keep yourself and keep your individuality and self-respect."'[20]

In an attempt to raise funds for her and Nicholas, Marguerite put the rights for Caradoc's once controversial play *Taffy* up for sale,[21] advertising it in *The Stage* as a 'gold mine in Wales' and a 'money-making sure-fire touring proposition'.[22] But with the play's once controversial edge now blunted by time, her offer did not attract any interest.[23] In another money-raising effort, Marguerite and Gordon were featured in the *Birmingham Daily Gazette* beneath the headline '£75 Car does 90 miles to the gallon' and a photograph of the couple side by side in a tiny, low open-topped vehicle. 'It looks like something from the pioneer days of motoring,' the article reads, 'but the three-wheeler has been built by Mr. Gordon Hewitt, former Kenya coffee planter [who] made it for Mrs. Caradoc Evans (Oliver Sandys, the novelist).'[24] Gordon's vehicle, which he claims 'can be

put together in a fortnight by a handyman', sits improbably close to the ground, looking closer to a go-cart than a car. It did not look a promising prospect, least of all for its two undeniably elderly passengers. Nothing came of their valiant, impractical scheme.

Perhaps viewing it as another money-making prospect, Gordon became a firm convert to Marguerite's cult of the Miracle Stone, claiming it as the twin of one he had seen in Kenya where, kept in a cave on Mount Elgon, it was venerated locally as the Mahenge Mzuri or the Good Stone. Believed to originate in ancient Egypt, it looked exactly like Marguerite's Stone, he insisted, its flat edge suggesting they were two halves of the same stone. It was a theory to which Marguerite readily subscribed. Later, David Conway, a magician and son of a local *dyn hysbys*, also connected Marguerite's 'curious blue rock that sparkled in the flickering light like a giant piece of sapphire' to its Kenyan equivalent.[25]

The Stone became a collaborative venture, with Marguerite its keeper and Gordon her factotum. Gordon's role was to welcome the guests and drive them to the station or the bus stop. Taking inspiration from the Good Stone in the Elgon cave, Gordon put his manual skills to good use by carving a grotto out of the slaty rock at the side of the chalet. He made a separate approach to it through a side path too, so Marguerite would no longer have visitors trudging through the chalet into her study, where it had been kept. 'In less than a month with his two hands and spade' her 'soldier' had wheeled away tons of earth in barrow loads, had made the grotto, and had laid 'a slab of white marble inset, on which the Stone was to repose'. He also put up a sign outside the lodge for the benefit of passing traffic: 'Approaching Happiness Stone'. As the Stone's zealous custodian, he would daily take it to the grotto every morning at 9 a.m. and return it later to Marguerite's tiny bedroom-cum-study, to place it back in her improvised shrine at the foot of the Madonna and child.

Marguerite was convinced Gordon was Caradoc come back to be with her in another man's form. Although the accommodating

Gordon appears to have gone along with this notion, it is difficult to gauge the full extent of his enthusiasm for this notion. In *The Miracle Stone of Wales*, Marguerite quotes from a letter, apparently from Gordon, in which he agrees that it 'may be conceivable' that a person 'without a physical envelope' is able to enter the body of another, in which case: 'I am only too willing to be used by such a man as he was, but do not think or suppose there is not an intensely personal side in my regard for you.'[26] The chalet, her relationship with Gordon, and, in particular, the Stone all feature in her 1956 novel *Miss Venus of Aberdovey* (although, perhaps on the advice of her publishers, any mention of her late husband's possession of Gordon is tactfully avoided). For a work of fiction, it reveals a surprising amount of factual detail, beginning with its elaborate dedication:

My dear Gordon,

You have figured in so many guises in my later books – as pioneer, soldier, inventor, adventurer, all fact mixed with fiction, but this book belongs to you especially because the portrait this time is as near to being a true portrait as this pen of mine can make it, and it is also fitting that the Happiness Stone should be enshrined within the eerie grotto of scrub-oak trees in the very heart of our beloved Happiness Island.[27]

On the face of it, *Miss Venus of Aberdovey* is a simple, romantic tale of local beauty, Megs Owen, whose prize at a beauty contest leads to the offer of a Hollywood contract and a career as an actress. Yet it is the 'character' of the Happiness Stone which really dominates, guiding Megs towards a simpler, happier life in her native Wales. The Stone, we are told, 'is a very beautiful blue colour' and 'more like a sapphire than anything else', but its real value lies in 'the good it may do'. Unlike Marguerite's Stone, it does not originate in Egypt, but has come 'from the East'. Brought over during the time of the Crusades, it is believed to be 'a Holy stone of some kind'. Here Marguerite brings to the mix the more established local myth of the

Nanteos Cup, rumoured locally to be the Holy Grail. Owned by Margaret Powell, dowager of the Nanteos Estate and Marguerite's one-time landlord, it was believed to hold curative powers and was made available to those who sought its help during times of sickness.[28] (Today, the Nanteos Cup is on permanent display in the National Library of Wales, on the condition that it is freely available to those seeking help from its curative powers.)

Other factual details, including Gordon Hewitt's name along with his rank of captain and his past in Kenya, remain unchanged. While the woman he lives with is playfully known only as the 'lady novelist', it would be clear to readers that this is really the novel's author. The description of their home – a 'pink-and-blue wooden painted chalet on the side of the road facing the estuary' – also reveals enough detail to act as directions for any interested reader to find it. This was exactly what Marguerite intended: to put fiction into service for the part cult, part tourist attraction of the Miracle Stone. Behind the mystic haze lay a desperate need to make a go of another struggling venture.

In 1958, Marguerite left both Panteidal and Gordon abruptly and unexpectedly. Although her departure came after she had broken her ankle tripping and falling on the lodge's steep driveway, this did not explain why she also left Gordon. It was a complicated fracture which required a long stay at the general hospital in Aberystwyth, where she was treated by the NHS she had so loathed during its inception ten years earlier. 'I wanted to lie alongside my sisters in suffering,'[29] she said, implying that her bed in a public ward was her choice, rather than admit she could not afford a private room. As soon as she was sufficiently recovered, she left Wales and returned to Shropshire.

Around this time, she sent a letter to her friend Clifford 'Doggie' Hubbard. She gave her address as 51 Trinity Street – the two-bedroom red-brick terraced house in Shrewsbury she was now renting. Once the kind of house she would have loathed (and probably still did), it was now all she could afford. She had left Gordon abruptly 'for reasons too long to list'.[30] There appears to have been something in Gordon's behaviour that had alarmed her enough to make her leave him so abruptly. While the reason may have been their money worries, or Gordon's continuing marriage, or both, *The Miracle Stone of Wales* hints at far darker reasons.

Gordon's proclivity for nude bathing, in 'a pool the tide always leaves behind', had at first seemed innocent enough. Marguerite thought it modern and progressive. In those more innocent times, his ambition to build a pool on the island 'for children who wanted to bathe and picnic on it' might have appeared no more than a sweet and thoughtful gesture. His descriptions of the children in his village in Kenya, who went around naked and discovered sex 'quite naturally' and 'came to maturity like male and female flowers upon a plant'[31], also sounded perfectly innocent to Marguerite's ears. Today they would sound alarm bells.

Whatever the reason, Marguerite had suddenly and decisively ended her relationship with Gordon. The move had taken most of what remained of her savings. Alone, in an unfamiliar town and still recovering from the fall, she had to face another unpleasant reality. In a few weeks' time, she would be completely broke. Abandoning her pride, she put her craft to work on composing a series of begging letters to old friends. Among those who responded to her pleas were Monica Dunbar and her parents, who began sending a regular supply of ten-pound notes in the post.

Nicholas had left. Finally realising his ambition to travel, he had gone to America and had taken the Miracle Stone with him, with plans of making it the subject of a lecture tour. His picture appeared in a Los Angeles newspaper dated January 1959. 'Count Barcinski' [sic.], the report reads, 'is a guest at the home of a Dr. and Mrs. Smith' in the Palos Verdes Peninsula. Coming to California had been 'a long-time dream', he said, 'and I am so happy it is realized at last'.[32] The 'Count' also claimed to have served as an RAF pilot during the war. Nicholas – who had spent his war years in

220

Brynawelon – must have seized upon his trip to California as an opportunity to recast himself as a war hero. In America, 'Count Barcinski' emerged as a full-blown fantasist: a latter-day Walter Mitty or – as in the Keith Waterhouse novel published around the time of Nicholas's travels – another Billy Liar. Nor had his 'hosts', Dr and Mrs Smith, invited him as a house guest, as the article claimed, but had engaged him as a domestic servant and had paid for his passage on that basis. Not surprisingly, the arrangement did not last long and, later that year, a destitute Nicholas was seeking repatriation to Britain and even managed to obtain a free passage back to England as a 'journalist'.[33]

As for the Stone, its fate is not known. Marguerite claimed she had donated it to the Welsh Folk Museum (as it was then known) in St Fagan's, Cardiff, but the museum has no record of it. Nicholas said he had left it with a doctor in San Francisco. There were also rumours the Stone had got into the hands of the FBI (one of the more outlandish theories discussed in a 1985 BBC Radio Cymru programme about the Miracle Stone). The most likely explanation is that Nicholas had somehow lost, or left, it in America. Given his lifelong tendency to sell everything of any value – papers, books, even the rights to the works of his mother and Caradoc – it is likely he sold the Miracle Stone. Who knows? One day a translucent blue stone, 'roughly the size of a sheep's head and resembling quartz', could well turn up in an auction house or antique shop, or as a blue, curious-looking doorstop on a Californian porch.

After the disastrous American trip, Nicholas returned to Shropshire where, bitter and frustrated, he went back to living with – and off – his mother. His fragile self-esteem shattered, he began to drink heavily, becoming a regular at his local pub, where 'Count Nick' soon gained a reputation as something of a local character. At home, his behaviour towards his mother became intolerable. Her home help recalls how Nicholas would lounge about in his dressing gown, often giving vent to fits of rage, during which he would throw things at his mother, 'a sweet-natured woman always scribbling away

221

in her huge armchair'.[34] Once a victim of Caradoc's rages, Nicholas was now becoming him.

Perhaps fortunately for Marguerite, he did not stay long. After only a few months, he left to resume his itinerant life, flitting between bedsits and lodgings in London, Ruislip, Broadstairs and Aberystwyth – all places with some connection to his past. Rarely certain of where her son was living, Marguerite now saw little of him, if at all. Yet her fears for Nicholas, 'a lost soul on his own', continued to haunt her. In what was to be her final letter to Monica, it is Nicholas who dominates her thoughts. 'Luck for Nick which with his happiness is all I ask of God,' she writes.[35] Her prayers were not answered.

The journalist Lyn Ebenezer, who knew Nicholas in Aberystwyth during the early 1970s, recalls him as a lonely figure. Then in his mid-fifties, he had dropped the 'count' honorific, now using the name on his birth certificate, Nicholas Barczinsky ('always Nicholas, never Nick', said Ebenezer). Sporting a wide-brimmed fedora, cape and silver-topped cane, Nicholas would spend hours a day sitting on a display bench outside a hardware store near Ebenezer's flat. 'I felt a bit sorry for him – people in the town seemed to have forgotten all about him and his mother.' Later, Ebenezer struck up an acquaintance with Nicholas, and would visit him at home. 'He had a very cultured, actor-type voice,' said Ebenezer, 'and he seemed to live in a fantasy world of his own. I always enjoyed talking to him. I tried to get him to talk about his mother and his stepfather, Caradoc Evans, but he never wanted to.'

In 1981, the critic and one-time friend of Caradoc and Marguerite, Gwyn Jones, reported that Nicholas 'has recently appeared again in west Wales' and is 'at present pursuing or being pursued by the Occult'.[36] It was a nod to Nicholas's newfound devotion to the cult of Isis, the Egyptian goddess who was a 'god in female form'. For Nicholas, who became one of its leading and most well-respected devotees, the Isis cult was a benign force in his life. Its meetings and ritual worship gave structure to his life, as well as something he had never really experienced before: a sense of belonging to a wider community.

In Aberystwyth he became a regular face in the town's local paper, the *Cambrian News*, as his mother had before him. Where Marguerite would blur the boundaries between fact and fiction, Nicholas invented a fantasy past life for himself, with tales of his birth in Poland, a war career that the Official Secrets Act would not allow him to disclose, and a spell in Hollywood as an MGM scriptwriter. He had only returned, he claimed, to nurse his ailing mother.

Caradoc Evans's biographer John Harris, who knew Nicholas during the 1980s, also found him reluctant to talk about Marguerite or Caradoc. Harris was shocked to discover that he 'carried not one item belonging to his mother: no book, no letter, no photograph'.[37] It was as if he had decided to erase any memories of Marguerite or Caradoc. For Harris, it brought to mind the prediction, 'He'll never cry for you, so long as he lives', made about Jon, the overly-indulged son in Caradoc's novel *Kitty Shore's Magic Cake*.[38] Whatever the cause, Nicholas had become estranged from his mother. Why he took so drastic a step is not clear, but it seems that he and Marguerite had some major falling-out towards the end of her life. Theirs had been a complicated and, at times, stiflingly close relationship. She had left the teenage Nicholas for Caradoc and, when he did eventually come to live with them, she'd failed to protect her vulnerable son from Caradoc's rabid temper. Yet Marguerite had fretted over him, had had him in mind when setting up both her theatre companies, had continued to support him financially, even to the point of bankruptcy. As a mother, she had been clingy and inconsistent, over-supportive and overbearing. She had not been perfect. But it is difficult to imagine what prompted Nicholas to abandon her in her dotage – so firmly and decisively.

The critic Gwyn Jones, in a series of letters to Nicholas during the late 1970s, urged him to write down his reminiscences of Marguerite and Caradoc, 'the principals in one of the most remarkable Welsh literary chronicles this century'. He never received a reply and his letters were eventually returned with 'not known at this address' on the envelope.[39]

By the early 1960s, Marguerite was living alone in Shrewsbury, increasingly frail and with her savings all gone. Sales of her books – already struggling during the 1950s – had reached their lowest ebb. Television, changing tastes and the decline of commercial lending libraries had conspired to hit her hard.

Yet even at a time when more married women than ever were entering the workforce and the birth control pill was available on the NHS, the market for romance was holding up surprisingly well. Unfortunately for Marguerite, her books were not among its top sellers. They were being sidelined by the phenomenally successful new paperbacks – sold by newsagents on almost every street corner – published cheaply by Mills & Boon.

From the hospital and airline romances of Betty Beaty and others, to the exotic locations and Latin lovers of Violet Winspear, they so dominated the market that any romance novel, regardless of publisher, would come to be known as a 'Mills and Boon'.[40]

Despite the difficulties of competing in this market, Marguerite continued to write as usual. She continued to evolve her style, too, as she always had. It is clear from her later works that she was influenced, for example, by Betty Beaty's hospital romances. As she was by now spending a great deal of time in either a hospital or a nursing home, this made a particularly apt setting for new work.

Marguerite was not frozen in time, but had always moved with it. If it had not been for her declining health, who knows, she could have been writing for Mills & Boon herself. Although she would dismiss her novels as 'fluffy romances', she would also have known they were more than that. She treated contemporary issues and contemporary myths with deft humour and the lightest of touches. From chorus girls on starvation wages, teetering on the edge of prostitution (*The Honey-Pot, The Pleasure Garden* and others), to traumatised victims of wartime shell shock or what would today be

224

called post-traumatic stress syndrome (*Black-Out Symphony*)[41], she did not flinch from sensitive or controversial topics.

In her 1960 novel *Black Harvest* she had even ventured into an exploration of the ethical issues of human artificial insemination, inspired by newspaper reports of experiments involving frozen sperm.[42] Despite this, during her later years her books, when they were noticed at all, were usually dismissed as anachronisms. Both the names Oliver Sandys and Countess Barcynska were quietly filed away with scullery-maids, cockney showgirls, empire, snobbery: the things people wanted to forget.

Then a moment of hope: Marguerite was rescued by a *deus ex machina* that might have come straight from one of her own novels. She received a telegram informing her she had been granted a Civil List pension for literary services.[43] Now in her seventies and with a career of more than half a century behind her, she was at last getting the literary recognition she had secretly longed for. Although, at around £2,500 a year at today's value it was not enough to retire on, that would have been of little concern to her. Writing was all she had ever known and all she wanted to know. Retirement would have been unimaginable. Even when feeling 'so weak and immobile' after a fall and the hip operation that followed, she continued to write from her hospital bed. Whatever difficulties she faced, writing sustained her. It was her gateway into a world of happy endings; her secret garden.

Her final novel, *Madam Adastra*, was set in the worlds of nursing homes and hospitals; the worlds she now inhabited as a patient. Its heroine, Felicia Diamond, had given up a nursing career to care for her elderly parents. (Her recent estrangement from Nicholas added a poignant subtext to this storyline.) Felicia had also adopted a six-year-old African boy, Timothy, whom she had found crying in the children's home when some of the white children wouldn't play with him. In the past, Felicia had worked in a lending library, until books were killed off by television (a contributing factor to Marguerite's own fall in sales). Later, finding a job in a dress shop, she was sacked when her boss overheard her telling a customer that a cheaper dress looked better on her than a more expensive one. Following her parents' death, Felicia returns to nursing, where she cares for Edward Dalrymple, who is receiving treatment for severe burns following a plane crash. It is later revealed that Dalrymple is also a well-known newspaper fortune-teller writing under the pseudonym of Madame Adastra. While he is in hospital, Felicia helps with his correspondence, which in turn leads to the inevitable romance and proposal of marriage.[44]

Throughout her career, Marguerite's ability to write through the most difficult of times was little short of miraculous. Even when struck down with another episode of 'nervous exhaustion', she would seek out, and find, a story that would somehow sustain her through the darkness. She had found miracles on the stage and in her two theatre companies, as well as with Caradoc and in Wales, her 'land of enchantment and faery'. Then, with the help of the Miracle Stone, she created her own myths and miracles. Yet, throughout, the real magic lay in Marguerite's writing. Even poverty, loneliness and ill health did not stop her writing cheerful, funny stories – as many as three or four of them a year, all populated by vivid, larger-than-life characters. Her heroines, in particular, were as complex and as driven as their creator: the irrepressible Maggy in *The Honey-Pot*; the spirited Vista of *Vista the Dancer*; or Lady Weybridge, the dashing, morphine-addicted con artist in *Chicane*. As she herself had acknowledged, she knew just how 'to make people laugh and smile and weep'. Her stories, and the speed at which she spun them, demanded a near-miraculous degree of grinding, relentless hard work: a regime that sometimes sapped her *joie de vivre* and took its toll on her mental health.

Madame Adastra was published posthumously, only months after she died of heart failure in Shrewsbury Hospital on 10 March 1964. She was seventy-seven and was reported to have completed the book just hours before her death, or, as she would have put it, before she passed over to the other side. The indefatigable Felicity, who kept on trying in the face of setbacks, makes an apt closing heroine. A trouper to the end, nothing short of death could separate Marguerite from her writing.

227

Epilogue
Return to Horeb

I think God likes all stories to end happily, and when
they don't I always imagine He is greatly distressed.
(Oliver Sandys, *Hollywood Honeymoon*[1])

It is fifteen years since my first visit to New Cross, when I first heard
the name Marguerite Jervis. Today I have returned with a bunch of
primroses, her favourite flowers, to lay on her grave.

The low lozenge-shaped gravestone looks like any other of its era,
except for its engravings. A book, an inkwell and a quill – writers'
emblems. Unlike its neighbours, the epitaph is not in Welsh, but in
English: 'Bury me lightly that the small rain shall reach my face and
the fluttering of the butterfly shall not escape my ear'. Marguerite
claimed the words were Caradoc's, that he had said they would make
an excellent epitaph. Yet the style of writing – closer to Marguerite's
flourishes than Caradoc's terse prose – would suggest Marguerite
as their true author. The grave is dated 1945, the year of Caradoc's
death, with 'Caradoc Evans' the sole name inscribed upon it.

Following Marguerite's death in 1964, in accordance with her
wish to be buried with Caradoc, Marguerite's body was taken from
Shrewsbury to lie here beside him. It is not known how many people
attended her funeral, but it was rumoured there were few. Her son,
Nicholas, was not among them. He had descended into alcoholism
and ill health and never got round to adding her name to the stone.

And so the woman who had resolved to 'never be dependent on
a man', who dreaded being buried as 'some man's Mrs Someone', lies
here today as Caradoc's nameless companion. The woman who

since childhood had dreamed of 'Making a Name', was now rendered anonymous in death. Caradoc, for all his faults, would not have wished it.

Yet during her lifetime she had made her name many times over. As Olive Bree, the wide-eyed, ambitious actress turned chorus girl turned jobbing Fleet Street journalist. As the young Mrs Armiger Barczinsky who fought back (and won) when her husband tried to steal one of her carefully-crafted names. As the New Woman journalist who was not above 'vamping' an editor, she would try on different names as easily as trying on costumes – Claudia Rayne, Constance Romanné-Jones, Olive Bree, Oliver Sandys.

As Oliver Sandys, she was the bestselling author of risqué novels for maids and shop girls. Her alter ego, the Countess Hélène Barcynska, was a grand Polish 'aristocrat' with a literary bent, tilting her pen at a more sophisticated readership. While Marguerite Evans was an actress on the silent screen, a comic foil to the legendary Gloria Swanson. Later, Countess Barcynska turned flesh and blood to take on a new role as proprietor of the real-life repertory theatre company, Rogues and Vagabonds – a Quixotic venture prompted by a desire to launch her son into his chosen career on the stage. Then with nothing more to prove, she wore her married name, Marguerite Caradoc Evans with pride, while Caradoc could barely disguise *his* pride in a wife who could write 'like the Angels sing – without effort'. After Caradoc's death, in a final burst of magic, she took on the mantle of wise woman, keeper of the 'Miracle Stone of Wales'.

Above all she was Marguerite Jervis, the bestselling author whose work was adored by millions of women. And while her 'countess' honorific was tenuous, in the realm of women's popular fiction, she was the uncrowned Queen of Romance.

Over her sixty-year career, Marguerite had adopted as many names as she had lived different lives. If she was to have an epitaph on that hillside, what would it be? What could do justice to a life so labyrinthine, so complex, so multi-layered? Perhaps her epitaph was the pleasure she gave her readers: the maid, the showgirl and shop girl, the New Woman who ventured into a male world, the typist, the 'lady' journalist and, yes, the sex worker too.

In her youth, Marguerite belonged to that army of women who shattered the old rules for 'young ladies' and invented new ones as they went along. In later years, she espoused romance, marriage and, by implication, dependence on a man, while much of her considerable earnings went on supporting a succession of men.

Warm and generous, snobbish and vain, sentimental and sincere, Marguerite has in turn amazed, amused and exasperated me. Possessed of remarkable talent, she could work it too hard and too fast for financial reward and the fast cars, luxurious clothes and extravagant theatre projects it bought her. She was a nurturing and caring mother who abandoned her son for her lover then smothered him as an adult. A seeker of love and romance who excused and adored the abusive Caradoc. A conservative and imperialist who loathed war and flag-waving of all kinds. Her entire persona, an assemblage of contradictions, embraced in her gloriously unique personality.

I arrange the primroses in a jar. Marguerite would have preferred the wild variety, her 'babies of the spring' that still grow in the hedgerows around Brynawelon. But it is early October and this shop-bought bunch is the best I can do. I wedge the jar onto the grave with a couple of nearby stones, then pause and reflect.

Author, actor, showgirl, theatre producer, mystic, forgotten celebrity. Among all her achievements, all her remarkable, almost superhuman energy, there was confusion, disappointment and pain. Her story did not end as happily as she would have written it. But then, whose story does?

Her lack of regard for the boundaries between fact and fiction could at times make her a frustrating subject. No matter how many layers were peeled away, there remained a sense that the 'real' Marguerite, if she existed at all, was evading scrutiny. Sometimes she would reveal a sliver of truth, or at least my best guess at it. Yet it was the layers and inconsistencies that made her the virtuoso storyteller she was. Stories were her life and her life, with all its evasions and secrets, she poured into her stories.

List of works by Marguerite Jervis

Abbreviations

C&H – Chapman & Hall
H&B – Hurst & Blackett
Hutch. – Hutchinson
R&C – Rich & Cowan

Oliver Sandys
The Woman in the Firelight. Long, 1911
Chicane. Long, 1912
The Little Mother Who Sits at Home [presented as 'non-fiction' with MJ as 'editor']. Edinburgh & London, T.C. & E.C. Jack, 1915
The Garment of Gold. H&B, 1921
Chappy, That's All. H&B, 1922
The Green Caravan. H&B, 1922
Old Roses. H&B, 1923
The Pleasure Garden. H&B, 1923
Sally Serene. H&B, 1924
Tilly-Make-Haste. H&B, 1924
Blinkeyes. H&B, 1925
Mr. Anthony. H&B, 1925
The Curled Hands. H&B, 1926
The Ginger Jar. H&B, 1926
The Crimson Ramblers. H&B, 1927
The Sorceress. H&B, 1927
Mops. H&B, 1928
Vista, The Dancer. H&B, 1928
SOS Queenie and Other Stories. H&B, 1928
Cherry. H&B, 1929
The Champagne Kiss. H&B, 1929
Bad Lad. H&B, 1930

Mr. Scribbles. H&B,1930
Sally of Sloper's. H&B, 1930
Jinks. H&B, 1931
Misty Angel. H&B, 1931
Butterflies. H&B, 1932
Squire. H&B, 1932
The Five-Hooded Cobra [revised version of *Where There Are Women*, Barclay, 1915]. H&B, 1932
Just Lil. H&B, 1933
Sir Boxer. H&B, 1933
Happy Day. H&B, 1934
Spangle. H&B, 1934
Tiptoes. H&B, 1935
The Curtain Will Go Up. Hutch., 1936
The Show Must Go On. Hutch., 1936
Angel's Kiss. Hutch., 1937
The Happy Mummers. Hutch., 1937
Prince Charming. Hutch., 1937
Crinklenose. Hutch., 1938
Love is a Flower. H&B, 1938
Mud on my Stocking. H&B, 1938
Hollywood Honeymoon. H&B, 1939
Old Hat. H&B, 1939
Whatagirl. H&B, 1939
Calm Waters. H&B, 1940
Singing Uphill. H&B, 1940
Full and Frank: The Private Life of a Woman Novelist [autobiography]. H&B, 1941
Jack Be Nimble. H&B, 1941
Wellington Wendy. H&B, 1941
Lame Daddy. H&B, 1942
Meadowsweet. H&B, 1942
Swell Fellows. H&B, 1942
Merrily All the Way. H&B, 1943

No Faint Heart. H&B, 1943

Miss Paraffin. H&B, 1944

Poppet and Co. H&B, 1944

Deputy Pet. H&B, 1945

Unbroken Thread: An Intimate Journal of the Daily Life in the Welsh Countryside of England's Best-loved Woman Novelist [memoir], London: Rider & Co., 1946

Caradoc Evans [biography]. H&B, 1946

Learn to Laugh Again. H&B, 1947

The Constant Rabbit. H&B, 1949

Dot on the Spot. H&B, 1949

Shining Failure. H&B, 1950

Bachelor's Tonic. H&B, 1951

Kiss the Moon. H&B, 1951

Let's All Be Happy. H&B, 1952

Quaint Place. H&B, 1952

Shine My Wings. H&B, 1954

Suffer to Sing. H&B, 1955

The Happiness Stone. H&B, 1955

Dear Mr. Dean. H&B, 1957

The Miracle Stone of Wales [memoir]. Rider, 1957

A New Day. H&B, 1957

Butterflies in the Rain. H&B, 1958

The Tinsel and the Gold. H&B, 1959

The Wise and the Steadfast. H&B, 1961

The Golden Flame. Ward Lock. H&B, 1961

The Poppy and the Rose. H&B, 1962

The Happy Hearts. H&B, 1962

Laughter and Love. H&B, 1962

Madame Adastra. H&B, 1964

Countess Hélène Barcynska

The Little Mother Who Sits at Home [presented as 'non-fiction' with MJ as 'editor']. Edinburgh & London, T.C. & E.C. Jack, 1915

From Dug-out and Billet: An Officer's Letters to His Mother [presented as 'non-fiction' with MJ as 'editor']. H&B, 1916

The Honey-Pot: A Story of the Stage. H&B, 1916

If Wishes Were Horses. H&B, 1917

Love Maggy. H&B, 1918

Sanity Jane. H&B, 1919

Love's Last Reward. H&B, 1920

Pretty Dear: A Romance. H&B, 1920

Jackie. H&B, 1920

Ships Come Home. H&B, 1922

Webs. H&B, 1922

Tesha (A Plaything of Destiny). H&B, 1923

We Women! H&B, 1923

Twenty-One [short stories]. H&B, 1924

The Russet Jacket: A Story of the Turf. H&B, 1924

Back to the Honey-Pot: A Story of the Stage. H&B, 1925

Hand Painted. H&B, 1925

Decameron Cocktails [short stories]. H&B, 1926

Mint Walk. H&B, 1927

The Golden Snail and Other Stories. H&B, 1927

A Certified Bride. C&H, 1928

Milly Comes to Town. C&H, 1928

Running Free and Other Stories. C&H, 1929

He Married his Parlourmaid. H&B, 1929

Fantoccini. H&B, 1928

The Joy Shop. C&H, 1931

A Woman of Experience. H&B, 1931

I Loved a Fairy. H&B, 1933

Under the Big Top. H&B, 1933

Exit Renee. H&B, 1934

Publicity Baby. H&B, 1935
Pick up and Smile. Hutch., 1936
God and Mr. Aaronson. Hutch., 1937
Keep Cheery. Hutch., 1937
Hearts for Gold. Hutch., 1938
Sweetbriar Lane. Hutch., 1938
Writing Man. Hutch., 1939
That Trouble Piece! R&C, 1939
Let the Storm Burst. R&C, 1941
Black-Out Symphony. R&C, 1942
The Wood is my Pulpit. R&C, 1942
Joy Comes After. R&C, 1943
Love Never Dies. R&C, 1943
Astrologer. R&C, 1944
The Tears of Peace. R&C, 1944
Love is a Lady. R&C, 1945
We Lost Our Way. R&C, 1948
Gorgeous Brute. R&C, 1949
Conjuror. R&C, 1950
Bubble over Thorn. R&C, 1951
Those Dominant Hills. R&C, 1951
Beloved Burden. R&C, 1954
Miss Venus of Aberdovey. R&C, 1956
Angel's Eyes. H&B, 1957
The Jackpot. H&B, 1957
Two Faces of Love. H&B, 1958
Prince's Story. H&B, 1959
Black Harvest. H&B, 1960
These Changing Years. H&B, 1961
I Was Shown Heaven. H&B, 1962
Smile in the Mirror. H&B, 1963

Marguerite Barclay

The Activities of Lavie Jutt [with Armiger Barclay]. Stanley Paul, 1911

Letters from Fleet Street [with Armiger Barclay]. Palmer, 1912

Where there are Women, [with Armiger Barclay]. [Revised as The Five-Hooded Cobra, Sandys, 1932]. H&B, 1915

Peggy-Day-by-Day [with Armiger Barclay]. Simkin Marshall, 1916

Yesterday is Tomorrow. R&C, 1950

Sunset is Dawn. R&C, 1953

Films

As Oliver Sandys

The Green Caravan (Edwin J. Collins 1922: UK)

Chappy: That's All (Thomas Bentley, 1924: UK)

The Pleasure Garden (Alfred Hitchcock, 1925: UK)

Blinkeyes (George Pearson, 1926: UK)

Born Lucky [from the novel *Mops*] (Michael Powell, 1933: UK)

As Countess Barcynska

The Honeypot (Fred Le Roy Granville, 1920: UK)

Love Maggy (Fred LeRoy Granville, 1921: UK)

Jackie [wrongly attributed to Helena Buczynska] (John Ford 1921: US)

Rose o' the Sea [from the novel *Pretty Dear*] (Fred Niblo, 1922: US)

Tesha/A Woman in the Night (Edwin Greenwood, Victor Saville, 1928: UK)

We Women (W.P. Kellino, 1925: UK)

All books published in London unless otherwise stated.

Notes

Abbreviations
NLW – National Library of Wales
M – Marguerite Jervis
H&B – Hurst & Blackett

Prologue: A Virtuoso Storyteller

1. Carmen Callil, *Subversive Sybils: Women's Popular Fiction this Century* (London: British Library, 1996)
2. Oliver Sandys (1923), *The Pleasure Garden,* London: Hurst & Blackett
3. The inauthentic 'Burmese' scene was filmed around Italy's Lake Como.
4. This is in some large part thanks to the 2012 restoration by the British Film Institute.
5. Marguerite published 149 books during her career, around 100 of which are extant.
6. She did indeed bequeath her books to the National Library of Wales, where they make a welcome addition to its existing collection of Marguerite's works.
7. A large number of press cuttings, letters and other material on Marguerite also form part of the Caradoc Evans Collection at the NLW, bequeathed by literary critic and close friend of Caradoc and Marguerite, Gwyn Jones. (See Gwyn Jones Papers).
8. Sandys, *Madame Adastra* (1964),
9. George Orwell, 'Boys' Weeklies' (orig. 1939), see *George Orwell Essays* (1994), London: Penguin
10. Oliver Sandys (1946) *Caradoc Evans*, London: Hurst & Blackett, 11
11. Virginia Woolf, *Three Guineas* (London: Hogarth Press, 1938)
12. See Corelli's *The Murder of Delicia* (1899), for example,

which sold a remarkable 52,000 copies in its first year of publication.

13. Sandys (1941), *Full and Frank: The Private Life of a Woman Novelist,* London: Hutchinson

Chapter 1: From Raipur to Reigate

1. *Full and Frank, 21*
2. *Ibid, 9*
3. *Ibid,11*
4. *Ibid.*
5. The name that was given to a nanny employed by the British in colonial India.
6. *Full and Frank, 5*
7. British Library: India Office Family History Archive
8. Richard Gott (2011), *Britain's Empire: Resistance, Repression and Revolt,* London: Verso, 44
9. Anne De Courcy (2012), *The Fishing Fleet: Husband-Hunting in The Raj,* London: Orion
10. Literally, 'little master', the term adopted by the British in colonial India to refer to a new recruit.
11. George Orwell, 'Shooting An Elephant' (orig. 1936), *Essays* (1994), London: Penguin
12. De Courcy, 66
13. Ibid., 67
14. Known as Myanmar today
15. Rudyard Kipling (1889, 'From the Sea to Sea'), later published in the essay collection, *From the Sea to Sea and Other Sketches*
16. John Harris (2018), *The Devil in Eden*, Bridgend: Seren, 177
17. De Courcy, 261
18. *Full and Frank, 6*
19. Countess Hélène Barcynska (1923), *We Women!*, H&B
20. Ibid., 21

21. *Full and Frank,* 6
22. *Ibid,* 6-7
23. *Ibid,* 8
24. Ibid., 8-9
25. *Ibid,* 9
26. Barcynska, *The Honey-Pot: A story of the stage* (1916), London: H&B
27. *Full and Frank,* 9
28. Ibid., 182
29. Ibid. 9. Quoted in De Courcy, 33
30. David & Stephen Howarth (1994), *The story of P&O: The Peninsular and Oriental steam navigation company,* London: Weidenfeld & Nicolson
31. *Full and Frank,* 11
32. Saki (H.H. Munro) (1910), David Stuart Davies (ed.) 'Cross Currents', *The Best Short Stories of Saki* (2008), London: Collector's Library
33. Sandys, *Unbroken Thread: An intimate journey of the daily life in the Welsh countryside of England's best-loved woman novelist.* (1948), London: Rider & Co, 54
34. *Full and Frank,* 17
35. *Full and Frank,* 18
36. J Albisetti et al (eds.) (2010), *Girls' Secondary Education in the Western World,* London: Palgrave
37. Vera Brittain (1933), *Testament of Youth,* London: Victor Gollancz
38. *Full & Frank,* 18
39. *Homeward Mail from India, China and the East,* 13 Sept.,1897
40. *Bath Chronicle and Weekly Gazette,* 29 Oct., 1896
41. Charlotte Brontë (2006, first pub. 1847) *Jane Eyre,* London: Penguin
42. De Courcy, 36
43. *Full and Frank,* 22
44. Ibid., 23

45. Rosa Baughan, *Character Indicated by Handwriting* (1871), London: Upcot
46. Cheiro (1996, first pub. 1916), *Palmistry for All,* London: Prentice Hall Press
47. *Full and Frank*, 24
48. Ibid. 5

Chapter 2: From 'Cage' to Chorus Line

1. *The Honey-Pot*, 40
2. In 1906, when Marguerite enrolled at the Academy of Dramatic Arts it was awaiting the royal approval that was later given, so allowing it to be renamed the *Royal* Academy of Dramatic Arts.
3. Anxiety over women travelling alone sparked a number of lurid stories in the popular press about so-called 'white slavery', involving the kidnapping and subsequent sex trafficking of unaccompanied young women.
4. Michael Holroyd, *A Strange Eventful History: The Dramatic Lives of Ellen Terry, Henry Irving, and Their Remarkable Families* (2009), London: Vintage
5. 'School of Dramatic Art. Opening Ceremony', *Daily Telegraph & Courier*, 26 April, 1904
6. While remaining on friendly terms with the royalty of Europe, Lipton also befriended anti-imperialist leaders such as Arabi Pasha and Colonel Arthur Lynch.
7. James Mackay, *The Man Who Invented Himself: A Life of Sir Thomas Lipton*, (1998), Edinburgh: Mainstream Publishing
8. *Full and Frank*, 29
9. Mackay, 177
10. Olive Schreiner's novel, *The Story of an African Farm* (1883) addresses the call for women to have an education and career outside marriage and motherhood. Schreiner's *Woman and Labour* (1911), which makes the case for a woman's right to a

meaningful vocation, is regarded as a landmark feminist polemic.

11. *Full and Frank,* 29
12. Oliver Sandys (1911), *The Woman in the Firelight,* London: Long
13. M had delivered a recitation of an Adelaide Procter poem in Miss Cowper's School, some eight years previously. (Possibly she had selected the same piece for this performance.)
14. *Daily Telegraph and Courier*, 12 September 1906
15. Oliver Sandys (1912), *Chicane*, London: Long
16. *The Honey-Pot*, 22-23.
17. Ibid., 23.
18. Clement Shorter, *The Sphere*, 25 June 1921

Chapter 3: A New Woman on Fleet Street

1. *Unbroken Thread,* 54
2. Arnold Bennet, *Journalism for Women* (1898), London: John Lane
3. Another difficulty in quantifying the number of women journalists at the time was the tendency for many to adopt male pseudonyms (as M later did with her penname Oliver Sandys). e.g. Pearl Craigie, the first President of the Society of Woman Journalists, wrote as John Oliver Hobbes.
4. In 1702 the remarkable Elizabeth Mallett broke the mould when she launched *The Daily Courant,* Britain's first daily newspaper.
5. 'An Old Oriental', *Englishwoman's Review*, 1904, 151-153
6. Like a number of women authors of her generation (such as Berta Ruck, the Welsh, Indian-born bestselling romantic novelist, whose career so closely paralleled M's), M began her career writing for women's magazines.
7. H.G. Wells (2018, orig. 1909), *Ann Veronica: A modern love story*, London: Blackwell's

8. Frederic Harrison, 'The Emancipation of Women', Fortnightly Review, Vol. 50, 297 (Oct. 1891)

9. *The Honey-Pot*, 34.

10. Stephen McKenna, *Sonia: Between two worlds* (1917), London: Hutchinson 245

11. Wyllarde, Dolf, *The Pathway of the Pioneer* (1906), London: Methuen

12. The PMG's child prostitution campaign prompted the passing of the so-called 'Stead Act' in 1885, which raised the age of consent from 13 to 16.

13. *Daily Telegraph & Courier*, 7 December 1904.

14. *Full and Frank,* 32

15. Ibid., 34

16. *Answers: The Popular Journal for Home and Train*, 1908

17. *Full and Frank*, 34

18. 'Confessions of a Lady Swindler', *Answers: The Popular Journal for Home and Train*, Jan. 30, 1909.

19. Elaine Jackson, 'Sievier's Monthly: Pseudonyms and Readership in Early Twentieth Century Popular Fiction', John Hinks & Catherine Armstrong (eds.), *Book Trade Connections from the Seventeenth to the Twentieth Centuries* (2008), London: British Library & Oak Knoll Press, 247-8

20. Adeline Sergeant, *The Work of Oliver Byrd* (1902), London: James Nisbet & Co., 10

21. Literary critic and founder of *Tatler* magazine.

22. *Full and Frank,* 35

23. Ibid., 18

24. Wyllarde, *The Pathway of the Pioneer* (1906), London: Methuen, 36

25. *Full and Frank*, 35

26. Published jointly as Armiger and Marguerite Barclay, *The Activities of Lavie Jutt* (1911), London: Stanley Paul.

27. In her description of Armiger, M also uses the anti-Semitic trope. 'Jewish nose'. Written as it was during World War Two

(*Full and Frank* was published in 1941), it makes particularly uncomfortable reading.

Chapter 4: Tabasco Tales

1. *Chicane*, 10
2. *Full and Frank,* 164
3. Francois Meltzer, *Hot Property: The stakes and claims of literary originality* (1994), Chicago: UCP
4. Berta Ruck, *A Trickle of Welsh Blood* (1967), London: Hutchinson
5. Armiger Barclay, *The Kingmakers* (1907), London: Cassell & Co.
6. *Aberdeen Press and Journal* , Mar. 6, 1907.
7. *The Queen*, 21 May 1910
8. *The Woman in the Firelight* (1911), London: Long, 7
9. Elinor Glyn, the original 'It girl' went on to enjoy a successful career as screenwriter, and longstanding columnist for Cosmopolitan, imparting beauty tips and advice to women on how to keep their men.
10. *Full and Frank,* 62
11. Among the Winning Post's risqué offerings was their 'Adam and Eve' rhymes – e.g. 'Eve stood in the garden/(Mother of us all)/Examining her trousseau/fig leaves – that was all!/There stood poor old Adam/Up against the wall,/"What oh, said he, "There's work for me/when the leaves begin to fall!"'
12. As a comparison, *Punch*, which topped the circulation figures at 100,000, had taken over seventy years to reach that figure.
13. *Full and Frank,* 66
14. Jackson, 261
15. For instance, M's work appears in *The Winning Post Annual* 1913 under various pseudonyms: Claudia Rayne, O.S. [sic.], Olive Bree and Ganwar.
16. British Library: *Sievier's Monthly* 1909, *Winning Post Annual* 1913
17. Oliver Sandys, 'Letters from Space', *Sievier's Monthly*, Aug. 8, 1909.

18. Constance Romanné Jones, 'Lord Charles and a Suffragette', *Sievier's Monthly*, Oct. 10, 1909.
19. Jackson, '*Sievier's Monthly*'
20. In 1918, Sievier stood for Parliament as a Unionist candidate in the newly formed Shoreditch constituency. He came second with 3,414 votes, over 6,000 votes behind the winning Liberal Coalition candidate, Christopher Addison.
21. John Welcome, *Neck or Nothing: The Extraordinary Life and Times of Bob Sievier*, (1970), London: Faber, 247
22. *Full and Frank*, 72
23. *Chicane*, 23
24. Ibid., 53
25. Welcome, 184
26. *Full and Frank*, 71
27. During this period, most of her contributions to *Sievier's Monthly* were as Oliver Sandys.
28. NLW. Gwyn Jones papers 68/58
29. Jackson, 246

Chapter 5: Making a Name, or Two

1. Jackson, 246
2. Harris 2018, 180
3. *Unbroken Thread*, 54
4. Harris 2018, 180
5. Ibid.
6. The Military Service Act of 1916, which imposed conscription on single men aged 18 to 41, also exempted certain groups including teachers, clergymen, certain classes of industrial workers and the medically unfit.
7. Published by Hearst
8. Barcynska (ed.), *The Little Mother Who Sits at Home* (1915), London: TC&EC Jack
9. *Aberdeen Press & Journal*, 3 May 1915

10. Harris 2018, 180
11. *Full and Frank,* 85
12. In *Full and Frank*, Marguerite hides Walter Lovell's identity, referring to him only as 'Leslie'.
13. Harris 2018, 180
14. Countess Hélène Barcynska, *Tesha, A Plaything of Destiny* (1923), H&B
15. *Full and Frank,* 81
16. *Empire Boys: Adventures in a Man's World* (1991), London, Unwin Hyman, 44
17. Barcynska, *From Dug-Out and Billet: An Officer's Letters to his Mother* (1915), H&B, 6-7
18. Jane Potter, *Boys in Khaki, Girls in Print: Women's literary responses to the Great War* (2005), Oxford: Clarendon
19. M continued to write for H&B following their takeover by Hutchinson's (just after the Great War) until their demise in 1954.
20. *Pall Mall Gazette, 14 February 1916*
21. This is in contrast to today, when a book by a bestselling author can total several million.
22. See *Caradoc Evans*, 64
23. See Rupert Croft-Cooke, *The Numbers Game*, (1963), London: Putnam
24. Juliet Flesch, *From Australia with Love: A History of Modern Australian Popular Romance Novels*, (2004), Perth: Curtin University Books
25. Mary Cadogan, *And Then their Hearts Stood Still: An Exuberant Look at Romantic Fiction Past and Present*, (1994), London: Macmillan
26. Sandys, *Garment of Gold* (1921), H&B was adapted by M from her series of short stories of that name published in *Woman's Weekly*.
27. *Aberdeen Press and Journal*, 6 June 1921
28. *The Sphere*, 25 June 1921

29. *The Green Caravan* (Dir. Edwin J. Collins, 1922)
30. *Full and Frank,* 89
31. Ibid., 90
32. Ibid., 92

Chapter 6: A Dangerous Age

1. Sandys, *Chappy, That's All* (1922), H&B, 19
2. Harris 2018, 185
3. Rudyard Kipling, 'Beyond the Pale' (1888), *Plain Tales from the Hills* (2011), London: Penguin
4. E.g. see De Courcy
5. The £1,000 earned from first edition rights alone was almost seven times the average national income for 1926 [source: the Measuring Worth Foundation https://www.measuringworth.com/]. This was in addition to Marguerite's other earnings (second and third serial rights in the UK, the US, Canada, Australia and Brazil, plus film rights and income from magazine serialisations).
6. *Tesha / A Woman in the Night* (US title) (Dir. Greenwood & Saville, 1928)
7. M. Ball & M Williams (eds.), *British Women's Cinema*, (2010), London: Routledge
8. *Easy Virtue* (Dir. Hitchcock, 1927)
9. *The Loves of Mary, Queen of Scotts* (Dir Clift, 1923)
10. *Nell Gwyn* (Dir. Wilcox, 1926)
11. *The Constant Nymph* (Dir. Brunel, 1928)
12. E.g. film advertisement in *Gloucester Citizen*, Feb. 16, 1927
13. *Full and Frank,* 94
14. *The Pleasure Garden* was restored and released on DVD by the BFI in 2010, the only extant film adaptation of a Marguerite Jervis novel.
15. *Stage Struck* (Dir. Dwan, 1925)
16. For her film name of Marguerite Evans she borrowed Caradoc's

surname, which suggests their relationship was already established by 1925, eight years before their marriage in 1933.

17. *Full and Frank, 94*

18. Oliver Sandys, *Singing Uphill* (1940), H&B, 200

19. Berta Ruck, another prolific author (although not quite as prolific as M) wrote up to three novels a year, amassing a total of 90 books over her long career.

20. Oliver Sandys, *Old Roses* (1923), H&B

21. *Full and Frank*, 100

22. Suncrete was demolished in 1933 and four shops, with flats above, were built on the site.

23. *Full & Frank*, 101

24. *Caradoc Evans*, 91

25. *Old Roses*, 275

26. *The Sphere*, September 1929

27. Countess Barcynska, *He Married His Parlourmaid* (1929), London: Chapman & Hall

28. *Gloucestershire Echo*, 19 August 1929

29. EM Hull, *The Sheik* (1919), London: Eveleigh Nash

30. Ibid., *148*

31. Anita Loos, *Gentlemen Prefer Blondes: The Illuminating Diary of a Professional Lady,* (1992, first pub. 1925) London: Penguin

32. Sandys, *The Ginger Jar,* (1926), H&B

33. *The Sketch*, 6 October 1926

34. Patrick Hamilton, *Twenty Thousand Streets Under the Sky* (1999, first pub. 1943), London: Penguin, 143

35. Jackson, 246

36. Oliver Sandys, *The Sorceress* (1927), H&B

37. *Aberdeen Press and Journal*, 17 February, 1927

38. Marguerite later claimed that she had been with Tots before she died, and when writing *Chappy, That's All* she would read a chapter to her aunt each night to comfort her during her final illness.

[39.] Sandys, *Blinkeyes* (1927), H&B
[40.] *Full and Frank*, 100
[41.] *Full and Frank*, 91

Chapter 7: Marguerite and 'the Man'

[1.] *The Honey-Pot*, 30
[2.] *Caradoc Evans*, 91
[3.] The label, 'the best-hated man in Wales', originated in a *Western Mail* article by Martin Sewell Stokes, 25 July 1924. It was one that stuck and which Caradoc himself embraced and repeated many times over.
[4.] *Caradoc Evans*, 92
[5.] Harris 2018, 174-5
[6.] *The Honey-Pot*, 7
[7.] Harris 2018, 177
[8.] 'Letters from Caradoc' in *Caradoc Evans*, 143-145
[9.] Harris 2018, 214-5
[10.] T.P. O'Connor died in November 1929.
[11.] *Caradoc Evans*, 110-2
[12.] NLW. Gwyn Jones papers
[13.] *Caradoc Evans*, 94

Chapter 8: Wales, 'The Setting of my Soul'

[1.] Oliver Sandys, *The Happy Mummers (1938)*, H&B, dedication
[2.] *Full and Frank*, 107
[3.] NLW. Gwyn Jones papers [undated scrapbook cutting].
[4.] Glyn Jones, *The Dragon Has Two Tongues: Essays on Anglo-Welsh Writers and Writing*, (1968), London, JM Dent & Sons, 61
[5.] *Caradoc Evans*, 64
[6.] NLW. Gwyn Jones Papers
[7.] Ruck, 162

8. Glyn Jones, 61
9. Ruck, 163
10. *The Collected Letters of Dylan Thomas*, Paul Ferris (ed.) (1985), London: Dent
11. Dylan Thomas, letter to Pamela Hansford Johnson, October 1934', in *The Collected Letters*
12. Sandys, *The Miracle Stone of Wales* (1957), London: Rider, 14-15
13. Glyn Jones, 61
14. *Caradoc Evans*, 10
15. NLW. Gwyn Jones Papers
16. *Caradoc Evans*, 54
17. Harris 2018, 182
18. *Caradoc Evans*, 11
19. 'English Plays in Rural Wales', *Western Mail*, June 20, 1935
20. John Harris, 'A Venture of Love and Youth and Spring', *Ceredigion Journal*, Vol. 16 (2012), pp. 133-170
21. Ibid.
22. *Western Mail*, May 1935
23. *Cambrian News*, 18 October 1935
24. When not performing at Aberystwyth's Quarry Theatre, Rogues and Vagabonds toured the nearby towns and villages of Aberdyfi, Machynlleth, Talybont, Borth, Lampeter, Aberaeron, Newquay, Aberporth and Llandrindod Wells.
25. Sadly, the script for *Hell Freezes* has not survived.
26. Thomas S. Hischak, *Broadway Plays and Musicals* (2009), London: McFarland & Co.
27. Harris (2012)
28. *Western Mail*, 26 June 1935
29. Ibid.
30. NLW. Gwyn Jones Papers
31. Ceredigion Archives, reference written by 'Countess Barcynska' on behalf of Rogues and Vagabonds, October 1936
32. Harris (2012)

33. *Full and Frank*, 130
34. NLW. Gwyn Jones Papers
35. *Full and Frank*, 6
36. Caradoc's Journal, *Caradoc Evans*, 125
37. NLW. Gwyn Jones Papers
38. Ibid.
39. 'Caradoc Evans: 100-year-old literary storm returns', 7 November 2015 https://www.bbc.co.uk/ [Accessed 11 June 2018]
40. *Full and Frank,* 127
41. NLW. Gwyn Jones Papers
42. Ibid.
43. Marguerite estimated her total losses for the 1936 season at £1,300 (see Harris 2012, 255)
44. NLW. Gwyn Jones Papers
45. *Western Mail,* April 1936
46. *Cambrian News*, 23 October 1936
47. Sandys, *The Happy Mummers* (1937), Hutchinson
48. Sandys, *The Show Must Go On* (1936), Hutchinson
49. Sandys, *Hollywood Honeymoon* (1939), H&B
50. Barcynska, *Pick Up and Smile* (1936), Hutchinson
51. *Daily Mirror*, 16 March 1939
52. NLW. Gwyn Jones Papers
53. Ibid.
54. *Hollywood Honeymoon,* 73
55. *Full and Frank*, 132
56. Ruck, 163-4
57. *Caradoc Evans*, 114
58. Ruck, 164

Chapter 9: Broadstairs and Ruislip – Brief Theatrical Interludes

1. Emlyn Williams, *Night Must Fall,* (pub. 1935, 1982) London: Heinemann

2. The original wooden steps that Buchan claims inspired him to write *The 39 Steps* were replaced with concrete ones during the 1940s.

3. *The 39 Steps* (Dir. Hitchcock, 1935)

4. *The Pleasure Garden* (Dir. Hitchcock, 1926)

5. Harris 2018, 282

6. This author's grandmother, who worked as a nanny in London during the mid-1930s, had spent a number of summers at Broadstairs in the employ of the family of the magician Jack Barnett and his daughter, the child magician Lucille Barnett.

7. *Uxbridge & West Drayton Gazette*, 10 December 1937

8. *Daily Herald*, 18 February 1938.

9. *Caradoc Evans*, 120

10. *Daily Herald*, 9 February 1938

11. Harris 2018, 10

12. *Daily Herald*, 9 February 1938

13. The script for Marguerite's stage adaptation of her Sandys novel *Chappy, That's All* (1922) is sadly not extant.

14. *Uxbridge & W. Drayton Gazette*, 15 October 1937.

15. *Caradoc Evans*, 119

16. *Full & Frank*, 123

17. Ibid.

18. Harris 2018, 259.

19. 'Kitty Shore's Magic Cake' was eventually published in 1949 by Rich & Cowan (one of Marguerite's publishers) as *Mother's Marvel*, apparently at Marguerite's request. (See Harris 2018 , 259).

20. *Caradoc Evans*, 121

21. Joyce later defected to Germany where he broadcast wartime Nazi propaganda to the UK, his sneering, upper class voice earning him the unflattering nickname 'Lord Haw-Haw'. After the war, he was captured by the British and later executed for treason.

22. *Thanet Advertiser*, 19 April 1938

23. *Radio Times*, 18 July 1938
24. *Full and Frank*, 123
25. *Thanet Advertiser,* 27 June 1939
26. *The Stage*, 29 June 1939
27. *Caradoc Evans*, 'Caradoc's Journal', 125
28. The then popular – and now unacceptable – act consisted of white male performers 'blacking up' in a burlesque parody of the black American minstrel performers. Uncle Mack (James Henry Sommerson) ran his show in Broadstairs for over fifty years. Today, he is a well-known (and controversial) figure in Broadstairs' history. In 2005, a plaque commemorating the 'joy and laughter' he gave 'to young and old' prompted a group of local people to form a petition to have it removed, stating that it represented 'a memorial to colonial-era bigotry and racism'. The petition attracted sixty-four signatures, not enough to topple it from its seafront pedestal, where it still stands today.
29. Frank Muir, *A Kentish Lad*, (1997), London: Bantam, 37
30. Barcynska, *Writing Man* (1939), Hutchinson
31. Sandys, *Calm Waters* (1940), H&B
32. See Chapter 8 for examples of other Sandys and Barcynska novels set in a repertory theatre.
33. *Aberdeen Press and Journal*, 29 May 1940.
34. *Daily Mirror*, 18 April 1940.
35. Barcynska, *Sweetbriar Lane* (1938), H&B
36. *Calm Waters,* 12
37. *Mother's Marvel* (1949), London: Dakers
38. *The Observer*, for instance, called it 'a somewhat slimy satire' (28 August 1949).
39. Harris 2018, 286
40. *Caradoc Evans*, 'Caradoc's Journal', 125

Chapter 10: Hill of Tempests

1. Nacio Herb Brown and Arthur Freed, 'We'll Make Hay While

the Sun Shines' (1933), New York: Robbins Music
Corporation

2. Oliver Sandys, *Meadowsweet* (1942), H&B
3. *Full and Frank,* 205
4. NLW. Gwyn Jones Papers: Letter to Nell Dunbar, 23 August
1939
5. *Caradoc Evans*, 'Caradoc's Journal', 127
6. NLW. Gwyn Jones Papers: Letter from M. to Margaret Powell
7. *Caradoc Evans*, 15
8. Ibid., 9
9. Letter to Pauline Block, 7 October 1978, Glyn Jones Papers
10. Harris 2018, 317-18
11. Ibid., 314
12. Letter to Pauline Block, 26 May 1942, Glyn Jones Papers
13. Sandys, *Jack Be Nimble* (1941), H&B
14. Sandys, *Swell Fellows* (1942), H&B
15. Sandys, *Wellington Wendy* (1941), H&B
16. *Wellington Wendy,* inner sleeve publicity.
17. Barcynska, *Astrologer* (1944), London: Rich & Cowan
18. Barcynska, *Black-Out Symphony* (1942), Rich & Cowan
19. NLW. Gwyn Jones Papers.
20. *Spiritualism and British Society Between the Wars*, Jenny
Hazelgrove (2000), Manchester: MUP, 212-222
21. Harris 2018, 318
22. Ibid., 317
23. *Full and Frank*, 180
24. Pauline added that the Evanses also obtained black market
brandy, gin and whisky for Marguerite's insomnia.
25. Letter from Pauline Black, 1978, Glyn Jones Papers
26. ETA Hoffmann, 'Councillor Krespel' (orig. 'Rat Krespel', circa
1818), *Tales of Hoffmann* (1982), London: Penguin
27. *Caradoc Evans*, 140
28. *Full and Frank*, 171
29. Ibid.

30. Trudel Losch, a fictionalised Pauline (and highly sentimentalised portrait of a Jewish German refugee), appears in the novel *Meadowsweet* (Sandys, 1942).
31. NLW. Glyn Jones Papers
32. Ibid.
33. Ibid.
34. *Full and Frank*, 154
35. Jan Struther, *Mrs Miniver* (1939), London, Chatto & Windus
36. *Birmingham Daily Gazette*, 13 February 1940
37. Ruck, 162

Chapter 11: After Caradoc – 'The Unbroken Thread'

1. *Unbroken Thread*, Foreword by Hannen Swaffer, 10
2. *Caradoc Evans*, 17
3. *The Miracle Stone of Wales*, 22
4. *Unbroken Thread*, 144-145
5. *Caradoc Evans*, 64
6. *Western Mail*, 17 January 1945
7. *Unbroken Thread*, 41
8. NLW. Gwyn Jones Papers
9. *Unbroken Thread*, 12
10. Rider & Co. (a Penguin imprint today) still covers similar subject matter, although with titles now listed as 'Inspirational' or 'New Age'.
11. Harris 2018, 137-8
12. What happened in the rest of the séance is not known as the organist, who had been instructed to play when the audience began to leave, drowned out the remainder of the otherworldly message with his music.
13. *Unbroken Thread*, 57
14. *Unbroken Thread*, 68.
15. Sandys, *Learn to Laugh Again*, (1947) H&B.
16. *Unbroken Thread*, 53

17. Ibid. 55
18. Ibid. 56
19. David Conway, *Magic Without Mirrors: The Making of a Magician* (2011), Salem MA: Logios Publishing, 158
20. *Unbroken Thread*, 139-40.
21. Barcynska, *We Lost Our Way*, (1948), Rich & Cowan
22. NLW, Clifford 'Doggie' Hubbard Papers,
23. Ibid.
24. Harris 2018, 346
25. *The Stage*, 5 June 1947
26. See Harris 2012
27. *Unbroken Thread*, 146
28. According to Marguerite's account, her only friendly neighbours were Olwen Jenkins, 'the beautiful, blue-eyed housewife' and Miss Jenkins, who had cared for her brother following his breakdown.

Chapter 12: A 'Miraculous' Ending

1. *The Miracle Stone of Wales*, 2
2. Ibid., 85
3. Ibid., 82
4. Nicholas Sandys, *Starset and Sunrise* (1951), New York, Sheed & Ward
5. NLW. Gwyn Jones Papers
6. Harris 2018, 346
7. *The Miracle Stone of Wales*, 34-6
8. Sadly, the documentary *The Secret Arts* has been lost.
9. *Western Mail*, 26 April 1955.
10. Ibid. 2 May 1955.
11. *The Miracle Stone of Wales,* 108.
12. It is likely that Keidrych Rhys still bore a grudge against Marguerite following his unsuccessful defamation suit, claiming she had libelled him in her novel *Conjuror* (Sandys, 1950).

13. Harris 2018, 347
14. *The Miracle Stone of Wales*, 52
15. Ibid., 49
16. The only source available for this and all letters M received from the 'pilgrims' of the 'miracle stone' is *The Miracle Stone of Wales,* which contains a number of M's selected (and unreliable) excerpts from the correspondence.
17. *The Miracle Stone of Wales*, 52-3
18. NLW. Postcard with picture of the stone, with inscription: 'THE HAPPINESS STONE AT PANTEIDAL LODGE, ABERDOVEY, MERIONETH' (circa 1959). Publisher unknown, but the card is likely to have been commissioned by M. as publicity material for the stone.
19. Harris 2018, 347
20. NLW. Gwyn Jones Papers: letter to Pauline Block, 7 October 1978
21. *Taffy: A Play of Welsh Village Life in Three Acts* (1923), London: Andrew Melrose
22. *The Stage*, 9 April 1953
23. With the exception of a 2006 script-in-hand reading at Chapter Arts Centre in Cardiff, *Taffy* has not been produced since the 1930s.
24. *Birmingham Daily Gazette*, 6 January 1954
25. David Conway, 42
26. *The Miracle Stone of Wales*, 74
27. *Miss Venus of Aberdovey* (1956), Rich & Cowan
28. See Juliette Wood, 'The Miracle Stone and Welsh Legend Formation', www.juliettewood.com/papers [Accessed 21 June 2018]
29. *The Miracle Stone of Wales*, 125
30. NLW. Clifford 'Doggie' Hubbard Papers
31. *The Miracle Stone of Wales*, 78
32. *Palos Verdes Peninsula News*, Volume XXXXVII, Number 15, 22 January 1959

33. Harris 2018, 347
34. Ibid.
35. Ibid.
36. NLW. Gwyn Jones Papers: letter to Pauline Block, 7 October 1978.
37. Harris 2018, 262
38. Ibid.
39. NLW. Gwyn Jones Papers: GJ letter to Nicholas Sandys, 29th September 1978,
40. Jay Dixon, *Romantic Fiction of Mills and Boon, 1909-1995* (2016), London: Routledge
41. Barcynska, *Black Out Symphony* (1942), Rich & Cowan
42. Barcynska, *Black Harvest* (1960), H&B
43. Circa 1960, although the exact date when M first received her Civil List pension is not know.
44. *Madame Adastra* (1964), H&B

Epilogue: Return to Horeb

1. *Hollywood Honeymoon*, 256

Acknowledgements

Writing a biography is a long process that is never really completed. Even as this book goes to press, I am discovering new facts about Marguerite's extraordinary, complex life. If it had not been for the help I have received from numerous people along the way, this book might never have been completed in any sense.

Firstly, my thanks must go to John Harris, the biographer and expert on Marguerite's second husband, the author Caradoc Evans. For his generosity in sharing his extensive knowledge of Marguerite and Caradoc, often over a cup of coffee, I owe him a huge debt. As the copyright holder of Marguerite's work (and that of Caradoc's until the copyright expired in 2015) Harris has also very kindly granted me permission to use her material. As if that wasn't enough, when *The Devil in Eden*, his impressive biography of Caradoc was published in 2018, it became my Bible during the final phase of my research. (Although, as they say, any errors are entirely my own.)

If it were not for the extensive facilities at the National Library of Wales, not least its large collection of Marguerite's works and the invaluable Gwyn Jones archive which holds a great deal of material on Marguerite (and Caradoc), this book would have been far more difficult to complete. Thank you as well to the ever-patient and welcoming library staff. While on the subject of libraries, I would also like to thank the staff at the British Library, Ceredigion Archives, Shropshire Archives, Kent Archives, Brent Archives, Gloucestershire Archives and the Country Records Office in Buckinghamshire.

Thank you as well to *Planet – The Welsh Internationalist* for publishing what I had assumed would be a one-off article on Marguerite. And a special thank you to the avid Marguerite reader from Presteigne, who very kindly offered to give me her collection of Marguerite's works. Sadly, she died shortly afterwards and, to my shame, I have since mislaid her letter and her name with it.

I am also grateful to David Russel Hume for sharing his collection of Nicholas's letters and to Elaine Jackson for sharing her research on Marguerite's early writing career and to Tony Burgess for his copy of the 'Aberystwyth Celebrities' cartoon. Thanks as well to the Women's Archive of Wales, *The Cambrian News*, Ceredigion Museum, the *New Welsh Review*, the Society for Theatre Research, and to Heike Roms, Peter Stevenson and Angela V. John. I must also thank my ever-supportive friends who for five years have patiently endured my stream of consciousness on Marguerite's life and times.

As Marguerite has no surviving descendants, I am particularly indebted to those people who have been able to share first-hand anecdotes with me. I would like to thank Llinos Jones and John Evans for coming forward with their childhood impressions of Marguerite. Thank you as well to Caroline Clark and Suzy Cellan Hughes for their recollections of Marguerite's son, Nicholas. And special thanks to Lyn Ebenezer, who shared his vivid portrait of the gentle, eccentric, and somewhat lonely Nicholas whom he befriended during the 1980s. Diolch o galon.

I have been privileged to work with Honno Welsh Women's Press and to experience first-hand that author care for which they are renowned. I would like to thank editor and Honno committee member Janet Thomas for encouraging me from the start and helping me get my initial proposal into shape. I would also like to thank my editor Caroline Oakley for her attention to detail and keen eye for a story. Caroline's critiques of my work were thorough, frank, and invariably correct, for which I am very grateful. Thank you as well to Helena Earnshaw, Stephanie Tillotson, Rebecca John, Lisa Shakespeare and all the staff and committee at Honno. Thanks as well to the freelance copy editors whom I have never met, but whose meticulous editing is greatly appreciated.

I was fortunate to receive not one, but two bursaries – from The Authors' Foundation (2016) and Literature Wales (2017). While both bought me some much-needed writing time, it was also gratifying to know that others were willing to invest in my work. I am very grateful for their timely support and hope the outcome does not disappoint.

Also, a huge thank you to my husband, Simon, for his unfailing support, endless cups of tea, and for reading more work-in-progress than I care to remember. And I mustn't go without thanking my daughters, Sian and Rachel, for cheering me up and cheering me on.

Honno Press and Liz Jones are grateful to Topfoto for permission to reprint the photograph of Mr and Mrs Caradoc Evans (picture section 1).

Honno has made a 'diligent search' for the Estate of Evan Walters to request permission to reprint his portrait of Marguerite Jervis. However, we have been unable to contact the Estate and would ask that the copyright holder please be in touch so that permission can be obtained retrospectively.

About the Author

Photo: Sian Wroe Jones

Liz Jones is a writer of creative non-fiction and creative writing tutor. Shortlisted for the 2017 New Welsh Review writing award and runner-up in the 2019 Hektoen International essay award, she has written for everything from literary journals to women's weeklies. She holds a doctorate in stage to screen adaptation – the result of her longstanding fascination with hidden histories of theatre and cinema. She lives in Aberystwyth with her husband where, winter or summer, she can be found splashing about in the Irish Sea. This is her first biography.

Index

267

270

Hear from renowned Welsh women writing
about their own lives:

Betsy Cadwaladyr: A Balaclava Nurse
An Autobiography of Elizabeth Davis
By Jane Williams (Ysgafell)
Edited by Deirdre Beddoe

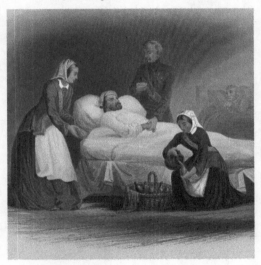

WELSH WOMEN'S CLASSICS

Betsy Cadwaladyr: A Balaclava Nurse

An Autobiography of Elizabeth Davis

Edited by Jane Williams (Ysgafell)
With an introduction by Deirdre Beddoe

Elizabeth Davis – known in Wales as Betsy
Cadwaladyr – was a ladies' maid from Meirionnydd
who travelled the world and gained fame as a
nurse during the Crimean War.

Great fiction from Honno:

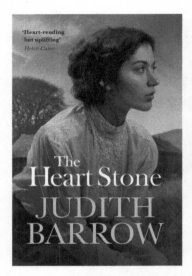

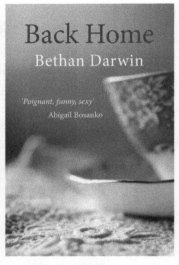

Find out more at www.honno.co.uk

Looking for more biographies on
great Welsh women?

*The Greatest Need: The creative life and troubled
times of Lily Tobias, a Welsh Jew in Palestine*
by Jasmine Donahaye

'Lily did not follow the traditional path set out for
her ... She made her own way, becoming a novelist,
dramatist, essayist and fierce campaigner. A
complex and extraordinary individual.'
Eluned Gramich, *New Welsh Review*

Hear from renowned Welsh women writing
about their own lives:

The Nightingale Silenced
and other late unpublished writings
By Margiad Evans
Edited by Jim Pratt

WELSH WOMEN'S CLASSICS

The Nightingale Silenced
and other late unpublished writings
Margiad Evans
Edited and with an introduction by Jim Pratt

'With the appearance of these late unpublished
works, Margiad Evans is once again given voice,
showing her defiant spirit to be ultimately
unsilenceable' Jon Gower, *Nation.Cymru*

Looking for more biographies on
great Welsh women?

Absolute Optimist: Remembering Eluned Philips
by Menna Elfyn

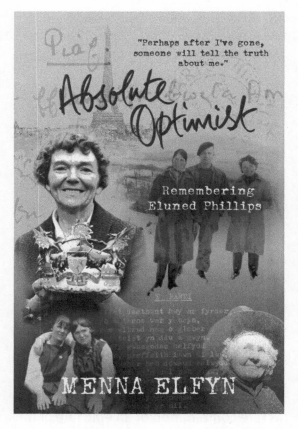

'[an] impassioned account of an extraordinary
woman and writer.'
John Barnie Gwales.com

Hear from renowned Welsh women writing
about their own lives:

One Woman Walks Wales
By Ursula Martin

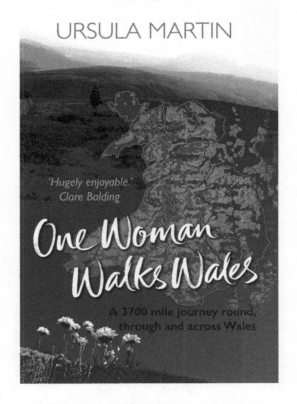

'A rare combination of an epic tale of an
extraordinary adventure and a delicately woven
study of the kindness of random strangers.
Hugely enjoyable' Clare Balding

Honno Voices: Bringing the past to life

A series of titles featuring vital firsthand testimonies from women of all walks of life, from important points in history, giving an intimate portrayal of real women's lives in different eras.

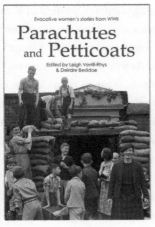

'A marvellous compilation' *Time Out*

'a book to treasure' The Big Issue Cymru

'fascinating, transporting and bound to capture the imagination of anyone' New Welsh Review

ABOUT HONNO

Honno Welsh Women's Press was set up in 1986 by a group of women who felt strongly that women in Wales needed wider opportunities to see their writing in print and to become involved in the publishing process. Our aim is to develop the writing talents of women in Wales, give them new and exciting opportunities to see their work published and often to give them their first 'break' as a writer. Honno is registered as a community co-operative. Any profit that Honno makes is invested in the publishing programme. Women from Wales and around the world have expressed their support for Honno. Each supporter has a vote at the Annual General Meeting. For more information and to buy our publications, please write to Honno at the address below, or visit our website: www.honno.co.uk

Honno, D41 Hugh Owen Building, Penglais Campus,
Aberystwyth University, Aberystwyth, SY23 3DY

Honno Friends
We are very grateful for the support of all our Honno Friends.
For more information on how you
can become a Honno Friend, see:
https://www.honno.co.uk/about/support-honno/